# HOSPITALITY LEADERSHIP

Food preparation with a flair in the institutional cooking kitchen of Martha Van Rensselaer Hall before 1950.

# HOSPITALITY LEADERSHIP

## The Cornell Hotel School

By Brad Edmondson

EDITED BY JOHN MARCHAM

ℬ

CORNELL SOCIETY OF HOTELMEN

ITHACA, NEW YORK, U.S.A.

CORNELL SOCIETY OF HOTELMEN, ITHACA, NY 14853

© 1996 by Cornell Society of Hotelmen.
All rights reserved.

Library of Congress Catalog Card Number 95–083075

ISBN 0–9649921–0–8

Text is composed in Adobe Minion, Adobe Myriad, and
Monotype Poppl-Residenz

Imageset in the United States of America

Printed and bound by Tien Wah Press, Ltd. of Singapore

Printed on Nymolla Silk

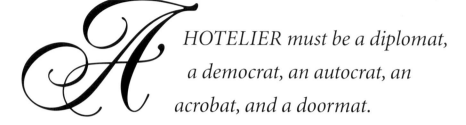 HOTELIER *must be a diplomat,*
*a democrat, an autocrat, an*
*acrobat, and a doormat.*

*He must be on both sides of the political*
*fence and be able to jump the fence.*

*To be successful he must keep the bar full,*
*the house full, the storeroom full, the wine*
*cellar full, the customers full and not get*
*full himself.*

*To sum up: He must be outside, inside,*
*offside, glorified, sanctified, crucified, cross-*
*eyed and, if he's not the strong, silent type,*
*there's always suicide.*

—unattributed

# Contents

# Foreword

BY ANYONE'S STANDARDS, Cornell University is among the great universities of the world. As one who has received three degrees from this institution, I am of course highly biased.

Ezra Cornell was an educational rebel. His dictum was, "I would found an institution where any person can find instruction in any subject." This was certainly revolutionary in 1865! Whether he said this, or even believed it is debatable, but he must have, among educational disciplines, foreseen the possibility of the inclusion of studies in the field of public hospitality. Although at the time of the publication of this book there are some 600 programs of hospitality management offered in colleges and universities in the United States; in 1922 the notion of such a field of study at a first-rate university must have been considered heretical.

Instruction in the field of hotel management as a formal curriculum leading to a bachelor's degree was established for the first time anywhere in the world at Cornell in 1922. The American Hotel Association was at that time embarking on an extensive educational program and the four-year college course was to be its climax. A committee of distinguished hotelmen negotiated with the authorities at Cornell and in September 1922 the School of Hotel Administration was founded.

The late Ellsworth Milton Statler, a prominent member of the hotelmen's committee, in creating the Statler Foundation indicated in his will that the income from the foundation should be used "for financing and carrying on research work for the benefit of the hotel industry of the United States, not only as regards the construction and operation of hotels, but also in training and making more proficient men and women to be workers in hotels for the benefit of the hotel industry as a whole."

Thus, it would appear that the charge to the school was clear. It was under the obligation to provide adequate education and training to prepare young men and women for leadership in the field of public hospitality. In addition, the school must use its resources and facilities as a necessary support for teaching, and as a desirable and much needed service to the industry and to the men and women who operate them.

An early *Announcement* of the school asserted, "Management of a hotel or restaurant calls for a wide range of capabilities. Guests must be received with cordiality and provided with comfortable, well-designed, and tastefully decorated surroundings. They need appetizing, wholesome food that has been wisely bought, properly stored, skillfully prepared, and graciously served. Various other conveniences in public areas, conference and exhibit rooms, communications systems, and travel services are required for proper guest service. Further, a staff of employees must be recruited, trained and motivated to provide hospitable service. Moreover, all must be successfully coordinated to return a profit to the establishment's investors."

A curriculum that will prepare a person to plan, direct, and oversee such a complexity of equipment and services must draw upon nearly every branch of science, technology, and the liberal arts. The Hotel student at Cornell studies accounting, advertising, chemistry, communications, computers, economics, engineering, finance, food preparation, law, literature, marketing, meat products, nutrition, personnel management, psychology, public relations, and sanitation among other subjects. In addition, the student has ample opportunity to partake of an extensive variety of subjects through the elective program.

Most courses are approached in the light of their specific bearing on the hotel and restaurant business, but the breadth is such that while they are receiving thorough preparation for their chosen careers, Hotel students are also achieving a basic liberal education. Prof. H. B. Meek's philosophy was to introduce the student directly to hotel subjects rather than spend one or two years studying "general subjects" and then specialize. His thesis was to start right out "specializing." He felt that if a student was interested in hotel administration, then, by goodness, immerse him in it. To paraphrase, "any subject in which a student is interested must be a worthwhile subject." From the school's point of view, he felt that any program in higher education has two major responsibilities to its students: (1) to fit them for effective work in the economic society of the future in order that each may justly claim from that society a reasonable standard of living; and (2) to provide them with an adequate cultural background against which to receive and enjoy the living so earned.

The School of Hotel Administration has been considered the preeminent institution of its kind in the world (this may be debatable). What are the factors that have contributed to this performance? Perhaps the major factor has been the relationship between the university administration and the school. As some wag once put it, "Cornell University is composed of a group of schools and colleges held together by an underground steam line" (now augmented by an underground chilled water line—ah! progress!). This relationship might also be compared to the old American Federation of Labor and its constituent international unions as described by its first president, Samuel Gompers, as "held together by a rope of sand."

Thus, from its inception, the Hotel school was to be the master of its own fortunes. The school was able to make its way independent of university interference or control. No demands or even requests have ever been made on the university's budget. The school has paid rent for its quarters, paid for accessory instruction as used, paid for all utilities and supporting services—in short, it has pulled its own weight in the boat.

Whereas other schools of hospitality management for the most part were a division or department of another school, the Hotel school at Cornell was able to preserve its autonomy, set its own goals, and seek its own destiny. Such an academic policy is not given to many! Another factor has been the loyalty and support (both moral and financial) of the alumni of the Hotel school—the Cornell Society of Hotelmen. Before and during my tenure as dean, almost three-quarters of the alumni paid dues to the society. This, to my knowledge, is a remarkable phenomenon. During my twenty-year tenure as dean never once did I call upon an alumnus for support but that I received it and more.

A great debt is owed to Professor Meek, to his early faculty, and to the devotion of the students in the early years of the school who established strong bonds (an old boy and girl network) at school and continued to maintain close ties after graduation.

What factors make a school great? Surely the faculty, students and administrative staff, but the School of Hotel Administration is, if not unique, highly unusual in having the loyalty, devotion, and support of its alumni, and through them its close relationship with the hospitality industry. As a professional school the Hotel school at Cornell has been outstandingly successful.

In 1939 Cornell University's football team went undefeated and was rated number one in the nation. In those days when players were expected to play both on the offense and defense and a total of perhaps twenty players saw action in a game, no fewer than fourteen of the regular varsity players were enrolled in the Hotel school, then a department of the Home Economics college. When Cornell defeated Ohio State, the Big Ten Champion that year, one news report read, "Never in the annals of football has a Big Ten Champion been defeated by a team, two-thirds of whom were enrolled in the College of Home Economics." In 1940, Ohio State came back with blood in their eyes, only to be defeated again, and never since have they had the temerity to approach the Home Eccies again.

The School of Hotel Administration at Cornell University is a great institution with a great history and a great future!

*Robert A. Beck '42*
*Guilford, Connecticut*

# Preface

WE ARE PRIVILEGED to bring you this history of the School of Hotel Administration at Cornell University. A project of this size cannot be the work of a single person, or even two or three. So we formed a committee of alumni of the school in the spring of 1994 and sorted through previous efforts to write a Hotel school history, with attention to objectives and to the audiences we were trying to reach.

We needed to set down the rationale for a hotel management school in the first place, and why Cornell University became the place to establish it. We wanted a history that would record the tenures of the program's four deans, H. B. Meek, Robert Beck, John Clark, and David Dittman, and the contributions they made.

It also seemed appropriate to present the story in terms of the school's impact on the hospitality industry and vice-versa and how marching through time together, they both evolved, grew, and became more important on the world's stage.

We were conscious of the audiences of alumni, friends, hospitality industry leaders, and others who might read this history.

To add to the book's relevance and interest, we decided to include separate accounts throughout that focus on events and individuals important to the industry. After reviewing the history of the hospitality industry we were proud to observe how many of the industry's leaders worldwide have been alumni of the School of Hotel Administration.

It has been a pleasure to co-chair this effort. We thank the many contributors of stories, photographs, and memorabilia. We especially want to thank our living former deans, Beck and Clark, and our present dean, Dittman, for being willing to be interviewed. We owe a debt of gratitude to our committee members who worked tirelessly to bring this history to a successful conclusion. These include Sue DeGraba '76, Norm Peckenpaugh '72, Howard Heinsius '50, Don Buch '67, Glenn Withiam *74, Susan Shellenberger '77, MS '81, Fred Rufe '48, and Gerry Lattin, PhD '49, associate.

Finally, we want to thank our professional staff for their fine efforts in support of this project: writer Brad Edmondson *81, designer Phil Wilson, MFA *69, and photographer Sol Goldberg *46. Special thanks must go to John Marcham *50, our tireless editor, without whose patience, diligence, and good humor we would not have been able to finish this.

This book has been a learning experience for us all. We hope you treasure reading the book as we have treasured the opportunity to put it together.

*Michael W. N. Chiu '66, project chair*
*George M. Bantuvanis '51, Richard W. Brown '49, and*
*Richard H. Kennedy '56, project co-vice chairs*

# Acknowledgements

*A* HOST OF ALUMNI helped at all stages in the book's preparation, providing reminiscences and photos, and reviewing a first draft of its manuscript. Many alumni and faculty gave interviews or answered questions, including Lois Jean Meek *47, daughter of the first dean; Jan Beck, wife of the second dean; Ed Whiting '29; Bob Beck; Mary Wright '45; Bill Keithan '50; and George Bantuvanis. Editorial research was provided by Ira Apfel, a Penn graduate living in Ithaca.

Photo research was provided by Apfel, the sterling university photographer Sol Goldberg, and Sarah Suplee. Gould Colman *51 and Nancy Dean of University Archives unlocked many important resources. Glenn Witham, editor of the *Cornell Hotel & Restaurant Administration Quarterly*, was invaluable as a guide to sources and away from errors, as was his associate Fred L. Conner *78. Marjorie Sharpsteen and other staff members of the school were also of aid. Indexing is by Jane Dieckmann; proofreading by Barbara Hall *43 and Barbara Rowan.

Several previous histories of the Hotel program were used during the preparation of this effort. The author and editor acknowledge a partial draft history by Prof. Helen Recknagel and a memoir by Prof. Charles I. Sayles '26, *From a Closet under the Stairs*. A selection of Hotel materials from the Cornell archives by Joan Livingston *75 saved many hours of inspection of primary materials. A full draft history of the program and school by History Associates Inc. of Rockville, Maryland, commissioned by the Cornell Society of Hotelmen in 1990, was also helpful.

Photo identification is by the editor, from notes attached to some of the photos, captions in periodicals including the *Bulletin of the Society of Cornell Hotelmen, Cornell Alumni News, Cornellian*, and publications of the Hotel school. Photographers' names where known are included in the Sources section.

Alumni designations are by class numeral or advanced degree for alumni of the Hotel school, by class or advanced degree plus an * for other colleges of Cornell, by highest graduate degree where an alumnus was not an undergraduate. *ss* indicates a special student in Hotel, generally not working toward a degree. *SpHot* indicates a matriculated student in a special program. Alumni names were checked by the Hotel Alumni Office. Others are checked against Cornell alumni directories and records at *Cornell Magazine*, successor to the *Cornell Alumni News*.

The writer of this history is Brad Edmondson, editor-in-chief of *American Demographics* magazine. The designer is Phil Wilson, an Ithaca graphic designer. The editor is John Marcham, retired editor of the *Cornell Alumni News*.

*John Marcham*
*Ithaca, New York*

# Underwriters

K EY FINANCING FOR THIS BOOK has been provided by a group of alumni and friends of the school and society:

| Underwriter | Business | Country |
| --- | --- | --- |
| Anonymous | | USA |
| Anonymous | | Japan |
| George M. Bantuvanis '51 Ann A. Bantuvanis | | USA |
| David W. Bentley '64 | Nordeman Grimm, Inc. | USA |
| Guglielmo L. Brentel | H&G Hotel Gast Ag | Switzerland |
| Richard W. Brown '49 Muriel Welch Brown *47 | Banfi Vintners | USA |
| William J. Caruso '70 | William Caruso & Associates, Inc. | USA |
| Jennie C. Chiu '91 | Prima Donna Development Corp. / Prima Hotels | USA |
| Michael W. N. Chiu '66 Shirley N. Chiu | Prima Donna Development Corp. / Prima Hotels | USA / Hong Kong |
| Donald M. Coe '62 | Hiram Walker and Sons, Inc. | USA |
| John F. Craver '52 | Horizon Hotels, Ltd. | USA |

| Underwriter | Business | Country |
| --- | --- | --- |
| William V. Eaton '61 Phyllis W. Eaton Pamela Eaton-Hanley '91 | Cini·Little International, Inc. | USA |
| Michael S. Egan '62 | Alamo Rent-A-Car, Inc. | USA |
| Fred J. Eydt '52 | Medallion Hotels, Inc. | USA |
| Richard D. Fors Jr. '59 | Resser Management Corp. | USA |
| Robert A. Freeman '63 | California Café Restaurant Corp. | USA |
| Peter R. Galliker | Galliker Restaurant | Switzerland |
| David P. Hanlon '66 | International Game Technology | USA |
| Erik Lars Hansen '71 | Arthur Andersen, LLP | USA |
| Bjorn R. L. Hanson '73 | Coopers & Lybrand Hospitality Consulting Group | USA |
| Hilton Hotels Corporation | | USA |
| Richard A. Holtzman '76 | Carefree Resorts | USA |
| Margelia L. Jones '78 | The Plasencia Group, Inc. | USA |
| J. William Keithan '50 Faye Y. Keithan | | USA |
| Richard H. Kennedy '56 Kay P. Kennedy | R. H. Kennedy Co. | USA |

| Underwriter | Business | Country |
|---|---|---|
| Caren Whiteman Kline '75 | Wyndham Hotels & Resorts | USA |
| J. Peter Kline '69 | Bristol Hotel Company | USA |
| Charles A. LaForge Jr. '57 | Beekman Arms | USA |
| Joseph A. Los '66 | Financial Consultant | The Netherlands |
| John Marcham *50 | | USA |
| Jane H. Marcham *51 | | |
| Virginia Mariani '82 | Banfi Vintners | USA |
| The Mexico, Central, and South America Region of the Cornell Society of Hotelmen | | Central and South America |
| Robert W. Miller '55 | Search International, Ltd. | Hong Kong |
| Judith H. Monson '69 | Seagram & Sons | USA |
| Rudolf W. Muenster '62 | RWM Hotel Consult GmbH | Germany |
| Charles J. Mund '51 | Service Dynamics Corp. | USA |
| Drew A. Nieporent '77 | Myriad Restaurant Group | USA |
| Norwegian Group of the Cornell Society of Hotelmen | | Norway |
| Rolf Oberloskamp | Büro für Bauplanning | Germany |
| Thomas V. Pedulla '60 | The Pedulla Company | USA |

| Underwriter | Business | Country |
|---|---|---|
| Philip Pistilli '54 | Raphael Hotel Group | USA |
| | Radisson Hospitality Worldwide | USA |
| Philip D. Rowe Jr. '48 | Dempsey Restaurants, Inc. | USA |
| Deiv Salutskij '71 | Elanto Cooperative | Finland |
| Eugenia Brown Sander '66 | EBS Enterprises | USA |
| Rudolphe W. Schelbert '55 | Sophisa / Hôtel Fleur du Lac | Switzerland |
| Paul A. Schoellkopf '41 | | USA |
| Carola Schumacher | | Germany |
| Heinz Schumacher | | |
| Leslie W. Stern '60 | Sullivan & Company | USA |
| Madeline Stern | | |
| Frank T. Stover III '65 | The Chicago Club | USA |
| Carol Gibbs Stover '65 | | |
| Fred Tschanz | | Switzerland |
| Madeleine E. White, MPS '81 | M.E. White Hospitality Enterprises, Inc. | USA |
| Yuji A. Yamaguchi '61 | Fujiya Hotels Co., Ltd. | Japan |

# A Project Too Big to Refuse

ONE DAY EARLY in the twentieth century, John McFarlane Howie had an idea. Howie owned the Touraine, a hotel in Buffalo, New York, but he was always thinking about new ways to promote the hotel industry. His idea came during a tour of the University of Illinois. Here, said his guide, is the college where we train engineers. Here is another school where we turn young men and women into librarians. Here is our Law School. And Howie thought: this is just what the hotel business needs.

Universities of the day were bursting with new ideas that hotel owners could put to use. At Cornell University, for example, the Home Economics department offered courses in quantity food preparation and nutrition. "Microbe hunters" in biology departments across the country were discovering the connections between bacteria and diseases. And a

The United States Hotel in Saratoga Springs, New York, in 1922 already showing the increased importance of the automobile in delivering customers to hotels.

John ("Uncle Jock") Howie, an early booster of the idea of college training for the hotel industry, particularly at Cornell, and his Touraine hotel in Buffalo, New York.

growing number of programs in business management taught accounting, personnel management, and other skills modern hotel managers needed to know.

Howie believed that college-trained managers could improve the state of hotels, many of which were using operating methods that were decades or even centuries old. Twentieth-century American travelers deserved better than to sleep on straw mattresses in drafty inns with the noise from a tavern coming from downstairs. That was the sorry standard, and Howie was one of the men who wanted to improve it.

John ("Uncle Jock") Howie was fond of grand gestures, big ideas, and doing things right. The flamboyant Scotsman "could quote Burns and Shakespeare by the yard and was also quite an actor," remembered Mrs. Cornelius Betten, widow of the Cornell Agriculture school's vice dean. "In my [husband's] office one day, he gave quite a performance. . . 'Now this is the way some men will order a meal,' [said Howie], and he gave a fine imitation of a man, slightly intoxicated, ordering a meal. 'Now,' he said, 'I'll show you how it should be done,' and he proceeded to order a meal in the fashion of a man of elegance and discrimination." When Howie was convinced of how something should be done, he always let you know it.

Howie always insisted that the big idea for Cornell's Hotel school had been his. In the last seventy-five years, several others have also been named as the school's intellectual founder. But the credit deserves to be shared. Around 1900, several leading American hotel owners simultaneously realized that college-level hotel instruction was an idea whose time had come. Between 1900 and 1920, the hotel and restaurant industries went through a wrenching period of growth and change. Hospitality became a big business whose early owners desperately needed new managers who could give their hotels a professional image.

Howie and his peers worked for almost a decade to convince Cornell University to train hotel managers, and at one point their efforts were almost abandoned. But the idea of formal training for hotel managers had success written all over it. Someone was going to do it; Cornell, to its credit, was the first to take the chance.

## The "Science" of Hotels

To understand how early twentieth-century hotel education raised the standards of the hospitality industry, one must first understand nineteenth-century standards. In October 1829, the Tremont House opened in Boston and was immediately promoted as the best hotel in the world. Each of its 170 guest rooms came with a washbowl and soap, individual room keys, a buzzer that rang the front desk, and room service. The dining room seated 200 and had printed menus. One of the twelve public rooms was stocked with books and newspapers from around the country. These were revolutionary improvements that were soon copied by other hotels.

Twenty years later, the Tremont had several competitors. In 1849 the editor of the *Liberty Hall and Cincinnati Gazette* declared that "there are no hotels in London or Paris that can be compared, in any respects, with the Astor, the Revere, the St. Charles, the Irving, and others." Americans, according to the ebullient journalist, had raised hotel management to a "science."

Science may be too strong a word, but like scientists, some nineteenth-century American hotel owners developed a habit of dissecting their operations, analyzing their methods, and making incremental changes. Their search for improvements in efficiency and cus-

tomer service was driven by necessity, just as it is today, because adapting quickly is the key to survival in any rapidly changing industry. And in the hospitality business, rapid change is a constant.

In the 1840s, for example, railroads replaced boats and stagecoaches as the primary means of travel. Hotel dining room managers suddenly had to cope with hordes of hungry guests who arrived at the same time. They adapted by teaching waiters to follow an intricate military-style dining room "drill" that allowed them to

A formal dining room in Chicago's Palmer House in the late 1880s typified a level of service that marked the best early American hotels.

ONE of America's most famous resorts is The Greenbrier in White Sulphur Springs, West Virginia. Presidents and monarchs have frequented the resort to take advantage of its therapeutic waters. The hotel is also famous for its rustic, mountainous, secluded setting. But a century after The Greenbrier began, its seclusion almost proved its undoing.

Because The Greenbrier is so isolated, accessibility was a problem. When it was founded in 1778, visitors sometimes spent two weeks in an uncomfortable coach to arrive there. But the owners and local politicians knew the value of the property, and they shrewdly utilized new modes of transportation to solve the problem.

First, Greenbrier owner James Calwell willingly permitted the new James River and Kanawha Turnpike to run through his property in 1821. Next, a canal connecting Richmond, Virginia, to the Ohio River was used until quicker railroad transportation made travel by water obsolete.

When a special convention of 300 delegates from thirty-four counties voted to support extending the Virginia Central line to the Ohio River, a critical decision was made to pass the line right by The Greenbrier. Another possible route that would pass by a rival resort was rejected. The rival resort, Sweet Springs, was condemned to obscurity, while The Greenbrier became the internationally known destination it is today.

Rail travel also brought the resort a new class of guests who were not as wealthy or connected as original guests had been, but were willing to spend good money to hobnob with the elite. The royalty may have grumbled, but The Greenbrier and other rail-connected resorts thrived on a new market of middle-class families. *See page 84 for a Cornell Hotel connection.*

serve dozens or hundreds of meals quickly and efficiently. Headwaiters used voice commands, bells, or music as signals for various movements that squadrons of servers executed in perfect time and step. Foreign travelers were fascinated by this homegrown spectacle. In 1843, a French tourist reported that dinner at New York's Astor House was "conducted with the regularity of maneuvers on board a frigate."

Still, even the best hotels of the late nineteenth century would probably be repulsive to late twentieth-century travelers. Consider the food in a hotel dining room of the period, which was plentiful but laden with fat. According to food editor Joseph Vehling, a formal fourteen-course dinner of 1880 would consist of seven meat dishes, six kinds of sweets, and one "cold dish, with greens." The morning after such a feast might have made guests feel even worse as they faced the reality of Gilded Age plumbing. In the 1880s, "the bowl and pitcher and slop jar [were] in evidence in the bedrooms of nine out of ten hotels," wrote John Willy, editor of the 1935 *Hotel and Motel Red Book*. "The toilet was 'down the hall,' the bathtub was a public one (usually one on each floor), raised on four legs and encased in wood paneling."

In 1900, many upper-class American homes had flush toilets and tubs with piped-in hot water. Yet only a few luxury hotels of the day offered similar levels of comfort and privacy, so even well-to-do travelers had to settle for what they could find. Hotels were also slow to serve a new kind of customer who came alone, traveled light, and usually stayed only one night. The growth of interstate commerce put thousands of salesmen and other business travelers on the road, and the road was an uncomfortable place.

Business travelers were a large and lucrative market by the turn of the century, but they were not well-served by hotelmen until 1908. The man who finally served their needs made a great fortune, and his fortune eventually helped endow the Cornell Hotel program.

## Statler: Faster, Better, and Cheaper

Ellsworth M. Statler, the eighth child of an itinerant preacher, was born into poverty in 1863. At age 9, he quit school and went to work at a glass factory outside of Wheeling, West Virginia, stoking the glassblower's "glory hole" for 50 cents a day. At 13, he found a better job as a bellboy for the Hotel McLure, then the tallest and most elegant building in Wheeling. Statler was a boy to whom pennies and nickels meant wealth. He set about accumulating more and more of them. The tools he used were a keen power of observation and a small black notebook.

When Statler saw something that needed improvement or heard a useful idea on hotel management, he wrote it in his black book. The McLure became the teenager's personal training ground, and the student, though self-taught, used the same deductive reasoning and research methods students at the Cornell Hotel school use today. Despite his youth, the ambitious Statler soon left the bell stand. He became a night clerk, then a day clerk, then head clerk. With the earnings he saved, he bought a partial interest in the hotel's failing billiard room. He turned it into a success by lowering prices and hiring his sister to bake fresh pies. He used the profits to buy a bigger hall offering bowling and billiards.

Statler's first real venture into the hospitality business began on July 4, 1895, when he opened the Ellicott Square Restaurant in Buffalo. It took six hard years of trial and error to make the restaurant profitable, and Statler nearly went bankrupt several times as he learned the business. As soon as he was in the black, however, he made an even riskier move: he built and operated a temporary 2,084-room hotel at the Buffalo Pan-American Exposition of 1901. The exposition was jinxed. It struggled to attract crowds, then collapsed after President William McKinley was assassinated there in September. But while the organizers and backers suffered great losses, Statler and his backers netted a modest profit.

Statler's notebook continued to be the key to his success. He had an uncanny ability to improve customer service while cutting costs by carefully observing hotel guests and thinking of creative solutions to chronic problems. For example, each guest in the temporary hotel in Buffalo needed a way to summon a bellboy for such things as ice water or fresh linens. Rather than install an expensive buzzer system, which was the rule in luxury hotels at that time, Statler devised a system in which guests could raise different flags outside their rooms to signify their wants. Bellboys were stationed in every hallway to watch the flags. In the days before minimum wage laws, Statler only needed to pay them pennies an hour. He got a cheaper building and his guests got better service.

Young Ellsworth M. Statler about 1890 in Wheeling, West Virginia, where he was learning about hotels and entrepreneurship at the Hotel McLure.

Statler's genius for innovation reached a peak in his first permanent hotel. In 1908, Buffalo was a major port, an important rail terminus, and the jumping-off point for most trips from the east coast to Chicago and points west. Every night, thousands of business travelers and tourists sought lodging there. They could choose an inn, which was probably inexpensive but could be loud, dirty, and unsafe. Or they could choose a full-service hotel like "Jock" Howie's Touraine, which cost more but offered a measure of privacy and a better class of guests. What they couldn't get, unless they were prepared to spend a lot of money, was a private bathroom.

All of this changed when the first Buffalo Statler opened in 1908 under the slogan, "A Room and a Bath for a Dollar and a Half." Such a luxury at such a low price proved irresistible to travelers. The hotel was a huge success, and it became a prototype for the modern commercial hotel.

Private baths are taken for granted today, but they were almost unknown in commercial lodging in 1908. A few luxury hotels offered private baths by running separate water and sewer lines to each room, but these rooms were too expensive for middle-class travelers. Statler did the same thing for much less by solving an old problem in a new way.

In his book *Statler: America's Extraordinary Hotelman,* Floyd Miller imagines a crucial conversation between Statler and his architect, August Esenwein. Statler stands before the drawing board with a sketch pencil: "First off, of course, we eliminate the large public baths that would normally be installed on each floor. In their place we pair off the rooms and their private baths. See, like this. The baths of each adjoining bedroom would be constructed back to back, with the fixtures and pipes opening into a common shaft. Also, all of them would be vertically stacked so that each pair of bathrooms would be directly above those on the floor below and directly below those on the floor above. Also, each bathroom would have a large mirror over the washbasin which, when removed, would open the interior plumbing shafts to easy access and repair."

Two decades later, a suspicious Statler visited the new program for hotel instruction at Cornell. The Statler Plumbing Shaft had become the standard in every American hotel and high-rise apartment building. It was the most important of hundreds of innovations he had made in commercial construction and hospitality. Statler was a wealthy man, and he suspected—correctly—that Cornell wanted a substantial contribution. But on a day-long tour of Cornell's facilities, he saw that the instructors at Cornell had the same spirit of experimentation, questioning, and innovation that had secured his fortune. Shortly after that tour, he became the school's greatest benefactor.

**Wanted: An Innovation Foundry**

By 1910 the United States probably had 10,000 hotels and 300,000 hotel employees. Some analysts said that hotels constituted the fourth-largest industry in the country. Commercial hotels could be found near every major railway terminal, just as today's motels cluster at freeway interchanges. Resort hotels were served by specially laid track that delivered private rail cars and their well-to-do passengers to vacations in the mountains or on the seashore. During World War I, thousands of soldiers and families crossed the country for the first time. Henry Ford had revolutionized travel with the inexpensive Ford Model T. By 1920, tens of thousands of automobiles were on the road—and many of their passengers needed places to stay.

Henry Ford, king of the automobile, was the same age as Ellsworth Statler. Ford's success created more business for men like Statler, and the emerging hospitality infrastructure eased America's transition into the age of automobiles.

The hotel and restaurant industries grew at a torrid pace in the late 1910s and 1920s. The growth created great wealth for the nation's leading hotelmen and restaurateurs, but it also brought severe growing pains. In 1918 and 1919, for example, strikes in Chicago and New York pitted thousands of unionized hotel workers against managers. The newer high-rise hotels of that

Harvey House in Needles, California, in 1907, one of 33 hotels and 54 lunchrooms built to serve passengers along the Santa Fe rail line that stretched west across the country.

era had central heating, elevators, mechanized kitchens, and, of course, a private bath in every room. And in 1920, when Prohibition became law, a traditional profit center for hotels—the bar—became illegal.

Where would the new hotels find managers good enough to handle such complex jobs? Previously, chefs and managers had been lured from their posts in Europe, but the war and tighter immigration laws put an end to that. Clearly, America in the 1920s had to grow its own hotel and restaurant talent.

In 1917, hotel owners formed the American Hotel Association in part to address these problems. In 1919, the National Restaurant Association was formed for similar reasons. The industries were in their adolescence,

**Hotel M'Alpin**
Broadway at 34th St.
New York City

CAFE SAVARIN NEW YORK
UNDER SAME MANAGMENT

CABLE ADDRESS
HOTALPIN. NEW YORK

L. M. BOOMER
MANAGING DIRECTOR

July 8/1920

Mr. John Willy,
Hotel Monthly,
Chicago, Ill.

Dear Mr Willy:

Our Mr. Frank Ready, who has just returned from the Greeters Convention, tells me that you are advocating a hotel training course as a part of the curriculum of some of the larger educational institutions. Further, that your plan includes the very practical suggestion of instruction being given along the lines of actual operation, as well as in theory. To this end, that you would have built a small model hotel, perhaps on the campus of some university, where visitors to the university and members of the faculty could find accommodations and hotel services of the usual sort

I sincerely hope that your promotion of this idea will result in some practical accomplishment. The hotel fraternity should stand back of you to a man and give you every help and encouragement possible. I most emphatically indorse your plan, and hope to hear good news of its favorable reception. If I can do anything to help, count on me.

With kindest regards,

Very truly yours

Managing Director

LMB-D

Howie made his first pitch to Cornell five years before the American Hotel Association was founded. After hearing his plea for formal instruction in hotel management, university President Jacob Gould Schurman told Howie that the idea was "absolutely out of the question." But Howie was not easily discouraged. As a boy in Scotland, he had worked in a five-story walk-up hotel, carrying guests' trunks on his back. Also, his persuasive powers were legendary. Charles I. Sayles '26, an early faculty member of the Cornell Hotel program, remembers that Howie was "a staunch Democrat [who] once entertained in his home five or six Hotel students, all, as one might presume, rabid Republicans. When the meal was over, all except one repaired to the kitchen to demonstrate their skill in washing dishes. By the end of the evening there remained only one Republican—the guy who couldn't get into the kitchen."

Schurman's rejection did not deter Howie for long. He soon found three other Cornellians who formed a more sympathetic audience. In 1914, he met with Flora Rose and Martha Van Rensselaer, the codirectors of Cornell's Home Economics department, and their boss, Albert Mann, who was dean of the College of Agriculture. Mann's initial reaction was also negative. Training hotel managers at a college was an outlandish idea. It was even more outlandish to start the first training program at Cornell, because Cornell had no business school at that

and the new trade organizations hoped to hasten their maturity. Some association members thought that the quickest path to maturity ran through college campuses. They hoped to turn hospitality from a trade learned by apprenticeship into a profession learned in a classroom. "Jock" Howie was the most vocal member of this group.

time. After their initial meeting, Mann told Howie to take his idea to Harvard. But Howie had several good reasons to keep coming to Ithaca.

As early as 1906, the Home Economics department had attracted attention from the restaurant industry by offering courses in nutrition. Cornell was also the government-supported land-grant college of New York, the state where Howie, Ellsworth Statler, and many other industry leaders were based. Frank A. Dudley, for example, the president of the American Hotel Association (AHA), was also president of the Niagara Falls–based United Hotels Company of America. Lucius M. Boomer, a leading hotel manager in New York City, was chairman of the AHA committee on education and training. It may also have been significant that Boomer's predecessor at the Waldorf, George C. Boldt, was a former chairman of Cornell's Board of Trustees.

Philosophical reasons also drew Howie to Cornell. The university stood for the broadest possible conception of higher education; in the famous vow taken by its founder, Cornell is the place where "any person can find instruction in any study." Hotel education may have been a new idea, but Cornell was a place where new ideas were welcome.

Flora Rose was immediately drawn to Howie's idea. She soon became a passionate advocate for the Hotel program, and her close relationship with Martha Van Rensselaer ensured Van Rensselaer's support. Dean

Mann also became a convert, but he may have been interested for more prosaic reasons. By the 1920s, American agriculture was on the wane.

The 1920 census revealed that for the first time, more Americans lived in urban than in rural areas. Farm prices were so low for most of the decade that many small farmers could no longer make ends meet, and the pace of rural-to-urban migration quickened through the 1920s. Enrollment in the Agriculture college declined from a high of 1,704 in 1915–1916 to a low of 676 in 1928–29, and fewer than half of the Class of 1928 went on to earn a degree. Mann may have seen the hotel training program as a way to find more students, identify with a rapidly growing field, and ensure a steady supply of funds from the State Legislature.

On December 17, 1919, Mann convened a conference to determine "for what purpose buildings to be erected at Cornell in connection with the agricultural college should be used." Howie represented state and national hotel associations. A resolution from that conference stated that the "School of Home Economics shall offer the facilities for training men and women in the profession of hotel keeping." Another stated that "as an entering wedge to the course in Hotel Economics... short courses be developed for practical hotel men."

Howie left the conference in a state of bliss. In a letter of December 19 to Elmore Green, manager of New York City's Iroquois Hotel and president of the New York

State Hotel Association, he listed ways in which a university, with its dormitories and kitchen facilities, could be used to train hotel managers. Of Van Rensselaer and Rose he wrote: "Intelligent men and women coming within the radius of the personality of these two women will readily grasp their inspirational qualities of leadership." Rose returned the compliment, writing Howie to thank him for "the inspiration and benefit that your presence gave at the meeting."

Over the next four months, Rose and Howie exchanged a steady stream of letters on how Cornell and the hotel industry could help each other. Rose put the correspondence to good use in an address to the AHA at its 1920 conference the following April. The hotel business, she told the assembly, was "an extension of home ideals into the industrial field." She then outlined a college curriculum for hotel training, and ended her remarks with a challenge: "Is the industry to remain an apprenticeship industry or shall effort be made to include it among the professions?"

Rose was an accomplished speaker who had been briefed on the hospitality field by Howie. She was also the first ambassador from Cornell that many hotel owners had seen, and the effect on the industry was powerful. After her speech, college courses on hotel management became a popular topic of discussion in the industry. The 1920 summer edition of *The Hotel Monthly* featured the concept of hotels on university campuses, complete with architectural drawings and endorsements from hotel owners and educators. Years later, Howie wrote that the day of Rose's speech was when he "*knew* the battle was won." Rose, "with her whole imposing, brilliant, and beautiful personality literally *blazing*," had carried the day.

By January 1921, AHA President Frank Dudley was petitioning Cornell President Jacob Schurman to set up courses for hotel training. Schurman, a classical scholar, was not enthusiastic about a new program that smacked of vocational training. But he did not say no, so the advocates moved forward. Rose, Van Rensselaer, and Mann were ready to work with the industry. Three questions remained: Who would pay for the program? What would the program teach? And finally, who would be the academic leader?

On June 15, 1921, Frank Dudley called a meeting of hotel and university leaders to consider the financial question. He invited such well-heeled luminaries as Lucius Boomer, Ellsworth Statler, and John Bowman of Biltmore Hotels. This meeting added momentum to the idea, but it did not produce a clear financial sponsor. Statler, in fact, was a vocal skeptic.

After the June 15 meeting, the Cornell Board of Trustees approved a resolution to allow the Agriculture school to offer a course in hotel management, "provided that the State is willing on the request of the State Hotel Association to authorize the use of the plant and facili-

ties for that purpose and to provide means for so doing." Hotel and industry officials then requested an initial appropriation of $11,000 from the notoriously stingy State Legislature, but they were refused. In fact the program and school never have received significant support from the state, despite numerous requests for public funds.

Cornell wouldn't foot the bill either. On April 1, 1922, its trustees reiterated their support for the program, but only "on condition that the moneys requisite for same are provided from other than present university sources." That left the hotel industry as the only possible source of funds. Industry leaders were willing to support the program, but they were reluctant to pay until they saw a detailed plan for a curriculum that served their needs.

Dudley, Howie, and others on the AHA education committee had begun discussions about a curriculum for the hotel program in 1921. After a November meeting, Dudley was enthusiastic enough to give a verbal commitment of funds. He told Mann that state and national hotel associations would raise $25,000 to sup-

port faculty salaries, equipment, and staff for up to forty students. He also pledged the industry's support in finding qualified students and placing them in summer jobs with New York hotels.

The hotel owners and Mann also reached an understanding that Cornell would control the content of Hotel courses, but that it would do so, in Dudley's words, with "the close cooperation of a committee representing the hotel interests." This cooperation came in the form of meetings where ideas were exchanged, and also in more practical forms. Cornelius Betten, who reported directly to Mann, assigned several people to

Home-to-be of a hotel program at Cornell, the Home Economics building, left, behind the original College of Agriculture and Home Economics buildings, Stone, Roberts, and East Roberts. Home Economics was later renamed Comstock Hall.

gather information from the hotel industry in 1921. One was an engineering student named Frank H. Randolph *17, who left Ithaca to study the operations and design of large hotels. Randolph was to evaluate all aspects of hotel engineering, from boilers and plumbing to elevators and refrigeration, and report back with a proposed course of study. Another early researcher was Beulah Blackmore, a professor of home economics, who spent a year working in the linen department of the Waldorf-Astoria Hotel in preparation for a course on hotel textiles.

The dialogue between industry figures and academic figures did not always go smoothly. Betten "suggested a [Hotel] course in the Department of Vegetable Crops," according to his wife Alice, "but this did not at first meet with approval. One hotelman said, 'That wouldn't be needed. All my man needs to know about a cucumber is that it is nine inches long. If it is that long, he buys it.' [Betten said he] thought there was a good deal more to know about a cucumber than its length. A course was set up in Vegetable Crops, and one in Animal Husbandry."

It is often said that academics are only interested in knowledge for its own sake, while businessmen are only interested in the bottom line. It's also said that university faculty will tolerate almost anything except being told what to do. These stereotypes contain grains of truth, and they probably explain the friction that developed between the home economists and the hotel managers. By January 1922, Mann felt that the "cooperation" from the AHA was getting too close. He was particularly vexed by Lucius Boomer, the chair of the AHA education committee. Boomer was impatient with the university's emphasis on home economics. He wanted the courses to attack "business problems" like accounting, "the language of the hotel business." Mann was clearly annoyed. In a letter to Rose, he said that the Agriculture school "would not care to undertake" a hotel training program that was not centered around home economics.

Negotiations continued through the spring of 1922, with little improvement in tone. When the AHA insisted that the proposed director of the program be chosen "for his fitness as a hotel executive," as well as his academic achievements, Mann complained about the AHA's "arbitrary limits or restrictions." Yet he never broke off discussions with the hotelmen because they were the Hotel program's sole source of support. For their part, the hotelmen continued with Cornell because they sought its prestige. As the two groups continued to work together, they forged an unusually intense alliance that would become one of the Hotel school's greatest strengths.

As spring 1922 approached summer, the discussions finally bore fruit. On June 14, Vice Dean Betten finally released a memorandum to the AHA outlining a four-year course in institution management that would lead to a bachelor of science degree. In return for a promise that Cornell would pursue "the closest possible cooperation of the hotel executives," Cornell asked the AHA for $7,500 in the first year, and up to $10,000 a year for five years thereafter. The AHA agreed. The new program was formally announced a month later, and Cornell began accepting applications from students.

One problem remained. Who would run the program? In the spirit of close cooperation, Betten was assigned to evaluate candidates for their academic merit, while W. I. Hamilton, an executive at the Waldorf-Astoria, would look for an experienced hotel executive. To his surprise, Hamilton soon found someone who seemed to meet both requirements. In a conversation with Betten (reported by Mrs. Betten), Hamilton said, "I think I've got just the man for you."

Howard Bagnall Meek had taught mathematics at Yale and was the former director of a vocational course in hotel operations at Boston University. Moreover, he was the summer operator of the Ocean House hotel in York Beach, Maine. "I stayed there for a number of days, studying him and his methods, and I tell you the standards stuck out all over that hotel," said Hamilton. "There is only one thing wrong with him."

"What's that?" asked Betten.

"Well," replied Hamilton, "he's such a darn little runt."

Meek was indeed a short person, but Betten and a new Cornell president, Livingston Farrand, interviewed him and found him equal to the task. The final stumbling block concerned his salary. Mann wanted to pay him $3,500 a year, the market value for someone of his qualifications. Meek, however, had recently decided to leave his job at Yale. He said that he did not particularly want to reenter academe, and he certainly would not do so for less than $5,000. Mann offered $4,500, and said that Meek should not accept unless it was a "cordial acceptance." Meek continued to stall, but he did consent to be interviewed by Rose and Van Rensselaer at their summer home on Long Lake in the Adirondacks.

The trip must have shaken something loose in H. B. Meek. After an all-night, solitary, "rackety-bang" experience that involved a train, a truck, and a boat, he arrived at the women's camp in "very considerably disheveled condition," reported Rose. Still, Rose judged him "very satisfactory" and urged both sides to settle. On September 11, Meek telegraphed Mann: "Project too big to refuse. Accept in spirit you suggest. Decision once made ensure every effort."

With funding, curriculum, students, and a leader in place, the program opened on September 20, 1922. Within a year, the money would dry up and the curriculum would undergo drastic changes. But as Betten later said, the diminutive Meek proved to be "a mighty big man."

The Library of the Cornell School of Hotel Administration has a reputation as an indispensable information resource to the hospitality industry. One of its treasures is a collection of restaurant menus that was once owned by a legendary figure in the hospitality industry.

Six thousand menus were donated to the library in 1950 by one of the most singular characters in hotel history. Oscar Tschirky was mâitre d'hôtel at the Waldorf-Astoria from the opening of the new Waldorf until his death in 1950. Known to all as "Oscar of the Waldorf," he became a fixture in the New York City social scene.

Oscar began collecting menus after he emigrated to America from his home in Neuchâtel, Switzerland in 1883. He was only 17 when he arrived in New York and was anxious to find work. He started waiting tables at Hoffman House hotel, and later moved across the street to America's best restaurant, Delmonico's. He wrote to William Waldorf Astor when he heard the new Waldorf building was under construction. Oscar was told he had the job as head waiter, but hotel manager George Boldt had someone else for the job, so Oscar became mâitre d'hôtel.

At the Waldorf, Oscar came in contact with many figures associated with Cornell and the Hotel school. They included Boldt himself, who had been chairman of the university's Board of Trustees; Lucius Boomer, president of the Waldorf and an advisor to the school; and Prof Meek. When he made out his will, Oscar wanted to leave his menus to an organization that would treat them as a collection, not as individual artifacts. Cornell, its library already the industry resource, was the logical choice.

For his prodigious collecting efforts, Oscar was inducted into the Hobby Hall of Fame by the Hobby Guild of America. But the menus are more than just the fruits of one man's efforts. They trace the history of dining out from the mid-19th century until 1943, when he collected his last menu.

The Oscar Tschirky menu collection shows that healthful eating was not on people's minds when they went to a gourmet restaurant in the nineteenth and early twentieth centuries. It was common for such menus to feature twelve courses, and sometimes more. There was a strong emphasis on meat and game, and little interest in vegetables. Menus invariably featured some kind of turtle soup, oysters, caviar, and crudités. Because Oscar's menus were from high-quality restaurants and hotels, one can assume that the food at taverns and lesser hotels was even less nutritious.

Oscar's menus contained some unusual dishes. At a 1909 "Game Dinner" honoring Teddy Roosevelt, guests were served bear cub, among other things. His oldest menu, from a dinner honoring Governor Louis Kossuth on December 15, 1851, also featured the most gluttonous bill of fare. Printed on silk, it featured thirteen courses—not extraordinary, given the dining environment of that era. But other menus would be hard-pressed to top this spread: 2 soups, including the ubiquitous green turtle; 5 fish dishes, including "salmon with rashers of

pork"; 16 "relevés," including 7 roast dishes (among them "larded capons"); 6 boiled dishes (among them tongue and "sour kraut with partridge"); 3 baked dishes (among them "opossum with Madeira Wine" and "Calabash of Terrapin"); 6 "cold and ornamental dishes," including eel; 4 relishes, including anchovies; 17 side dishes, including game, fish, eel and beef; 15 vegetables, including 4 kinds of potatoes—"baked mashed," "mashed with cream," "baked sweet," and "plain baked"; 10 game dishes, including "red heads," "brandt," three duck dishes and partridge; 9 pastries, including "blanc manger" and "champagne jelly"; 10 ornamental confectionery dishes, including "Atlas Supporting the World" and "Kossuth's Residence at Kutaiyeh"; 9 "confects" or cakes; 5 preserves, including "chow chow"; fruit; and finally, coffee, liqueur and "anchovy toast"—to aid digestion, no doubt.

Though the food back then might have been hard on the stomach, the menus were a feast for the eyes. Restaurant managers took great pains to produce the most beautiful menus to match their gargantuan meals. Some featured individually hand-painted pictures; others were bound in leather; still others were decorated with gold leaf. One menu from 1923 dealt with Prohibition by including a small "entre nous" menu inside that featured "Cocktail LA," 1848 VVO Courvoisier, and 1869 Chartreuse.

# Meek Can Have Anything He Wants

WHEN PEOPLE SAY that Cornell's Hotel school is Number One, they usually mean that it is universally recognized as the best such program in the world. The phrase would have had a different meaning in 1922, however. The Cornell program was the nation's first experiment in hotel education. It began in obscurity, with an unreliable funding source and more detractors than supporters. During its first decade it was never more than one or two mistakes from oblivion.

Today, the memory of founding Dean H. B. Meek is revered by seven decades of Hotel alumni. But Meek commanded far less respect when he arrived at Cornell in the fall of 1922. The new head of the hotel education program was just 29, nine years younger than his oldest student. He was a dropout from academe who had decided to

Already an accepted part of the hospitality industry, Cornell Hotel faculty and students occupy a central table as guests of the Hotel Pennsylvania in November 1929, opening luncheon of the Annual Hotel Show in New York City.
*See Sources for names.*

An early food preparation lab, likely in the Home Economics building. Student John Courtney '25 is identifiable at right rear.

leave academe. "The salaries were very low, and I was restless," he says. "I was through with teaching and had a job lined up with a big restaurant organization . . . so I was not interested in coming to Cornell."

Meek's opinion changed after Cornelius Betten persuaded him to visit Ithaca after closing Ocean House. He was smitten. "I had been teaching in what was essentially an urban university," he said. "I came here in September to this beautiful campus. . .all the place was bustle and alive. It was kind of attractive looking." Meek was especially impressed by "Goldwin Smith [Hall] with its columns, which was the traditional academic kind of an atmosphere."

Meek met once again with Betten, and then with President Livingston Farrand. But he seemed most impressed by his interview with the dean of Agriculture, Albert Mann. "He was a very able person; keen eyes—

dark brown eyes. He was a real leader," Meek recalled. Mann arranged Meek's all-night trip from Ithaca to Long Lake to meet with Flora Rose and Martha Van Rensselaer. "I left [Ithaca] saying I wouldn't come," he says. "On the train, I decided I would. I think I had decided before I left that I would come, but I was too stubborn to admit it."

### Scrounging and Borrowing

On September 20, 1922, the Hotel program opened with twenty students. Six of them were the sons of hotelmen, five were sons of businessmen, three were doctors' sons, two were of college professors, two of lawyers, one was a farmer's son, and one was the son of a mechanic. Joseph H. Nolin '25 and his roommate decided to enroll as sophomores after spending a year in the College of Arts and Sciences. "We enrolled because it was a whole new experience," says Nolin. "I had worked in hotels; my first summer job was in Northern Michigan, and my second was in Montreal. That's what hooked me."

What the first students experienced was a far cry from the state-of-the-art facilities of today's Statler Hall. The Hotel program was not a new school, but a new program of study that relied heavily on existing courses and was taught at borrowed locations around campus. The curriculum had already been set by Mann, Rose, and the AHA education committee before Meek arrived. Students in their freshman and sophomore years took courses in chemistry, physics, biology, human physiology, and bacteriology in the College of Arts and Sciences. They also enrolled in two accounting courses offered by the Agricultural Economics department, three Home Economics courses in food, and courses in mechanical drawing, English, and economics. Four specialized courses were scheduled: Hotel Accounts, Hotel Organization, and Hotel Operations, all taught by Meek; and Hotel Engineering, taught by Frank Randolph.

Randolph was the young Cornell engineer whom Mann had enlisted to study hotels in the 1921–22 academic year. By the time the Hotel program opened, he had prepared a complete four-year course on the intricacies of hotel equipment, kitchen planning, plumb-

Hotel students are proud of their school's independent status. But for the first twenty-nine years, Cornell courses in hotel administration were offered as a specialization within the School of Home Economics, which was in turn part of the College of Agriculture.

The goal of college instruction in home economics is "to give the household arts and home economics the same practical encouragement which is now given to agricultural and the mechanic arts in State schools and colleges," according to an 1899 statement. Today the "household arts" of sewing, canning, and home accounting are largely neglected, but they were of vital importance to farm wives a century ago. Cornell's home economics efforts began in 1900 when Agriculture college instructor Martha Van Rensselaer began teaching illiterate farm women how to read. In 1904, she added additional courses on home management, literature, and women's work. By 1905, more than 20,000 women were enrolled in Van Rensselaer's "Saving Steps" home economics program.

In 1909, the Agriculture college created a Department of Home Economics and a four-year degree in the subject. Van Rensselaer became co-director of the department with Flora Rose, a Kansas State Agricultural College graduate with a graduate degree from Columbia. For the next two decades, Van Rensselaer concentrated on administration and Extension work while Rose focused on teaching and research. They remained devoted friends and professional partners until Van Rensselaer's death in 1932.

In 1911, over much opposition from the faculty, Van Rensselaer and Rose became Cornell's first female full professors. That same year, the first three women graduated from the Department of Home Economics. Two years later on December 8, the department moved to its own building, which would later be renamed Comstock Hall. And in 1919, the School of Home Economics was established.

Van Rensselaer and Rose worked hard to make a science of home economics. One of their crowning achievements was the 1920 Manual of Home-Making which gave good advice to generations of rural women. The manual taught food storage, the fundamentals of accounting, and other skills that were similar to the tasks of hotel management. Hotel managers needed a modern education in supervising, buying, cooking and decorating their buildings. Cornell's Home Economics school was, without doubt, the best place to start.

ing, heating and air conditioning, electricity, building construction, and hotel design.

"His equipment was practically zero at the start, but Randolph was a most persistent scrounger," writes Charles Sayles, a former student who later served on the Hotel faculty for forty years. "A lot of the more simple experiments were hand-crafted out of tin cans,

Students learn engineering practice in an early lab, likely in the basement of Roberts Hall.

rubber tubes, and glass tubes, while visits to local establishments provided laboratories." For one laboratory, the class went to the steam plant at the Cornell infirmary to see how an engine driving a generator supplied electricity and steam heat.

Randolph secured two vacant rooms in the basement of East Roberts Hall for his lecture space and prepared them with student labor. His textbook was a hodgepodge of mimeographed notes and excerpts from magazine articles. But what Randolph lacked in tradition, he made up in an insistence on discipline. This made him unpopular with some students. "He was a martinet, insisting that everyone hew the line—but always with a measure of fairness," writes Sayles.

Meek believed that scrounging and improvising for materials, if done well, would make the courses more interesting to students. "Just as soon as a student arrives on the campus, he ought to begin to get subject matter which is related to his interest," Meek said. He was opposed to "the general doctrine that everybody, no matter what he is to become, should study the same— follow the same freshman curriculum and the same sophomore curriculum. I think it's a great mistake."

The lack of specialized courses was a source of frustration for Meek. To learn chemistry, for example, his first students enrolled in a class with 2,000 other students. "They would be under the wing of some

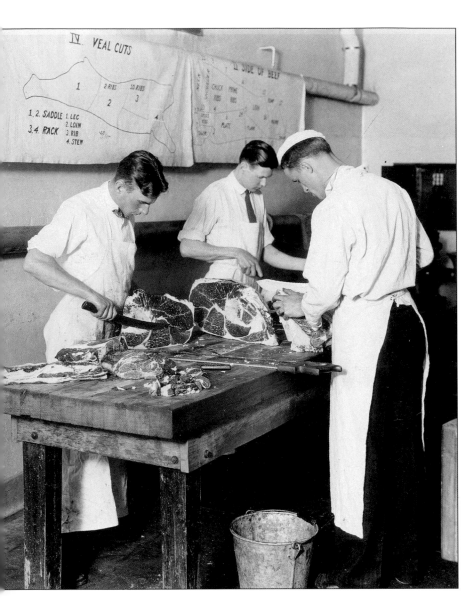

Early students butcher a steer, likely under Cecil Schutt in Wing Hall.

graduate student who had no more interest in hotel problems than I had in fleas in the Sahara Desert," he recalls. The purpose of a basic university course was to lay the groundwork for advanced study in chemistry or some other disciplines. This was "almost lost effort as far as [Hotel] people were concerned," said Meek.

The answer for Meek lay in building on his students' natural interest in hotel problems. "When I first studied inorganic chemistry, they gave us an exercise in which alcohol, glycerin, water, and some kind of oil were mixed in a test tube. We were to shake these things up and to see which would mix to try to get the notion of solutions and suspensions. Well, why not take vinegar, olive oil, and water, perform the same experiment, and discover, if you will, that French dressing is not a solution but a suspension? Why not work with the things?"

In the early months of the program, Meek worked with hotel managers and academics to create basic courses built around solving hotel problems. A traditional drafting course would begin with students manipulating abstract geometric forms; the Hotel program's course began with students designing a cocktail table. The course in hotel accounting started by settling the nightly tab at an imaginary restaurant. "I think that people grow and develop by doing things, by throwing their hat into things," Meek said.

The learn-by-doing philosophy was popular with hotel executives, and it occasionally saved Meek from hiring workers. Yet it also led to a few near-disasters. One Hotel student in a Home Economics kitchen used twenty cups of raw rice in a recipe that called for precooked rice. When the rice swelled, he had to clean his mistake off the floor with a shovel.

At other times, Meek's learn-by-doing philosophy endeared the early Hotel students—or "Hotelies," as they came to be called in later years—to industry leaders. Each year beginning in 1925, Hotel seniors went to New York City for the annual Hotel Show. In 1926, the Cornell group stayed at the Waldorf-Astoria Hotel as guests of Managing Director Lucius Boomer. They were chaperoned by the legendary Oscar Tschirky, given a tour of the facility, and welcomed by conference-goers as a new generation of hotel leaders. The students scored on three counts—they were learning by observing the industry, showing off the Hotel program, and promoting themselves.

## Help from Hotelmen

With no established faculty, curriculum, building, or funding source, Meek built the program by turning to his only source of strength—the hotel industry. He found a notable asset in his second faculty member, Louis Toth of the hotel accounting firm Horwath & Horwath. Toth kept his accounting job in New York City while he taught one day a week at Cornell. In fact, he was the first of several Cornell faculty members to work in New York and commute to Ithaca. He put up with the inconvenience because he loved teaching, and by all accounts he was very good at it.

Toth began with no textbook, but he quickly hired a secretary to record his lectures. An edited version, with tables and graphs, soon became the standard hotel accounting text. According to Sayles, Toth's class was enjoyable "partly because of the free exchange between teacher and student, [and] partly because of the wealth of examples Louis could bring to bear on the subject matter." Sayles relates one of Toth's favorite stories:

"The control of cash, particularly in the front office, is important. If otherwise, people stick their hands in. In one hotel I audited, the cash was considerably short. I found out the owner was quite accustomed to simply expropriating whatever he needed for a night on the town. I explained that it was his hotel and he could do as he pleased with the money, but it was very bad prac-

Prof. John Courtney '25, an early faculty member, teaches hotel accounting in 1928.

tice. He agreed. The next time I ran an audit, I found he had heeded my advice. Here was a note in the drawer signed by him that said, 'I took some money.'"

Toth continued the once-a-week arrangement until his retirement from Horwath, whereupon he moved to Ithaca and became a full-time faculty member. To Meek in the early years, he was a godsend: a top figure in the field who was willing to work for the price of a train ticket and a lecture. To generations of students, he was a mainstay.

Meek soon learned, to his delight, that Toth was not unique. Many hotel leaders were so flattered by an invitation from Cornell that they were willing to travel to Ithaca and give a lecture for free. Meek soon established a Friday afternoon lecture series followed by a

When Cornell's Hotel program began, many industry insiders were skeptical that a four-year college program could adequately prepare young men and women for the practical challenges of hotel administration. Conventional thinking of the day held that hotel-keeping was a skill best learned on the job. But Prof Meek was no conventional thinker. He knew that service, the "subtle anticipation of human needs," as he described it in the May 7, 1926, edition of *The Register of Ye Hosts,* could be taught as the scientific basis of outstanding hotel management.

The 1925–26 Hotel program curriculum reflected the present and the future of hotel administration. Students took courses to learn the correct way to provide service. ("We give it a place at Cornell," Meek wrote in *Ye Hosts.*) They also took courses in accounting and economics, as all hotel managers would need to keep a firm control on costs for the multimillion-dollar hotel chains that had begun to appear in the 1920s.

Food preparation courses balanced science with customer service. The students took quantity cooking classes to learn how to prepare and serve foods on a commercial scale. "The boys slaughter and butcher beef, veal, lamb, and pork," Meek wrote. They also took food chemistry courses to understand the foods they were preparing, as well as biology, physiology, dietetic and nutrition courses to understand customers' dietary needs.

Meek also anticipated the demands of the increasingly competitive hotel industry by having students take marketing, pricing, and commercial geography courses. Classes in textile selection and decoration assured that students would have the best aesthetic taste to match their strong business skills.

Ultimately, Meek believed that a four-year degree in hotel administration from Cornell would prepare hotel managers better than working up through the ranks. Seven decades of hotel leadership prove that he was right.

By 1925, most of the classes for junior and senior years were specialized Hotel courses. Meek had devised a curriculum strategy that would last, with only minor revisions, until 1970. One-third of the Hotel program's courses were in the liberal arts and sciences. One-third were in required hotel technical courses. Of the remaining third, twenty credit hours were in elective technical courses and twenty were electives in the arts and sciences.

One of the most important parts of the curriculum was Meek's requirement that Hotel students spend summers as he had. Each student had to perform three summers of supervised work in the hospitality industry. Students would submit detailed monthly reports on their job experiences; they were expected to progress to more difficult jobs each year, so they could move directly into a supervisory position upon graduation. Thanks to the many connections students made with industry leaders, Cornell graduates usually had little trouble finding such positions.

"The old line method of training men in the hotel business has its merits, but the cost in time and effort is fast becoming prohibitive," Meek wrote in a 1926 article. "To shorten the preparation for positions of responsibility by condensing some of the lessons of years of experience into a course of intensive training is the aim of the work at Cornell."

When the Hotel program opened, Cornelius Betten published an article in the *Cornell Daily Sun* that set out

coffee hour that allowed students to meet the top hotel operators of the day. (This series, known as "Hotel Administration 155" because it met at 1:55 p.m., continued in the mid-1990s. After Meek retired, it was called "brownies with [Dean] Beck," then "cookies with Clark" and "donuts with Dittman.")

Other one-day-a-week lecturers were recruited to give courses in hotel insurance, law, advertising, personnel, and real estate. The list of instructors soon became impressive, although the number of full-time instructors and, by necessity, the faculty salary line, stayed relatively small.

First full Hotel class to graduate in 1926. Second row, includes, from left, Professors Frank Randolph *17 and H. B. Meek, Director Martha Van Rensselaer of Home Economics, John Howie of the American Hotel Association, and acting dean Cornelius Betten of Agriculture and Home Economics. *See Sources for more names.*

its goals. "The complexity of the hotel business today makes it impossible for a manager to be skilled in every phase of the work of his organization, and it is manifestly absurd to expect a college course to do that. What the course can aim to do is to give the student some knowledge of the fundamental principles underlying the various phases of hotel management, some information of immediate and direct usefulness in the profession, and a basis of judgment on the standards maintained in the various departments.

"But skill in the application of these things must come with experience. It will be impossible to turn students into expert chefs, accountants, engineers or stewards, but it is within the range of possibility to teach them to think clearly in terms of the practices and problems the hotel profession must deal with."

In three years, Meek created a program that met these objectives.

### Where's the Money?

In many ways, the Hotel program was an immediate success. It began with 20 students, but 40 were enrolled by the end of the 1922–23 academic year. The total rose to 101 for 1923–24, 115 for 1924–25, and 125 in the fall of 1926. At the same time, enrollment elsewhere in the College of Agriculture was plummeting because of a depression in farm prices. By 1926, the Hotel program accounted for 22 percent of enrollment in the newly designated School of Home Economics.

The first ten graduates of the "Hotel Executive" program hit the job market in 1925, and eighteen more followed in 1926. According to the Agriculture college's annual report for 1926, all of them found management-level positions in the hotel industry. An American Hotel Association resolution praised the program as "eminently successful." Summer job placement also was 100 percent. In 1928 the newly-formed alumni association the Cornell Society of Hotelmen, found that the original graduates were earning an average gross salary of $3,543 a year, respectable income for a young man of that time.

Meek took great satisfaction from the budding careers of his "boys," as he called them. And as the years went by, he also found great personal satisfaction in a young family. Soon after he arrived at Cornell, Meek began seeing Lois Jean Farmer, an assistant professor in institution management who also ran the cafeteria at the College of Home Economics.

"My mother graduated from the University of Minnesota with degrees in cookery and nutrition," said daughter Lois Jean Meek *47. "She and a friend came to Ithaca in 1921 to manage the cafeteria where my father ate. There weren't many unmarried faculty men who ate in the cafeteria. They were married in September of 1924."

Like her husband, Mrs. Meek was short and had auburn hair. Baby Lois was the first-born, followed by a boy, Donald. The family lived in a house in Cornell Heights, just across the street from Risley Hall. In 1929, Meek took a sabbatical from the Hotel program to go to Yale and finish his Ph.D. dissertation in economics, an early work in the theory of pricing.

A year after the newly minted Dr. Meek returned from New Haven, Mrs. Meek returned to work part-time as an instructor in quantity foods preparation. With the children settled and the family together again, the Meeks became enthusiastic hosts. Deans have always been expected to host dinner parties for lecturers and donors, but the Meeks' home in Cornell Heights also became a social center for students and faculty of the young Hotel program. At their regular Sunday evening buffet, guests gathered after the meal for singing around the piano while a fire blazed in the grate. The Meeks also attended hotel conventions and trade shows frequently, and their seven-passenger red Buick touring car rarely left town with an empty seat. One student of the 1920s recalls hearing Meek "singing snatches from Gilbert and Sullivan to a carload of hungry undergraduates on their way to a feast at Krebs [a restaurant in Skaneateles]."

With a new family, adoring students, and growing recognition for his work, Meek must have been a happy man. But success was bringing its own problems, and one of the most basic was an acute lack of space. Meek's first office was a closet under the stairs on the fourth floor of Home Economics (later Comstock) Hall. His furnishings were a beat-up desk, a bentwood chair, and an orange crate. His secretary worked in the hall. "At the end of the day this equipment was moved into the 'office'—a rather pointless procedure, for there wasn't any door," writes Sayles.

Meek was not one to complain, and his office had what he needed to get the job done. But classroom space was another matter. The program's first lecture hall was in a heated barn that stood at the present site of Mann Library. The barn had creaking floors, no chairs, and no bathroom, but it was available and student labor transformed it into an acceptable lecture hall. "In such surroundings people like the manager of the Waldorf were asked to lecture," writes Sayles. Shortly after that, rooms in Roberts Hall became available for Frank Randolph's engineering courses and a growing library of hotel literature.

Another classroom space was created in the basement of Bailey Hall, the university's largest auditorium. The auditorium's sloping floor leaves seven or eight feet of headroom at the back of the basement, although there is only a foot near the stage, and this strange space became a lecture hall for the Hotel program. The room was "blocked off with columns, inadequately heated in winter and overheated in the summer," Meek wrote. "There was an escape of steam which kept the humidity around 98 [percent]. This was the kind of place we had. Any place that was dirty, dank, or dark or noisy and nobody else wanted it. Then we could have it, providing we put in lighting fixtures."

After the Bailey basement was cleared, no more space could be found. Meek was forced to declare that the program would stay at its 1926 enrollment level of 125 students until conditions changed.

The program's low-rent conditions were one symptom of its biggest problem, which was the lack of money. The American Hotel Association had agreed in

## EARLY HOTEL CURRICULUM

Here's the list of course requirements and electives published in the *Announcement* of the Hotel program for the year 1925–26.

The philosophy behind the curriculum is explained by the program's head, Prof. H. B. Meek, in excerpts from an article on page 26. Note the relatively small number of electives over a four-year course of study.

### Freshman

Required: | hours
---|---
Orientation | 1
Biology 1 | 6
Human Physiology 303 | 3
English 1 | 6
Foods 15 | 2
Foods 16 | 2
Mechanical Drawing 2 | 3
Chemistry 101 | 6
Chemistry 880 | 2
| 31

Advised:
French
Physics 3 ............ 3
Physics 4 ............ 3

### Sophomore

Required: | hours
---|---
Accounting 121 | 3
Accounting 122 | 3
Economics 2 | 6
Foods and Nutrition 17 | 4 or 3
Physics 3 | 3
Physics 4 | 3
Bacteriology 3 | 2
Textiles 51 | 2
Decoration and Furnishing 35 | 3
| 29

Advised:
Meats 20 ............ 3
French
Public Speaking

### Junior

Required: | 
---|---
Hotel Operation 151 | 3
Hotel Organization 152 | 3
Mechanism of Hotel Machines 161 | 4
Hotel Power Plants 162 | 3
Hotel Accounting 181 | 2
Hotel Cookery 115 | 4
Hotel Psychology | 4
Meats and Meat Products 20 | 3
| 26

Advised:
Biology 7 ............ 1
English
History
Philosophy

### Senior

Required: | 
---|---
Hotel Auxiliary Equipment 163 | 3
Business Management 125 | 3
Money and Banking 11 | 5
Law as related to Innkeeping 171 | 4
Commercial Geography 206 | 2
Hotel Accounting (Advanced) 182 | 2
| 19

Advised:
Special Hotel Problems 153 ............ 3
Hotel Engineering Problems 164 ............ 3
Accounting
Biology 7 ............ 1
Economics
English
Government
History
Philosophy

Required hours: 105

January 16, 1920 was a turning point for the hospitality industry. On that day, the Eighteenth Amendment to the U.S. Constitution, which prohibited the sale and consumption of alcohol, became law.

Overnight, the hospitality industry saw one of its biggest sources of revenue—liquor sales—vanish. The start of Prohibition sent many hotel and restaurant managers into a panic: How could they squeeze more profits out of other revenue sources? Prof Meek had an answer.

In the May 7, 1926 edition of *The Register of Ye Hosts,* Meek wrote an article describing the school's curriculum and justifying the need for a hotel school program to skeptics. "With the absence of old-time bar-room profits . . . the demands on [hotel managers'] energy and ability are enormous!"

Cornell students and other residents of Ithaca typified America's "civil war" over Prohibition. Ithaca had been a hotbed of temperance activity since the end of the Civil War. By the time the Eighteenth Amendment was passed and alcohol was banned, Ithaca reform groups had persuaded hundreds of members to take vows of sobriety. And at least eight towns in Tompkins County had passed "dry" laws.

Yet private citizens in and around Ithaca fought Prohibition by brewing, drinking and smuggling illegal liquor from Canada. Cornell students did their share of the drinking. "Every [fraternity] house on campus was making beer," says Edward J. Vinnicombe Jr. '33. "When you walked down the street, you could smell the fermentation."

Fraternities were where Cornellians most frequently flouted Prohibition. The fraternities "would get big fifty-gallon crocks to make beer," said Vinnicombe. "And when it stopped fermenting, they'd add more raisins or yeast to make the liquor content higher. Then they'd filter it; most had a contraption to put dry ice in them. They'd put a piece of dry ice in and cap it. That gave it head. Then they'd lay it down on its side to make sure it didn't explode overnight. If it didn't explode by morning, they'd drink it. We'd also send it over to some Chemistry grad students in Baker Hall to see if it had anything in it that'd kill you. And sometimes we made gin by buying juniper berries in the local pharmacies."

Cornell students could also find liquor off campus. Vinnicombe says there was an Italian restaurant on Cayuga Lake called Aresty Villa that served red wine, as well as several speakeasies in Elmira (he knew of none in Ithaca). "They were typical speakeasies," he says. "You rapped on the door and someone looked through a peephole, and if he thought you looked okay, he let you in. But we weren't drunks. We did it for parties. The word I would use is to describe it is 'dignified.'"

Tompkins County authorities did their best to stop bootleggers. They netted "30 stills, thousands of bottles, and cases of beer," in a raid on June 6, 1922, according to the *Ithaca Journal-News*. At last, on December 5, 1933, the Eighteenth Amendment was repealed. Most leaders in the hospitality industry breathed a sigh of relief.

June 1922 to contribute $7,000 to $10,000 a year to the program. A year later, no money had arrived and AHA counsel L.S. Hawkins was questioning the group's legal obligation to pay. Deans Mann and Betten eventually arranged an August meeting between AHA President Frank Dudley and Cornell President Livingston Farrand, whereupon Dudley reaffirmed his support for the program "in the strongest language" and "personally guaranteed" the expenses for the coming fiscal year.

The College of Agriculture was tuition-free to all New York residents. But AHA money was uncertain, the State Legislature would not pay Hotel expenses, and bills had to be met. The university trustees imposed a $200 tuition charge for Hotel students in the fall of 1923 in an effort to slow the program's losses. Negotiations with the AHA continued, and in January 1924 Farrand and Dudley signed a memorandum of understanding. Cornell would assume the program's administrative and overhead costs, and the College of Agriculture would not charge for teaching Hotel students in existing classes. The AHA would pay for additional teachers, equipment, and other direct expenses.

The association's bill for 1923–24 came to $20,050. But by the summer of 1924, it had paid nothing. The root of the problem was a struggle for control of the AHA. Some members, including Frank Dudley and John Howie, believed that promoting hotel education was of paramount importance. But another group of hotelmen led by E.M. Statler wanted the AHA to deflect its energy and funds into efforts to repeal Prohibition laws. Dudley was reelected AHA president in 1924, and he saw that the association paid its bill to Cornell in July. That act effectively ended Dudley's tenure at the AHA, because it infuriated Statler.

By 1920 Statler was the most powerful man in the hotel industry. Meek had solicited his support from the beginning, but this notoriously blunt man was initially hostile to Cornell. In November 1922, for example, Statler and John Howie attended a fundraising luncheon for the AHA educational campaign to fund the Cornell program. According to Howie, Statler said he would not support the program until he had answers to three questions:

"What can a student of the Hotel Management course at Cornell University get *now* that he could not get before this [program] was inaugurated?

"If Cornell University has all the needed mechanism for teaching the hotel business, then *why* come to hotelmen seeking financial assistance when I as a taxpayer am entitled to as much aid from a state institution of higher learning as any other taxpayer. If we are to do this, why not request a fund of two millions of dollars to educate men for the legal profession?" And finally, "What knowledge does an employee of a hotel like [Statler's] Pennsylvania gain at a vocational school that he or she can not gain at the hotel?"

In time, Statler would be convinced that the Hotel program was worthwhile. But in May 1923 he refused to place Cornell students in summer jobs at the Hotel Pennsylvania. And when the AHA made its first payment to Cornell in 1924, Statler and the manager of the Buffalo Statler, Elmore C. ("Morey") Green, temporarily withdrew their support from the association.

Politicians in Albany were equally unfriendly. After several petitions to the State Legislature, Betten and Mann were convinced that no money would ever come to the Hotel program from New York State officials. They saw an endowment as the only way for the program to become stable. Time proved them correct.

Meanwhile, the 1924 payment had driven the AHA deeply into debt. At its 1925 meeting, Dudley was ousted in favor of Thomas D. Green, an ally of Statler's who was manager of the Hotel Woodward in New York City. Green's campaign pledge was to cut expenses and wipe out the debt, which seemed ominous to Cornell. But after several tense months, Betten and Meek were reassured that the program could develop adequate sources of funds with or without formal support from the AHA. Their confidence was based on the program's many informal and positive ties to industry leaders. Also, their first crop of graduates had quickly been placed in management positions. In a letter to President Farrand, Meek said that "endorsement and financial support seem to be coming from men who have had personal contact with the course or our students."

Meek knew that gaining Statler's support would unlock a huge source of funds, both from Statler and from the many hotelmen who followed his lead. So Meek made a study of the man. "Statler was a very able person, a profound person, but not a communicative person," he said. "He was a poker player in everything he did. I think there are few people, indeed, who could read Mr. Statler's mind and know what was in it. I have to deduce. I think that he was interested in [Frank] Dudley's [idea for a] research program.

"I was in [John Howie's Touraine hotel] when Statler and I started to make a tour. We went into a bedroom. Statler went into the bathroom and turned on the tap and took out a stopwatch. He measured the time that it took to fill the tub. He pulled out the plug and started his stopwatch again and timed the time it took the tub to empty. He shook his head. He said, 'Much too slow. You put three-quarter-inch pipe in that drain when it should have been an inch. People aren't going to stand for this.' Well, this wasn't very pleasant for Howie, but it illustrates . . . the kind of research that Statler envisioned."

Perhaps it was the victory of Statler's forces in the 1925 AHA election. Or perhaps Cornell's emergence as a center for new ideas in hotel management finally got his attention. But whatever the reason, Statler's opinion of Cornell seemed to soften a bit in 1925. After an AHA Executive Committee meeting, Statler executive Morey Green wrote to Meek that it was his "pleasure" to "do anything I can for Cornell." Attorneys at the meeting told the group that the AHA had no legal authority to bind itself in a financial agreement with the university, so the group passed a resolution to raise money for the program by voluntary individual subscription.

Morey Green became chairnan of a Special Cornell Fund and began soliciting members for donations that would raise $53,000 and wipe out the "blot of this indebtedness" on the AHA. Statler pledged $4,200, and seven other leaders pledged at least $3,000 apiece. Green worked for a solid year on the campaign and eventually met the association's obligations. When a payment arrived in July 1926, Betten wrote to Green: "This is the first time we have been square in the account, and I certainly appreciate your own good work with respect to it."

The AHA's contract with Cornell was set to expire in July 1927, and it would not be renewed. In 1926, the Hotel program's tuition had increased to $300, but this alone would not make ends meet. More help was needed, and more promises were promptly made. AHA President Thomas Green, who had personally guaranteed the final payment to Betten in July 1926, called a meeting of the Executive Council of the New York City Hotel Association to seek $20,000 a year in pledges to

Cornell. He secured a total of $14,400 a year for the next five years, including $2,500 a year from Statler. But in 1927, he admitted to Meek that the $20,000 goal would not be achieved.

By this time, Meek and Betten had a realistic view of the fundraising prowess of their friends in the industry. They resolved to go about building their endowment themselves. They soon received another promise from Statler that would determine the future of the school.

### The First Hotel Ezra Cornell

Meek was not the only Hotel person with a flair for fundraising. Hotel students were just as ingenious when trying to meet their own expenses. Some students worked for their room and board by doing domestic chores or child care. Others worked for their meals as waiters, cooks, or stewards for fraternities or sororities. Hotel students were prominent in a student-owned corporation that distributed the *New York Times* and did laundry, catering, and part-time jobs. Experienced students often worked the night shift in Ithaca hotels.

Hotel students of the 1920s planned and schemed with the energy only college students seem to possess. "We intended to conquer the world, specifically the hotel world," wrote John Courtney '25. "We intended to organize corporations, to open new hotels, to really grab the hotel business by the tail and subdue it."

Such conversations often took place around a coffee urn, and the students found theirs in the experimental kitchens of Home Economics Hall. After the course taught by food science professor Jessie Boys and her assistant, Anna Driscoll, students would take a coffee and conversation break. The group became known as "The Coffee Hounds." That informal group soon became two formal student organizations — Ye Hosts, an honor society open to upperclassmen by invitation only, and the Cornell Hotel Association, open to any student.

In the fall of 1925, a Coffee Hounds discussion about the recent opening of a new hotel turned into something else entirely when Mrs. Boys proposed that the students operate one of the campus dormitories as a hotel for a day. "At that time, hotels were opening about every second week somewhere in the eastern part of the United States and Canada, and everybody was trying to outdo everybody else in larger and better openings,"

Formal invitation to the first Hotel Ezra Cornell and the dining room in Risley Hall, home of the opening banquet of the first and second Hotel Ezra Cornell, student-run "hotel for a day," in 1926 and 1927.

Board of Directors of an early Hotel Ezra Cornell (HEC), meeting in 1929 in the recently opened Willard Straight Hall. *See Sources for names.*

recalls H. Alexander MacLennan '26. "The idea was accepted immediately [and] the committee worked out some beautiful plans without giving too much thought as to how feasible they were."

The students secured the date of May 7, 1926 from a university committee on student affairs. "Being more enthusiastic than rational, Walt Bovard and I asked for permission to call on the president," writes MacLennan, "and that was a meeting indeed. . . certainly our plans were extensive and far beyond our capabilities, but we assured [President Farrand] at the same time that we would have the backing of the hotel industry." Sayles

adds that they also brought a delicious cake to the meeting to assure a friendly conversation. Farrand said that if the students could persuade one of the New York hotels to donate one of the most expensive items—an orchestra—they could go ahead. "I think the president felt that this was his best way out," writes MacLennan. Farrand thanked them for the cake and wished them well, expecting to hear no more of it.

MacLennan, using his summer job connections, approached the manager of the Roosevelt Hotel and asked for Ben Bernie and His Orchestra, one of the country's hottest bands. Charmed by MacLennan's presumption, Bernie and the manager agreed to play for free. Farrand was "dumbfounded" by the students' success, but he kept his word and gave the plan his blessing.

After an unsuccessful attempt to book the event into the brand new Willard Straight Hall, the students succeeded in booking Risley Hall for the evening. Risley was a women's dorm, so the students agreed to appoint John L. Slack '26 as their security officer to keep the upper floors inviolate. Financial backing for the event came from the students, who sold themselves shares of stock.

Three days before the event, with all the tickets sold and the food ordered, tragedy struck. "Ben Bernie advised me that the union would not permit him to carry out his agreement," says MacLennan. "We still had to have an orchestra, and that without cost. . . Walter Bovard '26 and I borrowed Professor Meek's new Buick sedan and drove it to Rochester. We walked up and down the main street, and what we intended to do there, heaven only knows." After a while, they screwed up their courage and walked into the Sagamore Hotel. They were "absolute strangers" to the manager, a genial man named Harry Somerville. "We told him our problem, and he did not hesitate. He not only gave us the services of the Art Taylor orchestra, he paid all their expenses."

After that close call, the event unfolded on a beautiful spring day that turned into a warm Ithaca evening. Chef Robert W. Boggs *26 opened the kitchens to the 600 invited guests that afternoon. Front office manager Fred L. Miner '26 and John H. Kahler *26, director of decora-

*Above:* Willard Straight Hall, student union opened in 1925, soon became home to Hotel Ezra Cornell.

*Below left:* Carrie Meyer '31, cigarette girl at a late 1920s HEC, and later head of housekeeping at the 1930 HEC.

*Below right:* Ralph Munns '27, a varsity wrestler and football player, looks every bit the Pinkerton "house dick" as head of security for the first HEC.

Industry leader E. M. Statler promised his support of the Hotel program at Cornell in 1927.

tions, transformed the Risley drawing rooms into an office, lobby, music room, reading room, and lounge, decorated with Jacobean furniture and rare Russian antiques from the collection of Andrew D. White. Guests packed the Risley dining room in two seatings, then retired to a 5,000-square-foot outdoor dance floor to enjoy the orchestra.

MacLennan and Bovard, general manager of the hotel, watched in amazement as the evening rolled on without a hitch. Virtually all of the 165 students in the program were at work in Risley that evening. They were making a powerful impression on some of the nation's top hotel operators, most of whom had never seen the program before. Thus began what came to be known as "the world's only hotel for a day," with the shorthand appellation HEC. Later, the young staff learned they had netted a profit of $5.62. (And on June 1, the Art Taylor orchestra cut its first record on the Brunswick label.)

## Ellsworth Comes to Ezra

Ellsworth Statler did not attend the event. His personal secretary, Alice M. Seidler, expressed his regrets to Meek and added a significant consolation: "Mr. Statler did want you to be assured that he was working with other hotel men to provide better things for the Cornell hotel boys."

Meek relayed the quote in a letter to Betten and added his thoughts: "A statement of this kind is interesting. He

and his group have been the last of the influential men to be won over to our present work. . . In view of little straws of this kind, I think, we can look forward to more favorable winds."

Plans for the second annual banquet were well under way when Statler wrote to Meek on March 22, 1927. "I cannot say positively about May 6 but I am keeping your letter before me and will get direct word to you nearer the date of the opening of the 'Ezra Cornell' for I should like very much to accept the invitation of the students."

According to biographer Floyd Miller, Statler was uneasy at the prospect of a spring weekend in Ithaca. He had several good reasons to be wary. First, he was a man of keen intellect who had no formal education. No university had played a role in his success, so why should he bother with one now? Second, Statler had a reputation in the industry as a coarse workaholic. He was known for wearing shabby suits, using obscene language, and generally telling his colleagues exactly what he thought of them. Spending a weekend with the other industry top brass, many of whom had had their ears singed by Statler, may not have seemed like a pleasant pastime.

In 1927, at age 63, Statler was the acknowledged king of the hotel industry—but his personal life and health were in terrible shape. His first wife had died two years earlier. He had a great deal of money but little time for their four adopted children. Now, as idly rich adults, the children were a constant source of frustration to the hard-driving tycoon. In truth, Statler had never been a happy person. He had endured extreme poverty as a child and extreme pain as an adult.

At the age of 40, Statler had been disabled for life when an exploding coffee urn scalded his chest, groin, and legs with fifty gallons of boiling water. For weeks, Statler lived with the pain of a severe burn over most of his body. After receiving thirty-one skin grafts, he managed his business for a year while confined to a wheelchair.

Hotels were the sole arena where Statler could exercise power and get a measure of comfort and satisfaction, so he worked ceaselessly. He became famous for his relentless spirit of innovation, and for his single-minded devotion to customer service. "Life is service," Statler once wrote in his company's newsletter. "The one who progresses is the one who gives his fellow men a little more—a little better service."

In April 1927, Statler married Alice Seidler. Seidler had been his personal secretary and friend since 1918, so she may not have been surprised when the groom forgot to bring a wedding ring to the ceremony. Nor did she express disappointment when their honeymoon was spent at the hotel convention in Atlantic City. After all, the hotel business was her life, too.

The newly married Statler said he looked forward to a life of sailing, travel, and less work. He may have been in an expansive mood when Leon D. Rothschild *09, owner of a department store in Ithaca and a close friend of Statler's for thirty years, phoned him with an invitation to a weekend of golf and an evening at the Hotel Ezra Cornell. Statler knew that Meek was stalking his fortune; he still had mixed feelings about an Ivy League college sponsoring courses in hotel management, and he may have suspected—correctly—that Rothschild was lobbying for Cornell. According to a fictionalized exchange in Miller's biography, Statler said, "All right, Leon, I'll come. But I'm not happy about it."

When Statler disembarked from the train in Ithaca, he was met by Rothschild and a contingent from the Hotel program. A game of golf was out of the question; the great man was expected to visit the program and observe all of its operations. Soon Statler was listening to Frank Randolph give a forty-minute lecture on the problems of heating a hotel with a coal-fired boiler. Randolph's speech became more and more technical, and several times he referred to British Thermal Units (BTUS).

At the conclusion of the lecture, Randolph asked Statler if he had any remarks for the students. "Boys," Statler replied (according to Miller), "you're wasting your time here. You don't have to learn this stuff to be a hotel man. When I have an engineering problem I hire an engineer. I don't know about British Thermal Units, and there's no reason for you to, either. Go on home and get a job."

Alice Seidler Statler, widow of E. M. Statler and a staunch supporter of the Cornell program.

H. Victor Grohmann '28 as headwaiter at the 1927 HEC. He is credited with escorting E. M. Statler around campus so well he left the previously skeptical hotelman convinced the Cornell Hotel program deserved his future support.

According to Sayles, Randolph responded to Statler's speech as follows: "Mr. Statler, what we've really been talking about is money, and in significant amounts, as you are aware. BTUS are basically the amount of energy that is in the coal you buy. Different coals have different BTU contents per weight. The only way to make a sound economic judgment is to know the BTU content. In the same units the efficiency of a boiler is measured— [and] if the heat content of oil, electricity, or gas is known, they can be compared one with the others. We do want our graduates to be able to make good economic decisions, and so that's why we teach them about BTUS."

"Mr. Statler assumed a thoughtful air. 'Maybe you have something. BTUS, huh?' Then he put on his old hat and left, along with the other bemused hotelmen."

Statler spent the weekend crisscrossing the campus in the company of a student guide, H. Victor Grohmann '28, thoroughly checking out the Cornell hotel operation. On the evening of May 6, he took his place at the head table of Risley Hall before the invited guests of the second Hotel Ezra Cornell.

Many legends have grown up around the actual events of that evening. Dean Meek remembered that the vegetable course was saved, and Statler's mind perhaps made up, by the quick thinking of chef Stephen W. Allio Jr. '29, whose father was chef at Statler's Hotel Pennsylvania. (In the book *The Best Ever: Memories of Hotel Ezra Cornell,* Allio is listed as chef for the HEC of 1928–29 and is not listed for the 1927–28 event. And in his account of the first HEC, written in 1950, MacLennan relates a similar story about salad dressing involving Chef Robert W. Boggs *26 and Lucius Boomer, director of the Waldorf-Astoria. Although memories recalled decades after the fact may be imprecise, Meek's story bears repeating.)

"The menu had asparagus with hollandaise sauce, but there were long delays and the sauce broke," recalled Meek. "Steve had to work up something else, so he found a recipe on a Wesson oil can which looked promising and doctored it up a little bit. Statler looked at it [on his asparagus] and said, 'This isn't hollandaise sauce!' and I said, 'Oh?' and he said, 'What is it?' and I said 'I don't know.' He said, 'Why don't you know?' I said, 'I don't know anything about it, the students are doing this.' 'The students are doing this?!' and of course I had been telling him this all along but he wouldn't believe it and he still didn't believe it.

"At the end of the evening he said, 'You say the students did this meal?' I said, 'yes.' 'Well, I want to talk to these students! Take me out to the students!' So I took him out to the kitchen and he pulled out his notebook and said, 'What was that sauce you served on the asparagus?' and Steve invented some name. 'How did you make it—it turned out all right?' and of course Steve was embarrassed and couldn't remember what he did but he did the best he could. Statler said, 'Well, I'm going to tell this to my chef,' and walked away. He got about five or six steps away and he turned to me and said, 'What did you say that boy's name was?' I said 'Allio. Stephen Allio. His father is at the Pennsylvania.' He said 'Oh yes,' so he turned around and went back and talked more with the kid.

"This is a tremendously significant thing as far as Statler is concerned, because in the morning he had been criticizing this whole project. Statler was by and large the best-informed hotel man of his time, all times if you want, but he didn't hesitate to take an idea from a 17- or 18-year-old kid. If it was a good idea, he was going to use it."

Statler went back to the head table with the dean of women and the president of Cornell "and all these high academic personalities," said Meek. "I think he was very much ill at ease because his education was very little and he was not the kind of hotel man who frequently mixed with his guests. So they asked him to speak and my recollection of it is that he didn't even say 'Mr. Toastmaster, Mr. President, and Dean of Women.' He

just got up and [said], 'Uhuh, uhuh, uhuh—Meek can have anything he wants!' and sat down."

Other accounts of the speech have Statler saying, "I'm converted. Meek can have any damn thing he wants." But all accounts agree that the speech was no longer than that.

Eleven months later, Ellsworth Statler died of pneumonia. His will left stock valued at about $100,000 to endow the Statler Foundation, for the purpose of "research work for the benefit of the hotel industry." About $8 million in cash and stock went to relatives. The rest—an amount that was never disclosed—went to the former Alice Seidler, who at 45 also became chairman of the board of Hotels Statler, Inc. In 1928, few if any other American women held such a powerful position. Until her death in 1969, she was also the Hotel school's most important benefactor.

It took years before the Statler Foundation began releasing money to the Cornell program. Even after the Statler money began to flow into the coffers, the Great Depression and World War II created financial and other hardships for Prof Meek and his students. But the 1927 Hotel Ezra Cornell remains a crucial turning point in the history of hotel education. On that evening, the young field's toughest critic was converted and the finances of the Cornell program were essentially assured.

# The Fulfillment of a Promise

**T**HE FIRST NOTABLE EVENT in the history of Hotel Ezra Cornell was E. M. Statler's conversion, but it was not the last. Events at those annual dinners often reflected the year's major themes. At the 1929 HEC, for example, University President Livingston Farrand spoke for many when he said, "The Hotel course at Cornell is now regarded as the fulfillment of a promise, and no longer a doubtful experiment."

Three years later, near the bottom of the Great Depression, the mood was different, the gathering smaller and more serious. Frank McKowne, the president of Hotels Statler, Inc. and the most important benefactor of the newly designated Department of Hotel Administration, brought a check for $12,000 and a reassuring message to the students: "Do not, because of economic conditions, turn back from the hotel industry. We need you and will absorb you as fast as we can."

Students get pointers on the hospitality industry during a study visit to the liner *Ile de France* in New York in 1938.

A year later, almost one out of four American workers was unemployed. The Hotel program was running a persistent deficit, Cornell's stock investments had lost almost half of their value since 1929, and many qualified students were unable to pay their bills. In March, millions gathered around their radios to hear a new U.S. president respond to the crisis. The Hotel department's students and alumni might have felt a special connection to the speaker, because Franklin D. Roosevelt had visited them in 1930 when he was governor of New York. He was even an honorary member of the student honor society, Ye Hosts.

The 1933 HEC "was not the extravaganza it had become in recent years," according to William P. Gorman '33, who served as its managing director. It had only 125 guests, most of whom were local hotelmen, alumni, and family. The star attraction was a seventy-pound scale model of McGraw Tower done in cake and icing. But the next HEC sold out, according to managing director Hubert E. Westfall '34. It was possible to coax big-city hotel executives to a weekend party in Ithaca, even during the Depression, because many leaders of the hospitality industry managed to endure. As long as salesmen still traveled and families still relaxed, businesses that served their needs could survive.

On May 8, 1937, dinner guests at HEC honored a familiar face. When he rose to acknowledge their standing ovation, H. B. Meek was only 44 years of age. But fifteen years at the head of the Hotel program had made him a well-respected man in the industry and a leading authority on hotel education. Meek did consider occasional invitations to return to the business world; only one year before, with the program's funding running dry, he had seriously considered leaving Cornell for the large restaurant firm that had almost hired him in 1922. But now he was fully committed to the Hotel department, and the long period of debt and uncertainty was over. He and his family would celebrate by taking a world tour of fine hotels, some of which were managed by his former students.

The next four HECs were increasingly elaborate. In 1938, students greeted some industry leaders in their hometowns and escorted them to Ithaca in specially-decorated rail cars. In 1939, managing director C. Oscar Strand '39 unveiled "the world's largest napkin," a banner made of 450 hotel napkins contributed by friends from every state and many foreign countries. In 1940, the weekend included the first HEC golf tournament and an appearance by "Stevie," a "robotic page boy" on loan from the Hotel Stevens in Chicago. In 1941, managing director Richard E. Holtzman '41 and Kenneth N. Jolly '41 flew to Cuba and secured a roomful of Pan-American decorations, along with a Cuban delegate.

A few months after the Pan-American HEC, the Statler Foundation announced that it would pay for a permanent building for the thriving department. American

Hotel Association president Bruce E. Anderson exulted at the announcement, calling it "one of the most important milestones in hotel history." But the foundation's promise was deferred by the onset of war.

In 1942, nearly 40 percent of the Hotel senior class left before graduation to join the armed services. The Hotel Ezra Cornells of those years were the smallest on record, and Statler Hall would not open until 1950. The Hotel department made slow progress during the Depression and war years, like a small boat sailing into the wind.

Anthony ("Bunny") Fertitta '39 demonstrates how to carry bags, when Hotel students take over jobs at the Hotel New Yorker in the 1930s.

## How the Industry Endured

Hotels of the late 1920s were often financed on the assumption that their rooms would rent for $5 a night and that the hotel would have 65 to 80 percent occupancy, according to Hotel faculty member Helen Recknagel. By 1932, the average hotel occupancy rate had fallen to about 45 percent. "You could walk into a hotel after 8 p.m., put two dollars down on the counter, and get a room almost anywhere. The room clerks had been told to fill rooms as best they could," said one business traveler.

The great hotel building boom of the 1920s crashed hard in the 1930s. By 1933, more than eight in ten U.S. hotels had filed for temporary relief from their debtors, including the Waldorf-Astoria in New York and the Stevens in Chicago. But relatively few hotels actually closed their doors; instead, the 1930s saw a massive shift in hotel ownership to banks, insurance companies, and other mortgageholders.

The new owners often relied on holding companies to operate their properties. One such company, National Hotel Management, was organized in 1932 by Ralph Hitz and operated 6,000 hotel rooms a year later. When these companies needed to find capable managers, they often came to Cornell. In 1932, J. Leslie Kincaid's American Hotels Company had sixteen Cornell graduates on its staff, which accounted for about 10 percent of the department's alumni.

"The banks would be looking for someone who knew something about [hotel operations] and they would hear about Cornell, so they would write to us," said Meek. "So the misfortune of others was the opportunity for the Cornellian." Newly minted Cornell graduates were a bargain for the banks because they had been trained to do everything. They could plan menus, purchase supplies, fix plumbing, and even fix dinner if they needed to, and they often needed to.

Meek had another advantage in the relative health of his biggest patron, Hotels Statler. All Statler properties remained solvent during the Depression, thanks to the company's tight operating controls, relatively low mortgage costs, and shrewd founder. In the years before his death, Ellsworth Statler was already preparing for a downturn in the market. He cut back on construction after 1925 and began building up his savings, intending to buy new hotels when prices fell. When the crisis came, the company survived on the savings.

The hotel industry improved slightly in the last half of the 1930s. Prohibition was repealed on December 6, 1933, allowing bars and nightclubs to regain their traditional place as hotel profit centers. Yet median hotel occupancy languished. It was 66 percent in 1936 and 62 percent in 1939, according to surveys by the industry's leading accounting firm, Horwath & Horwath. In 1939, the industry's total sales were 18 percent lower than they had been in 1929.

There were a few profitable niche markets in hospitality in the 1930s, and smart hotel operators found them. Low-cost package vacations to the Century of Progress Fair filled Chicago hotels to capacity in the summers of 1934–35. More daring vacationers took long-distance auto trips on newly built federal highways. Travelers on the tightest budgets stayed in tourist cabins and cooked their own meals. Those with a little more money chose a new option in lodging called the motor court, or motel. These travelers often ate good, reasonably priced food from the new chain restaurants like A & W Root Beer, White Castle, Marriott's Hot Shoppes, and Howard Johnson's.

The 1930s were a time for new ideas in the hotel and restaurant business. Businesses could survive only by placing tight controls on their inventory, standardizing procedures, and demanding peak productivity from their employees. Restaurant chains that mastered this formula were poised for explosive growth when the war ended, and that growth was often managed by Cornell graduates. By 1939, a number of Hotel alumni were managing restaurants.

As the decade wore on, bankers looked for buyers who would relieve them of their hotel stocks. Conrad Hilton began his hotel empire by buying out bank-held hotels and standardizing their operations, just as Statler had done three decades earlier. Hilton eventually employed many Cornell graduates, including his right-hand man,

Joseph P. Binns '28. Another eager stock buyer was Ernest Henderson, the founder of Sheraton Hotels. Henderson's expansion was made possible by many Cornell-trained employees, including Sheraton vice president Robert M. Brush '34.

Market research often thrives during an economic downturn, and a few hospitality firms supported Cornell's first efforts in hotel research in the 1930s. At mid-decade, for example, the Hotel department surveyed business travelers for a New York advertising agency. They found that the customer's strongest desires were for prompt, courteous service, a comfortable room, and good, wholesome food. Some things never change!

## Hard Times on the Hill

Cornell survived, but the hard times took a toll. By 1931, the market value of the university's endowment investments stood at 60 percent of their book value, and the endowed colleges were carrying a two-year operating deficit of more than $2 million. The state colleges were prohibited from operating at a deficit, so their budgets were reduced by more than 40 percent. Innovation, thrift, and hard work were the keys to survival on East Hill, just as they were in business.

In the struggle to survive, Prof Meek had several advantages over a typical academic department head. First, his department charged tuition. It was rare for students in a state college to pay tuition in those days. The Hotel program charged $400 a year because state legislators refused to give it any money. As a result, Meek was less concerned than many of his peers when the state's support decreased.

Meek also had no trouble finding qualified students who would pay to attend the Hotel program. Enrollment grew from 163 in September 1929 to 250 in 1937, and another 250 applicants had to be turned away. In a report that year to the AHA, Meek said that enrollment had reached the maximum current facilities would allow. Five years later, enrollment exceeded 300.

The Hotel program could also rely on a strong group of dedicated alumni and friends. In 1939, for example, Meek reported a gift of $10,000 from the estate of Thomas Bland, $12,500 from the F & M Schaeffer Brewing Company, and several "lesser scholarships" and bequests. Hotel professionals continued to serve as part-time instructors and unpaid lecturers, which saved on faculty salaries. Whenever he could, Meek used industry facilities and connections to keep his costs down.

The Hotel department's impressive record of placing graduates in good jobs meant that Meek never had to worry about student recruitment. But during the Depression, everyone was acutely concerned about the students' struggle to pay for room, board, and tuition. Fortunately, Hotelies of the 1930s had great entrepre-

neurial instincts. Edward Vinnicombe '33, steward of his fraternity house, got his father, who was still in the hotel business, to send food to his kitchen. Many fraternities and sororities realized the value of having a Hotel student with parents in the hotel industry. Vinnicombe says that in his first three days at Cornell he pledged his fraternity, was inducted, and made steward.

"That period was really tough on all the students," he said. "Six of my fraternity brothers' fathers committed suicide in 1929. But Cornell was unbelievably good to people. Meek let the students who couldn't afford it stay."

Many Hotel students washed dishes, waited tables in local restaurants, or made sandwiches and sold them in student dorms. Others, as Sayles wrote, "offered accounting services, mowed lawns, did house cleaning—anything to make a nickel and buy the next meal or to help with the rent."

During an alumni reunion in the 1950s, one Hotel alumnus watched a middle-aged man walk into "Pop's," a restaurant in Collegetown. "I came to pay off a loan," said the man. "It was $5 and here is ten, figuring the interest and so on." After the man had left, the alumnus asked Pop whether that kind of thing happened often. "Second time this month," the owner replied. "Times were tough then. I couldn't let people go hungry."

Charles Sayles was a young professor of Hotel engineering in those days. He remembers a $10 bill that was pinned to one of the Hotel program's bulletin boards. "Any student could borrow it for a short time by signing the accompanying card on the reverse side," he wrote. "If the money was not returned within three days, the card was turned over, exposing the delinquent's name. The device worked for a considerable length of time with only a few replacements required."

In 1931–32, the Hotel department had only five scholarships available for nearly 200 students, along with a small loan fund from the Cornell Society of Hotelmen and a $50 writing prize. By 1935 there were just nine scholarships, two loan funds, and two prizes. The need for assistance was so great that some of the more generous scholarships were divided. That spring, McKowne appealed to his peers that the benefit of helping a "hard-pressed boy trying to work his way through school is far greater than the net cost to the donor." By 1941 there were nineteen scholarships for some 300 students.

"Tuition was $400, an unattainable amount for some," writes Sayles. "It was distressing, indeed, to see a student crying because he didn't have it."

Virtually all of the Hotel students were working their way through school in the 1930s. Students raised on farms harvested produce and sold it to fraternities, sororities, or restaurants. Hotelies often catered parties, cooked for fraternities, or did the housekeeping and desk work at local hotels. Summer jobs were still part of the curriculum, and they also helped pay the bills.

In September 1932, Meek reported that the Hotel department had suffered a "relatively small loss by withdrawals from [juniors and seniors]. It was expected that lack of financial support would force a heavier shrinkage over the summer months than usual, but instead there was less. Apparently the greater ability of the Hotel student to get work in the summer, and the greater demand for his services at self-supporting activities such as waiting on table, has made it possible for him to cope with financial difficulties better than his fellow student at other colleges."

Directors of the 1942 HEC meet in the Hotel Seneca in Rochester in April 1942. *See Sources for names.*

### Struggling With Statler

Meek had another advantage most of his peers did not possess—the general promise of "anything he wants" made by Ellsworth Statler in 1927. Yet it took almost two decades for the promise to be fulfilled. First, Statler's will set up trust funds for each of his four adopted children, the income from which was earmarked for the Cornell Hotel program. This amounted to a check for $12,000 a year from 1928 to 1933, usually presented by Statler President McKowne at the Hotel Ezra Cornell. But the deepening Depression cut the next payment in half, and that was the last Cornell would see from that source.

On their 1938 study visit, students watch a manager check bellmen's gloves on the *Ile de France*.

The second, more significant provision of Statler's will was the eighth paragraph, which set aside 10,000 shares of the company's common stock to endow the Statler Foundation. His intent was to support "research work for the benefit of the hotel industry in the United States, not only in the construction and operation of hotels, but in the training and making more proficient of workers in hotels, for the benefit of the hotel industry, as a whole, to the advancement and improvement of which business I have devoted my life."

When Statler died in 1928, each share of his company's stock was worth about $10. McKowne, one of the will's three executors, soon made it clear that he intended to fulfill the promise his boss had made at the 1927 HEC. But three obstacles stood between Cornell and the money. The first was a probate dispute with the government that was resolved in 1932, when the university trustees won the right, on the basis of Cornell's nonprofit status, to have the value of the foundation stock deducted from the value of Statler's gross estate.

The second obstacle was the second executor, Alice Statler, who stepped in at the conclusion of the probate dispute. She charged that the eighth paragraph was void and that she was entitled to the foundation's stock, which had split and was now worth $335,000. McKowne and the third executor, Edward H. Letchworth of the Marine Trust Company of Buffalo, denied her claims. After two more years, the three parties reached an ami-

cable settlement and recast themselves as the trustees of the Statler Foundation. Alice Statler never discussed her reasons for contesting the will, and she remained one of the university's most important benefactors until her death in 1969.

At the 1934 HEC McKowne announced that all of the income from the foundation's 20,000 shares, now worth $2 million, would go to Cornell. But the Depression was a third obstacle, and the only way to remove it was to wait for it to end. For the next five years, Meek found himself in a familiar position. He had many promises of support, but the cash was slow to come.

"We all took cuts in pay," he said. "Mrs. Meek tells about the chance we had to buy a Chippendale extension-top table which she wanted very much. I told her I didn't think we had better do it because I didn't know how much longer we would be able to stick it out."

Deficits had been a near-permanent condition of the Hotel program in the 1920s, and they continued in the early 1930s. In several years the red ink came to about $20,000, or one-third of the program's income. While Agriculture college Dean Albert Mann tolerated the deficits, he was acutely aware that state legislators might object to them. In February 1930, he wrote to Vice Dean Cornelius Betten: "We are traveling on a most uncertain

June Miller '39, managing the candy shop in the Hotel New Yorker for a day when students took over operation of the hotel, tries to make a sale to Prof. H. B. Meek.

omen have majored in hospitality management since the founding of the program. However, they were not always treated as equals by their male counterparts. The reasons given were typical of attitudes toward women years ago: Hotel administration was said to be "a man's profession," while a proper major for women was home economics.

Prof Meek also opposed having women in the hospitality program. In interviews, he said that it was because the industry denied them opportunity. But the few women who did attend the Hotel program sometimes thought differently. About Meek, Dorothy Daly Johnson '26 said, "He had not wanted *any* women in the course and he gave all five of us a particularly hard time." When a housekeeper for the Hotel Vanderbilt failed to send in a report on Johnson's summer work assignment, Meek "never missed a chance to tell me that I was 'not in good standing' and, as far as he was concerned, no longer in the program."

Hilda Longyear Gifford '26 said later that "[the American] Hotel Association had told Professor Meek not to train any women." Longyear had transferred into the program. "Had I applied for admission direct from high school, my application would have been turned down," she told Charles Sayles. But Longyear played a key role in the first Hotel Ezra Cornell. At that time, the program did

not have proper banquet facilities to entertain industry VIPs. Longyear asked her boss, Anna Grace, director of Cornell's dining services, for the use of Risley Hall. Grace said yes; Longyear had saved the day.

Some early women alumni of the Hotel program found considerable success as hospitality executives, breaking new ground in an industry dominated by men. Hilda Longyear, for example, eventually donated more than $250,000 to the Statler Hall capital campaign with her husband, John P. Gifford '29. Mary Wright '45 managed hotels in Upstate New York and Massachusetts, worked in accounting for Horwath & Horwath and other firms, and taught hotel operations at several colleges.

Students around a table of desserts with one of the original instructors in the Hotel program, Prof. Jessie Boys, left.

Margaret McCaffrey Kappa '44 consulted for thirty-five hotels after a long career as director of housekeeping at the Greenbrier (*see pages 4 and 84*). But in 1940, she was a frightened first-year student from a third-generation hotel family. Before Kappa was allowed to enroll at Cornell, her mother talked to Prof Meek at a Hotel Show in Chicago. "He said not many women entered and that they either flunked, left, or got married," she remembers. At her mother's urging, however, Meek allowed her in.

"I had a really bad inferiority complex" upon arrival at Cornell, said Kappa. She overcame it with the help of professors like Thomas Silk and Charles Cladel, and with encouragement from her housemother, Gladys Barteau. "I know I never would have had the success I have enjoyed without my Cornell degree," she said.

As more women entered the program and excelled, the neglect and sexism of the early years gradually faded. In 1985, Elizabeth A. Harlow '85 became the first female managing director of HEC. "I never felt discriminated against," says Harlow, now a marketing director for a private club in Philadelphia. "I felt my treatment was pretty evenhanded. There might have been a word or two mentioned about how I was the first female managing director when I was at a speaking engagement, but that was it."

basis. It is not simply that we carry a perpetual overdraft, but that there is a constant uncertainty as to how the overdraft is to be liquidated."

"I think Dean Mann felt that we had sufficient backing so that in a pinch we could make it up," said Meek. "But

he did put himself out on a limb, to an extent, to help us out." He remembers that "it was especially difficult in 1932–33. That was touch and go." But a management style Meek called "rigorous economy" pulled them through. In September 1933, Meek reported to the AHA that "the deficit in its present form has now been completely liquidated." A year later, the Statler Foundation gave Meek the safety net he had always needed.

The Statler funds ensured the Hotel department's future. But they had a strange and unfortunate effect on John Howie, the Cornell program's earliest advocate. Howie was a bitter foe of Statler's in life, and his animosity continued after Statler's death. The bad feelings may have stemmed from a disagreement about alcohol. According to Meek, Howie "had a great devotion to the U.S. Constitution. When the Constitution was amended and Prohibition came in, he accepted it and espoused it." Howie used his considerable public speaking talents at temperance rallies, where he would get before audiences of 1,000 or more and, as Meek put it, "spread the American Eagle in great shape." This made Howie unpopular with many of his peers in the hotel and restaurant business. It was especially grating to Ellsworth Statler, who was spending a lot of time and money on efforts to repeal Prohibition. "This, plus the natural professional jealousy of the two men operating in Buffalo, is the reason for their parting of the ways," said Meek.

In August 1934, Howie wrote an indignant letter to Meek in response to Meek's public statement that the Hotel courses were made possible "through the financial assistance of the heirs and trustees of the late E. M. Statler." Howie reminded Meek that nine years before

Students take over the Hotel New Yorker for a day in the early 1930s. Sorting bedding, which the hotel laundered itself, are Edna Mullen SpHot '29–31, Frances Hicks '32, and Janet McGregor SpHot '30–31.

Since its beginning, the Hotel school has endured a steady stream of criticism from various Cornellians. In the 1920s, professors and students mocked the program for being part of the Home Economics school, which was traditionally for women. Charles Sayles related a typical wisecrack that Hotel students used to hear: "Boy, you're going to make some girl a good wife."

Critics also did not believe a "trade school" should be associated with Cornell. Ezra Cornell's founding philosophy behind the university, that Cornell was a place where a student could receive an education in any subject, was forgotten by those who liked to indulge in old-fashioned Ivy League snobbery.

When Hotel school students attended classes outside the program, they were often greeted with scorn. In one such class, the instructor asked all the Hotel students to stand up. When the five students rose, he told them they should consider dropping the course because he could not guarantee they would pass. The other students cheered.

In addition, the Hotel curriculum was felt by some to be too easy. They gave the courses fake names like Handshaking 1, Mashed Potatoes 2, Elementary Hamburgers, and Psychology of Tipping. The fact that the school had more than its fair share of athletes also helped promote the perception that it was easy.

Most Hotelies responded with an energy and good humor characteristic of the school. Hotel students were especially active as participants in campus parties, fraternities, and sororities, where their hospitality training was put to good use.

What finally silenced the critics—at least to a degree—was the Hotel school's reputation. As the years went by, it got harder to ridicule the world's top hotel management school.

that announcement, Statler was "moving heaven and earth to destroy" the Hotel program. He felt that Statler's wealth had allowed him to "horn in and grab all the credit," while such stalwarts as Frank Dudley, E. M. Tierney, and Howie himself went unrecognized.

Despite numerous efforts to placate him, Howie grew more and more embittered as the influence of Statler's money increased. Near the end of his life, he stopped communicating with Meek and began calling him an "ingrate" and a "mere academic pimp for the Statler crowd." There was never a reconciliation. Howie died in 1948, and his influence on hotel education was largely forgotten.

## The School Gets Stronger

The financial uncertainty of the early years had little effect on the program's progress within the university. In June 1931, Hotel Administration was organized as a department of the College of Home Economics, with Professor Meek as the department head. "This was merely a temporary status," Dean Mann wrote to Meek. "Undoubtedly we would be bringing to the council before long a recommendation that this work be given the status of the School of Hotel Administration." The "temporary status" lasted until 1954.

In 1934, the Hotel department moved into a suite of four offices in the brand-new Martha Van Rensselaer Hall. Finding classroom and lab space was a continuing problem, however, because so many of Meek's ideas quickly became popular courses. In the spring of 1928, for example, he announced that the program would offer short summer courses for hotel professionals in accounting, food preparation, and engineering. Despite the short notice, the program's first effort at executive education attracted 29 students from as far away as Florida and California. The next year, 100 professionals enrolled. By 1937, the program offered fourteen courses to 188 students from thirty-three states and Canada.

Also in 1928, Meek proposed a decrease in the number of required courses in the endowed colleges to make way for the increase in hotel-specific courses.

And on May 2, 1929, he outlined his goals for hotel research. They included an annual survey of hotel finances, an annual survey of traveler preferences, a study of payroll practices, a study of the effect of "tourist wayside lodging" (i.e., motels) on hotels, and an index of hotel rates. The first goal was soon achieved when Prof. John Courtney '25 published the first financial survey of the industry, *A Study of Fifty Hotels.*

Courtney was hired to assist Louis Toth in accounting instruction, along with Charles E. Cladel '29. All three men were former or current employees of the accounting firm Horwath & Horwath. In 1930, Courtney expanded the study to seventy-five hotels. In 1934 it was taken over by Horwath & Horwath and renamed the *Annual Report on* 100 *Hotels.*

Courtney was also known as "the grandfather of the [Hotel] program," according to Charles Sayles, because he was some years older than Meek. Sayles remembers him as "Uncle John," a serious but good-natured person who served as treasurer for many school organizations. Courtney was also known as "putt-putt," said Sayles, because of the sound he would make whenever he was puzzled.

Courtney is a beloved memory to many alumni because of his charming but absent-minded personality. In an incident that became legendary, he drove to a meeting in Syracuse, then forgot his car and rode back on the bus. When his wife asked him where the car

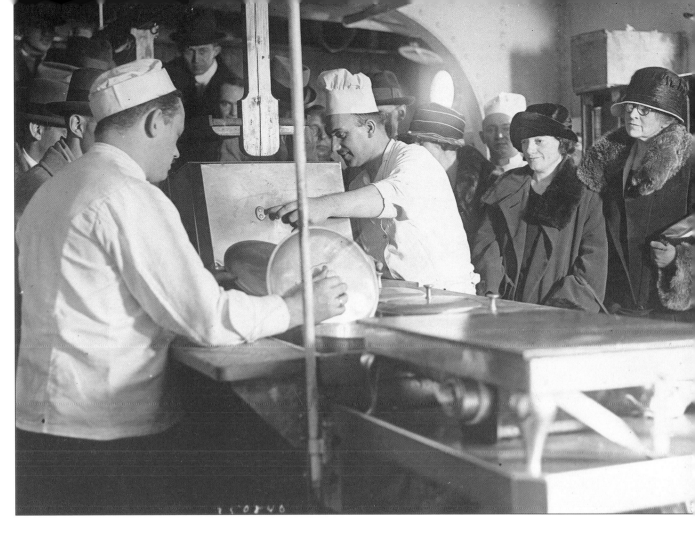

Men and women watch a kitchen operation. Lois Meek, who taught food preparation several years in the Hotel program, wife of Prof. H. B. Meek, is second from right. Place, time, and occasion unknown.

was, he remembered—so he went to the Greyhound station and, to retrieve his automobile, bought a round-trip bus ticket.

"One morning at a one hour lecture in a room with a platform across the front, [Courtney] strode back and forth while explaining some of the intricacies of hotel accounting—but these went unheeded by the class," writes James P. Duchscherer '36. "The problem was that one leg of his trousers was caught in his garter on one side. When he walked from left to right, this did not show. But when he went from right to left, the sight was comical to say the least. He remained oblivious to this sartorial mistake throughout his lecture, even though the entire class emitted muffled chuckles at regular intervals."

The Hotel school has produced many industry leaders. One reason is that the program has had leading faculty in their fields. Students of the late 1990s might not recognize names like Charles Sayles, Helen Recknagel, or John Courtney, but many students from earlier generations revere these professors.

**Charles I. Sayles** (1903-1991), a 1926 graduate of the Hotel school, grew up at the summer resort his father owned in the Adirondack mountains. Sayles maintained the property after he started teaching property management and electrical engineering at Cornell. These skills came in handy when he supervised the construction of the original Statler Hall. He served two terms as acting dean of the school, led the way in applying data processing to the hotel industry, and in 1989 wrote a memoir of the program, *From a Closet Under the Stairs,* which is cited throughout the early chapters of this book.

**Charles E. Cladel** (1906-1985) transferred from Columbia University to the fledgling hospitality program at Cornell and graduated in 1929. He joined the faculty as an instructor in 1933 and taught hotel accounting for forty years. During World War II, he taught all five accounting courses to military personnel—a seventy-hour course load. In 1953 he was made a full professor.

**John H. Sherry** (1902-1984) taught innkeeping law for forty years, starting in 1935. Sherry commuted from his law practice in New York City for all those years. He missed only one train during his commuting years; fortunately for him, a blizzard that day forced Cornell to close because of weather the first time ever. Sherry is remembered for his seminal text on hospitality law, *The Laws of Innkeepers.* (*See photo,*

Summer school students in an accounting class with Prof. John Courtney.

*page* 87.) Upon his retirement in 1975, his post was filled by his son, John E. H. Sherry, who revised and updated the law text.

**John Courtney** (1880-1957) graduated first in the first class in 1925. He worked at the accounting firm of Horwath & Horwath, taught accounting at Cornell, and was secretary-treasurer of the Cornell Society of Hotelmen from its founding until his death. He developed the hotel operation ratios that are models today, and wrote such standard texts as *Basic Accounting Principles* and *Normal Hotel Operations.* (*See page* 53.)

**Helen J. Recknagel** (1910-1992) was the first female professor in the Hotel school and taught there for thirty years. Born in Oklahoma of Cherokee ancestry, she was assigned to teach "business communications," a largely secretarial course. She soon turned it into the Hotel program's first course in sales and marketing. In 1960 Recknagel became the founding

editor of the *Cornell Hotel and Restaurant Administration Quarterly.* (*See page* 86.)

**Jeremiah J. Wanderstock** (1920-1972) a graduate of the Agriculture college in 1941, began his teaching career there. In 1953 he transferred to the Hotel school and became an authority on meat science, management, and menu planning. He was a faculty advisor to three university groups, secretary of the Ithaca Chapter of the Cornell Society of Hotelmen, and a founder of the fire department in neighboring Cayuga Heights.

**Louis Toth** (1893-1977), a Hungarian emigre, taught hotel accounting at Cornell for thirty-four years. He became a partner at Horwath & Horwath in 1926 after earning the highest possible score in the American Institute of Accounting exam. Two years before that, Toth had been teaching such courses as Interpreting Financial Statements and Hotel Accounting, also the title of a book he wrote, considered the definitive text on the subject. (*See page* 25.)

Duchscherer eventually got a job as Courtney's teaching assistant. "After leaving the lab one day, he telephoned me from his basement office and asked, 'did I leave my glasses up there?' I searched but could not find them, but since class was then over, I went downstairs where the good professor was still looking for his spectacles. Just then he turned to me and said. 'Oh, here they are,' and they were all right—right on top of his head!"

The growing enrollment in the Hotel program meant that some courses taught by Home Economics faculty were dominated by Hotel students. After Jessie A. Boys's introductory course in food preparation, students were required to take courses in quantity food preparation taught by Mrs. Meek and Irene Dahlberg. Courses in textiles were taught by Beulah Blackmore, who had spent an internship with the housekeeper of the Waldorf. Design was taught by Annette J. Warner, whom Meek described as "a character in the fullest sense of the word."

The list of part-time and visiting faculty had grown to impressive lengths by 1935. One of them was a young attorney named John H. Sherry, an expert in the burgeoning field of hotel law. Sherry traveled from New York to Ithaca once a week for forty-five years to teach Hotel courses. At the end of his career, he was recognized as a leader of that field and was much in demand—but he still rode the train to Ithaca once a

Hotel housekeeping leaders study at a Hotel summer session class in the 1930s.

week. Allan H. Treman *21, a prominent Ithaca attorney, was another lecturer in the program.

Other part-timers in 1935 included Henry A. Carey *12, who taught a course in insurance; Albert E. Koehl '28 of the Hotel New Yorker, who taught advertising; Daniel H. McCarriagher *13, operator of two Buffalo hotels; Ernest N. Smith of the American Automobile Association, who taught a course in tourism; Victor Grohmann '28, marketing executive, Statler's erstwhile guide in 1927; and Joseph D. Vehling, food editor of the *Hotel Bulletin*.

It was inevitable that many faculty would be alumni in those early years, given Cornell's low budget and the lack of facilities for hotel education at other schools. But the alumni involvement was also evidence of the intense loyalty felt for the school, and the close-knit relationship alumni had with each other.

Alumni at a meeting of the Cornell Society of Hotelmen in New York City at the Commodore in October 1938.

Hotel alumni stuck together partly because they were forced to find their own opportunities. When success came to them, they often felt an intense gratitude to Cornell. Needham, for example, cofounded an advertising firm with Grohmann that handled many hotel accounts. He also taught a public relations course in the Hotel department, did free publicity work for Meek and Hotel Ezra Cornell, and was an early leader of the school's alumni organization. Needham died in 1939, a relatively young man. While on his deathbed, he asked that he be authorized to establish a "Land-of-the-Hereafter" chapter of the Hotelmen. He joked that his would eventually become the largest and most active chapter, but that he would not be able to send back reports of its activities.

The Cornell Society of Hotelmen (CSH) was organized in May 1928, with John M. Crandall '25 as president and Professor Courtney as secretary-treasurer. Its influence increased along with the power and influence of the school and its alumni, so that it soon became far more than a social organization. Beginning in the 1930s, the CSH began sponsoring smokers, later receptions, at the annual hotel shows in New York and Chicago. These soon became major industry gatherings that attracted hundreds of guests each year, and they were still going strong in the 1990s.

From the beginning, the CSH helped graduates find jobs. It has also been a major source of loans and schol-

## The Cornell Society of Hotelmen

The bond felt by early alumni grew partly out of adversity, according to a reminiscence published in 1935 by a charter graduate, W. R. Needham '25. "We found that [in the job market], mention of Cornell hurt rather than benefited us," he wrote. The earliest graduates "had no alumni to point to as successes," and the prevailing attitude of employers went as follows: "Why did you fellows waste four years and your old man's money studying the hotel business at Cornell when you could have been down here working in this hotel and getting paid at the same time?"

arships, and it publishes a directory and a quarterly *Bulletin*. Local chapters began forming as soon as the group was organized. By 1935, there were chapters in New York City, Ithaca, Philadelphia, Cleveland, Chicago, and Pittsburgh. By 1941, new chapters had been added in San Francisco, Minneapolis, New England, Washington, D.C., and Western New York. As the school approached its seventy-fifth anniversary in 1997, forty-seven chapters of the CSH were in operation in Asia, Africa, Europe, and North and South America.

Alumni influence is probably the main reason for the Hotel program's impressive record of placing its graduates in good jobs. In 1932, for example, all nineteen graduates found positions within a week of graduation, despite the devastated job market. In June 1934, only one of 231 living graduates was reported out of work.

In 1937, very few Hotel alumni had reached the age of 40. Yet a survey taken that year showed that more than one-third of the program's living graduates were in upper-level management positions. Twelve alumni owned or leased their own hotels or restaurants, 60 managed hotels or clubs, 33 were assistant managers, 19 were in sales promotion, 28 in hotel accounting, 28 in room or front-office positions, 42 in hotel or restaurant food departments, and 15 in related fields such as hotel advertising or education. Only 18 were unemployed or unaccounted for. And from the beginning, the Hotel

## NEEDHAM & GROHMANN

No advertising firm that specializes in the hospitality industry is more respected than the oldest agency in the business, Needham & Grohmann. It was founded by two Hotel graduates, H. Victor Grohmann '28 and William R. Needham '25.

Hotel advertising was in its infancy in the early twentieth century. "You had a sketch of the hotel, some copy that said 'Fireproof' and '600 Rooms,' and that was about it," says longtime associate Howard A. Heinsius '50, who bought Needham & Grohmann in 1981.

Soon after graduating from Cornell, Needham and Grohmann saw that the industry needed a more professional attitude toward advertising and promotion. In 1931, the firm opened in a sub-sublet office with one secretary and one artist. It also had one client, The Croydon Hotel, which soon prospered on the strength of the firm's imaginative advertising and promotion. Among the innovations was an elevator for guests with dogs.

Needham & Grohmann grew steadily through the Depression, thanks in part to the firm's Cornell connections. "As Mr. Needham and I had both graduated from the School of Hotel Administration at Cornell University and had worked in numerous hotels, we soon acquired other accounts in the field," Grohmann wrote in 1970. Hal Needham died unexpectedly in June 1939, but the firm's growth continued.

In 1939, Needham & Grohmann acquired the Colonial Williamsburg and Rockefeller Center accounts. Eventually, it would count the Rockefeller family's Rockresorts chain as its client. During World War II, it conducted several award-winning advertising campaigns for national defense. At one time, Hilton Hotels used Needham & Grohmann exclusively.

"They changed advertising for the hospitality industry," says Heinsius. "What they really did was make it more sophisticated."

school's presence was global. Alumni in the 1930s were working in Canada, Bermuda, Mexico, Japan, South Africa, and Yugoslavia.

As the decade ended, Hotel alumni began going overseas for a different reason. In October 1941, Meek reported that a capacity group of 300 students had enrolled in the department, despite heavy on-campus recruiting by the Army and Navy. So many of the 1941 students were children of hotel families that "a roll-call of the Cornell student body sounds like a list from the offices of the American Hotel Association." But the times were already changing. Each male Hotel student was required to take two years of course work in Military Science and Tactics.

Hospitality industry leaders meet with faculty and the head of Cornell's Hotel program in 1934, in Willard Straight Hall on campus.

Those eligible were encouraged to take two more years and earn commissions as reserve officers. Sixty-five graduates were serving in the armed services.

As the campus and nation prepared for war, Meek was preoccupied with a happier development. The Statler Foundation stock had finally begun paying dividends. Meek remembers that early in 1941 Frank McKowne asked him what he would do with $40,000. "Our most critical need is some kind of building," Meek replied, "because we are squatters and tenants at will. Any time there might be a change in university administration, we would be out on our ear . . . if you would start a building fund and give us $40,000, perhaps I could get someone else to contribute and make our building."

As the year went by, the Statler Foundation and Cornell worked on a plan to finance the building. They agreed that all of the foundation's income less expenses would go to the Hotel department's building fund. Cornell would save the money until both the trustees and Statler agreed that the time was right to build. Further, the Statler Foundation agreed that all of its income would go to Cornell until the building costs were covered; the university would pay the extra costs up front, and Statler would pay them back as its income permitted. The agreement was signed on December 4, 1941. "I announced it to the class [155] on December 5," said Meek, "and everybody was very happy."

On the morning of December 7, Meek noticed that the Navy's chief of staff had told the *New York Times* that the U.S. was ready for anything. Later that day, he said, "I was driving along with the radio on, listening to the Boston Symphony. The announcer interrupted it to say that Japan had attacked Pearl Harbor, and cafluey! went our building plans. They were not resumed until 1945."

## The War Years

All at once, the Depression ended and the war began. Cornell became an armed camp devoted to various forms of Navy training, and the campus community struggled to switch to the new rules. One alumnus recalls his return to Ithaca after being inducted: "The Navy issued uniforms, but there were no tailors around to make the alterations. On the first Sunday we were there and granted liberty, Professor and Mrs. Meek invited us to dinner at their house. The invitation contained a post-script—'bring any clothing that needs altering. I will have the sewing machine set up and ready.' What a life saver! Frank W. Carney '47, Richard N. Boland '49, Henry F. Dylla '47, and Robert D. Flickinger '47 came back to the barracks with perfectly altered uniforms, thanks to Mrs. Meek."

"It was a sad time," writes Sayles, "a time for introspection and even tears. Classrooms gradually emptied. Those students remaining found no stomach for serious study, each concerned with his or her own position. Meek was faced with a reduction in tuition income as well as a surplus of instructors."

The number of Hotel students and graduates dropped abruptly during the war years. In 1944, there were virtually no graduates out of a class of seventy-four. Many students in the wartime classes returned to graduate later, and were counted with their original class. But for the duration, the rule was austerity, rationing, and nighttime blackouts. Civilians often chafed under the strict military rules. Once a group of students in uniform reported to a two-and-a-half hour laboratory soaking wet from a sudden downpour. The instructor, in the privacy of the lab, suggested that everyone take off his pants and hang them on the radiators. The Navy officials on campus were "fit to be tied," writes Sayles, but they could not punish the instructor because he was a civilian.

*Above:* Guests at the banquet of the 1935 HEC fill the Memorial Room of Willard Straight Hall, the university's student union.

*Left:* Alumni at a Cornell smoker in 1938 in New York City.

*Top:* Traditional Hotel Ezra Cornell waiters' derby becomes a waitresses' derby in wartime 1944. *See Sources for names.*

*Bottom:* The war over, men compete again in the annual waiters' race at the 1945 Hotel Ezra Cornell.

Meek did what he could to match his curriculum to the military's needs. Hotel graduates were soon running base facilities at airfields, supervising the housing and feeding of munitions workers, and serving as officers in the Quartermaster Corps and the Naval Supply Corps. But in a February 1942 letter to Dean Sarah Gibson Blanding of the College of Home Economics, Meek complained that "so far our training has had little official recognition" from the military.

Meek proposed to the Navy commander at Cornell that he be allowed to train officers of the Naval Supply Corps. But the Supply Corps already had a training facility at Harvard, and they had no interest in expanding to Cornell. In February 1943, Meek wrote to the chief of the Navy's Bureau of Supplies and Accounts to offer the Hotel department's assistance in a different

field—training commissary officers. The offer, once again, was politely declined.

Total enrollment fell to 245 in September 1942, and 122 in both 1943 and 1944. As able-bodied Hotel men left Cornell, they were replaced by a growing number of women students. Between 1933 and 1943, a total of 20 women had graduated from the Hotel department. In 1944, 41 of 122 students were women.

The increasing presence of women students did not please Meek. In April 1943 he was asked by Lucretia Battles of the University of Washington to summarize Cornell's experience in training women for hotel work. He replied that only four of the twenty graduates were currently employed in the hotel industry. "The hotel business seems to be one largely influenced by tradition, and they have been very slow to make opportunities for women," he added. "All of our women graduates have had positions open for them upon graduation, [but] their number has been small, most of them have married shortly after graduation, and many of the others have found more attractive positions in other fields." In 1943, marriage usually ended a woman's career.

"It has consistently been my policy to discourage the enrollment of women students, not because they are in any sense unwelcome but because we have felt that the public has been misled regarding the opportunities open to them in the hotel field," wrote Meek. "When a girl comes from a hotel family or has had hotel experience so that she is able to appraise the situation for herself, she is very welcome. The others I try at least to talk to, to be sure they understand the situation."

During the war years, however, the situation of women began to change. Some of the changes seemed superficial. For example, each year Hotel students would publicize Hotel Ezra Cornell by holding a "waiters' derby," where men wearing white aprons would dash 100 yards while carrying a full bowl of water on a tray. In 1944, the men were briefly replaced by waitresses in white uniforms and chef's caps. But other changes were more lasting, as women trained during the war made inroads into the male world of hotel management.

Meanwhile, Hotel alumni were serving their country. In October 1943, Meek reported that 7 in 10 Hotel alumni were on active duty. Of these, 435 were in the Army, 134 in the Navy, and 22 in the Marines. The vast majority were officers. In November 1944, 692 of 950 alumni were in uniform, 458 as officers. Ultimately, 27 Hotel alumni died in the war.

As Hotelies suffered through the war, their Cornell connections occasionally served them well. One alumnus, for example, found himself swimming toward the African coast after his ship was torpedoed off Cape Town. Once on shore, he had no money and no possessions. But he knew that many of the officers' clubs in the world's ports were run by Cornell Hotel alumni, and he

did have his name and rank in indelible ink on his shorts.

The sailor found the club manager and began trying to convince him that he was a Hotelie. The manager remained skeptical as the castaway mentioned the names of professors and classrooms, until the sailor mentioned that one instructor required that the definition of Portland Cement be learned verbatim.

"Did you take sticks and bricks?" asked the manager. "Certainly!" replied the sailor, who began to recite: "Portland Cement is the product obtained by calcining to incipient fusion an intimate and properly proportioned mixture of argillaceous and calcareous. . . ." The manager stopped the sailor, gave him a good meal and a loan, and the two became friends.

When the war finally ended, Meek had a new set of challenges. Hundreds of Hotel students shed their uniforms and returned to the campus to collect their degrees, so enrollment skyrocketed. All of his careful saving and planning during the war was finally coming to fruition, and it was time to break ground for a permanent building. When the war ended, the Hotel department's golden age began.

A. Wright Gibson Jr. '42 in uniform, H. Victor Grohmann '28, and Director H. B. Meek look at a flag with stars for Hotel alumni in the armed services during World War II. At the time 656 were serving, and 8 had died in service. Ultimately 27 Hotel alumni would die in the war.

# A Magnificent Addition…
## an Enduring Legacy

LICE SEIDLER STATLER was not accustomed to laying bricks. Her elegant black dress, veiled black velvet hat, white gloves, and double strand of pearls weren't suited for the job, either. But this was a very important brick, so she gingerly picked up the mortar-laden trowel. At noon on May 7, 1949, Ellsworth Statler's widow formally laid the cornerstone for Statler Hall. One year later, Cornell's Hotel program finally had its permanent home.

A great crowd of students, faculty, staff, and industry leaders gathered for the ceremony, which was the highlight of the twenty-fourth Hotel Ezra Cornell. Mrs. Statler was accompanied by Edmund Ezra Day, the university president who authorized Statler Hall as one part of a great building program; Neal Dow Becker, chairman of the Cornell Board of Trustees; and H. B. Meek, the beaming founder of the Hotel

Laying the cornerstone for the first separate home of the Hotel program, Statler Hall, in May 1949. *From left,* Neal Dow Becker *05, university trustee chairman; Director H. B. Meek, Cornell President Edmund E. Day, and Mrs. Alice Statler.

Plaque honors E.M. Statler for his support of the Hotel program.

Department who would soon be appointed dean of the Cornell School of Hotel Administration. But those four deserved only a portion of the praise, and they reminded the crowd of it in their remarks. Inside the cornerstone was a directory of alumni, a list of faculty, and a biography of Ellsworth Statler.

President Day said that Statler Hall had "significance in at least three notable respects." It was a "magnificent addition" to the university and its "richly deserving" Hotel program. It was a tribute to the "vision and wisdom" of Statler Foundation trustees Frank McKowne, Alice Statler, and Edward Letchworth. And it was "an enduring memorial to a truly great man," Ellsworth Statler.

Statler's "purpose and aim in life was to share with his fellow hotelmen," said his widow. "He was a strong believer in research, and gave liberally of any ideas. Always a friend of the young person in the hotel business, it was but natural for him to become interested, knowing that with such a school [as Cornell's] they would bring into the industry better people, people with better training, and thus improve the standards of the hotel industry."

Alice Statler could have added that Ellsworth Statler often acted like a tyrant, that he had mixed feelings about the value of academic training in hotel management, and that he pledged his support to the Cornell program only once and in the most general terms before he died. But she never would say those things. Since 1918, she and Frank McKowne had worked to round off their boss's rough edges and prepare his place in history.

## Executive Secretaries

Ellsworth Statler was the head of America's largest hotel chain, but he never had a secretary until he hired Frank McKowne in 1913. McKowne, fresh out of law school, proved a perfect foil for him. Statler worked with broad visions and grand plans, and he was prone to sudden temper tantrums. McKowne was an even-tempered detail man. Both of them could work tirelessly without complaint. McKowne later became Statler's executive vice president and took on the company's routine management duties. He and Statler came to rely most on C.B. Stoner, the company's treasurer; David Newton, advertising and promotion manager; and John L. Hennessy, chief steward.

One of McKowne's biggest challenges was finding ways to control his boss. Statler had a habit of roaming the halls. Whenever he was seized with a new idea, he would corral the nearest employee and begin dictating massive correspondence—a practice employees found highly unnerving. Although Statler didn't want a secretary, he clearly needed one.

In November 1918, McKowne received a job application from a 36-year-old unmarried editorial secretary. Alice Seidler was about to be laid off by the failing humor magazine *Life,* and she needed a job. When McKowne introduced her to Statler, he angrily refused to interview her. But it was clear, even to Statler, that his loose-cannon style was not good for the company.

A week later, Statler swallowed his pride. He summoned the woman to his office and began dictating a letter. "Dear Miss Seidler," he said, "it will be necessary for me to know your belief in your own qualifications and ability to do the following things. First and most important, [you must] be able to control an unruly, unsystematic, disorderly, inefficient business man." Statler proposed that Seidler set his engagement calendar, write letters for him, ensure that he was on time for appointments and deadlines, and be available to work at any time during hotel construction periods. She began work the following Monday.

Statler found another match in Seidler, and this time it was a pairing of a more personal nature. Both of them had grown up persevering in the face of hardship.

Seidler's father had been a wealthy designer of railroad sleeping cars, but after losing a contract with Pullman

The Hotel school's success is due to the vision of its founder, the talents of its faculty, and the brilliance of its students. But the school's success also depends on staff members whose important work receives far less attention.

One pillar of support was Edna Osborn, who served as administrative assistant to Prof Meek until his retirement, then continued in student services until the 1970s. "Eddy," as she was affectionately known to students and alumni, was the image of a good executive secretary. "She literally seemed to run the school when Prof was away," remembers George Bantuvanis '51. "She kept everything on an even keel."

Osborn was especially useful in providing support to the Cornell Society of Hotelmen when it was still a small, informal organization. She shared this task with her colleague Helen Ayers, who was administrative assistant to Prof. John Courtney. Courtney, in addition to his teaching duties, was secretary/treasurer of the Cornell Society of Hotelmen until his death in 1957, so Ayers and Osborn shared many of the practical details of keeping

alumni in touch with each other. In fact, the two women were co-editors of the *Bulletin* of the society for many years.

In the 1960s and 1970s, Osborn helped coordinate job recruitment at the school. "My fondest thoughts go back to her," said William Caruso '70, president of a restaurant consulting firm with offices in Atlanta, Buffalo, Chicago, and Denver. "I spent endless hours driving her crazy reviewing and re-reviewing what seemed like never-ending pages of information on companies, dates, and times. She almost went over the edge a couple of times." Caruso even called on Osborn in 1972, when he was a graduate student elsewhere, and help was cheerfully given.

Osborn lent a sympathetic ear—and sometimes more—to students who were having trouble with their graduation requirements. Osborn and Meek "reshaped the rules to allow me to receive my degree under extremely strained financial conditions," said Richard D. Fors '59. To John F. ("Jack") Craver '52, Osborn "believed my reasons for missing ROTC and provided me with the documentation that helped get through it all."

Edna Osborn in 1966, administrative aide to Deans Meek and Beck.

he blinded himself in a suicide attempt. The family plunged into poverty. Alice went to secretarial school at night so she could spend days reading to her father. She became a self-assured woman who was comfortable with wealth but not troubled by the lack of it. "She had the quiet confidence of a woman who had surmounted personal tragedy," according to Statler biographer Floyd Miller. The boss's tantrums and threats had little effect on her—or if they did, she didn't show it. She simply reminded him of his obligations, and eventually he met them.

Seidler's cool professionalism and McKowne's thoroughness helped the Statler empire run smoothly in the 1920s. The boss came to depend on Seidler's advice when writing speeches, attending business functions, and performing the other social duties of his professional life. Yet Statler's personal life also needed a guide. When his first wife, Mary, died in October 1925, Statler feared that he did not have the skills to be a good father to his four adopted children. In desperation, he turned to Seidler for advice and comfort.

The growing intimacy between the boss and his secretary delighted McKowne and other Statler executives. Seidler was one of their inner circle. If Statler married her, their long-term control of the organization would be assured.

Statler finally did propose on the morning of April 30, 1927. Seidler must have been prepared for it because the wedding took place that afternoon. That evening, the couple left for their honeymoon—at a hotel convention in Atlantic City.

"Did she love him? Certainly not with the heedlessness of youth, not with those illusions of perfection, of perpetual bliss," writes Floyd Miller. "For years she had spent more hours per day with him than most wives ever do with husbands, and since he was not a man to dissemble she knew him thoroughly. What she felt for him was affection, compassion, admiration, and pride. If that did not add up to the romantic concept of love, it was certainly a sound basis for marriage."

One year later Ellsworth Statler was dead. Frank McKowne became president of the company, and Alice Seidler Statler became chairman of its board. Statler's posthumous order to put a woman in charge of his corporation was almost unheard-of in the 1920s, but Mrs. Statler was well prepared for the job. She, McKowne, and the others kept the company solvent during the Depression and war years, then managed its rapid growth during the great post-war economic expansion. By the time Mrs. Statler sold Hotels Statler to Conrad Hilton in October 1954, the company was almost twice as big as it was before the war.

Alice Statler, McKowne, and Letchworth of the Marine Trust Bank of Buffalo (which held Statler's accounts) were the founding trustees of the Statler Foundation. While they were expanding the business in the 1930s and 1940s, they also worked with Meek and Hotel faculty on plans for a permanent home for the program. Sadly, McKowne never lived to see Statler Hall. He died suddenly of a cerebral hemorrhage three months before construction began.

Like her husband, Alice Statler was initially hostile to the Cornell Hotel program. But also like her husband, Mrs. Statler had a "conversion experience" that changed her opinion of Cornell when she attended her first Hotel Ezra Cornell weekend.

At the cornerstone-laying ceremony, Mrs. Statler remembered her first visit to Cornell in 1941. A tour of the facilities gave her the impression that the Hotel program was "a poor relative of the campus." She, McKowne, and Letchworth subsequently decided that "a building to house this school would be the very best way to carry out [Statler's] wishes." Six months later, they signed the agreement that endowed Statler Hall.

## A Hotel for Cornell

The idea of a "practice hotel" for Hotel students goes back to the beginning of the Hotel program. In 1923, Frank Dudley of the American Hotel Association proposed that a 200-room hotel be built adjacent to the Cornell campus and staffed by Hotel students. In November of that year, Agriculture college Dean Albert Mann met with two Ithaca businessmen to discuss a similar proposal. And in June 1929, Cornell trustee Sherman Peer proposed that the university back a mortgage for the "Cornell Inn Corporation" in exchange for 60 percent of the inn's stock. Peer promised Meek that the inn would net about $45,000 a year.

The Depression soon obliterated Peer's revenue projections and put the idea of a practice hotel on hold. But Meek's vision for the program never changed, and

Director Meek with a model of Statler Hall.

his patience was inexhaustible. When the economy improved a decade later, he raised the subject again.

Serious plans for a building began with the December 1941 agreement between the Statler Foundation and the university. But eight and a half years elapsed between that agreement and the opening celebration—long and tortuous years for Meek. It took all of his considerable powers of wheedling, threatening, and scheming to get the building built, and the result was not exactly what he wanted. Getting that was to take another eight years.

In July 1942 Meek presented Cornell and Statler officials with two summaries of space requirements, one for a hotel program that would enroll 300 students, and another for a program with 450 students. Meek clearly preferred the latter option. His wish list included a 450-seat assembly hall with an elevated stage, flat floor with movable seats, projection equip-

Removing faculty homes on East Avenue in 1948 to make way for the new home of the School of Hotel Administration.

ment, lecturer amenities, an outside entrance, and a connecting kitchen. The accounting rooms needed good light, writing surfaces, and ample chalkboards. After twenty years of making do with basements and spare rooms, drawing up these plans must have pleased him immensely.

In August 1942 Cornell and Statler officials agreed to hire the Chicago firm of Holabird and Root to design Statler Hall. After considering six possible sites, the principals decided that their first choice was for a 300-student facility on the south shore of Beebe Lake, just north of Martha Van Rensselaer Hall. It was to be a long, low building with lecture rooms and laboratories in the center section, a thirty-room inn at the east end, and an auditorium capable of holding all students at the west end.

Meek was not pleased with certain aspects of the firm's initial proposal, and his frustration grew as the plans progressed. He fussed over such details as the offices, which he wanted to face the lake; the student lounge, which he said should be centrally located to

promote community spirit; the roofs, which should be safe for the students who would inevitably sun-bathe on them; and even the coat racks, which in his view were insufficient. Worst of all, Meek felt that the building's out-of-the-way location would "impose serious burdens on the inn operation."

By 1944 several key aspects of Meek's plan were in danger. Support for the inn and restaurant operations had all but disappeared, possibly because of trustee concerns that they might jeopardize the university's tax-exempt status. Then President Day, worried that Statler support might disappear if construction did not begin soon, directed Meek to cut costs by reducing his request to the barest essentials. Meek did it under protest. In April he wrote to Day that "it is a genuine question, in fact, whether, in attempting to meet the pressure for area reduction, I have not perhaps gone too far, gone so far that future improvements in the program may be seriously handicapped, and whether the long-run interests of the university would not be better served if we were to revert to my earlier and ampler requisitions."

With his options narrowing, Meek thought of another plan. He served on a committee that was studying the feasibility of a faculty club. Cornell's 1942 master plan even included a site for the club on the east side of East Avenue. But the committee had concluded that a faculty club befitting Cornell would cost about $400,000, and as Meek put it in 1964, "no such money was in sight. So I turned to my associates on the committee and said, 'Supposing I can persuade the Statler Foundation to include a club area in the building. Would you agree to a proposition where the Hotel school would lease the area to the club and you would let the Hotel school operate your dining room?'" With a provision that would limit their possible losses, the committee agreed.

Meek then went to McKowne and pointed out that many hotels leased parts of their operations to clubs. Moreover, he said, the inn could sidestep the tax issues if its guests were limited to those on Cornell business. Reluctantly, McKowne agreed. To please his faculty, Day also agreed. The proposed structure would give the students crucial experience in restaurant management, food preparation, and innkeeping, which pleased Meek.

Early in 1945, the architects submitted plans for a building on East Avenue, between Sage Hall and Barton Hall. The building would include a faculty club, class rooms, and an inn. Meek felt that these plans weren't perfect, but offered "the best solution yet presented." On June 11, as the Allies were declaring victory in Europe, the Statler Foundation agreed. To pay for the club and inn, the university agreed to loan the operation $300,000. The architects began drawing detailed plans while the university began searching for a contractor and materials amid post-war shortages. After three more years of legal, financial, and philosophical wrangling, construction of Statler Hall began in August 1948.

Statler Hall under construction.

### Life During Construction

In 1948 and 1949 the dust and noise on East Avenue were hardly noticed. Statler Hall was only a small part of a huge expansion that began with the Day administration and continued under Day's successor, Deane W. Malott. Between 1936 and 1966, the university's physical plant more than doubled in size.

Once the building plans for Statler Hall began in earnest, Meek was joined by several of the brightest minds in the Hotels Statler organization. Probably the most important "volunteer" was Harold B. Callis, the company's specialist in design, construction, and layout. Arthur Douglas, who became president of Hotels Statler after McKowne's death, also had a major role.

*Top:* Statler Hall, home of the School of Hotel Administration, completed and dedicated in 1950.

*Bottom:* The East Avenue entrance.

Many of the furnishing and decoration decisions were made by Kenneth M. McCann, Ernest Wottitz, and Helen H. McQuillan of Statler's interior design division.

As with any large construction project, the first Statler Hall had its share of compromises and misadventures. After the plans were complete, for example, Meek noticed that they would destroy a beautiful old swamp oak tree. But if the building were moved twenty feet to the south, the tree would be preserved in the center of a courtyard, right outside Meek's office window. The building was moved. The tree was still there in the mid-1990s.

Soon after ground was broken, the construction crew discovered that the long-fabled source of a small stream, known on campus as "Wee Stinky," was actually deep under the site of Statler Hall in a large bed of quicksand. As Charles Sayles puts it, "The contingency fund immediately shrank."

A contingency of another kind arose when it was time to hang the ceiling in the main dining room. The crew noticed that a family of robins had built a nest on top of a drain pipe, and they refused to close in the ceiling until the baby birds hatched out. As Sayles recalls, they waited and did the extra work on their own time.

The fact that the inn would serve alcohol also caused some consternation. Meek insisted that a proper hotel training facility should have a bar, over the objections of some trustees. "For someone who drank only milk with an ice cube at cocktail parties, and who didn't know the difference between a manhattan and a Coca-Cola, Meek was quite persistent," writes Sayles. The problem was a New York State law that prohibited bars from operating within a certain distance of a church. According to the law, the Statler's bar was too close to Sage Chapel when measured on a straight line. The impasse was overcome by using the walking distance rather than the bee-line distance. "The bar came into being," writes Sayles, "and about that time the Hotelies acquired the dubious sobriquet of 'bartenders.'"

As construction progressed essentially without major problems, Statler executives had a rare opportunity to experiment with hotel design. One innovation of Callis's concerned the poured concrete floors.

Normally, each poured floor slab had a ceiling hung below it. Callis thought that if a pleasing surface could be created on the underside of the slab, the hung ceiling could be eliminated in the inn with considerable savings, and the height of each story would be reduced. The new method was a success. Another innovation in bed design meant that some of the inn's single beds converted into divans during the day.

The only real crisis in Statler Hall's construction came after most of the dust had settled. One week before opening day—which would coincide with the twenty-fifth Hotel Ezra Cornell—the laborers went on strike.

"There were trucks filled with furniture parked in the lot, there were empty guest rooms, there were laborers down by Cascadilla Creek carrying signs and walking around in a big circle," writes Sayles, "and there were some eighty students in a building-construction course, all of them familiar with the building through frequent inspection trips. The class as a group made a proposition to the general effect that, if they could be excused from Hotel classes, they would install the furniture." It was a perfect spring adventure for a group of budding capitalists who didn't like the strikers anyway, he recalls.

"Students in the Industrial and Labor Relations school were outraged. They wrote letters to the *Cornell Daily Sun* and complained to whomever would listen—to no avail. Nevertheless, the Statler organization and the furniture suppliers had done an excellent job. Each major piece was identified as to its destination, so the placement became easy.

"The university supplied trucks for removing cardboard cartons and crating material. The whole job moved with the greatest dispatch. Housekeeping managed to press and hang all the drapes, supply the linen, make the beds, and place the pin cushions—a Statler trademark—on the dressers; the rooms were now ready. In the kitchen, sharp edges on the equipment had been filed down (after fingers had been bandaged); dish, glass, and utensil racks filled, cutting boards placed, and supplies moved in; they, too, were ready.

"By noon on Friday the lobby and lounge rugs were laid and cleaned, the furniture placed and dusted, the draperies pressed and hung, and the floors cleaned. At 3 p.m. the place was full of flowers, and formal attire began to appear. As far as the building construction class was concerned, they were done. They were tired and proud and happy. Mostly they were tired. The class members went away and weren't seen for a week. They had learned more than they ever would learn in class.

"Nobody remembers what happened to the strikers."

Sayles's account of the Statler Hall opening weekend ends with Meek wandering around the building after

Latest decorative styles are reflected in the main dining room of the newly opened Statler Inn in May 1950.

New Hotel school library.

the guests had departed. He says that Meek stopped at a south-facing window on the fourth floor and said, "There's room down there for a big addition."

## Maturity in the Classroom

Statler Hall marked the beginning of a new, more professional era in hotel education. The Cornell program, though still the butt of jokes on campus, had gained international renown. Roughly twice as many students applied each year as could be admitted. In a typical year, between 10 and 20 percent of the entering class would come from other countries. The quality and seriousness of the student body had increased dramatically.

But the student transformation really began five years before the building opened. During the war, total enrollment in the program went as low as 122 students.

But the end of the war produced a deluge. Enrollment was 202 in the fall of 1945, 260 in the spring, over 300 the next year, and 360 in 1948–49. During the 1950s, enrollment stabilized at about 400.

The Hotel program's rapid growth was a small part of an enrollment explosion that forever changed Cornell. The G.I. Bill, signed in 1944, entitled each veteran to one year of educational benefits, plus an additional twelve months for each year served, and a stipend for living expenses. The response was staggering. When 1,027 veterans arrived in the fall of 1945, the Cornell student body immediately increased 18 percent in size. Another 2,900 arrived the following year. Over 10,000 students attended Cornell in 1946–47, nearly double the number who attended in 1944–45. Nearly two-thirds of students in 1946–47 were veterans, and men students outnumbered women 5 to 1.

Many quaint old traditions died suddenly in the new, postwar Cornell. Wilson Greatbach *50, who had been a Navy dive-bomber pilot, remembers that he and his fellow veterans had little patience for the long-standing tradition of freshman beanies: "After you've been on a dive-bomber, you're not going to let some sophomore tell you to wear a little hat."

Students in the postwar years were older than they had been in the 1930s, and their age and experience led to more discipline in class. Greatbach, for example, went on to medical school and later invented the implantable pacemaker for cardiac patients. Richard W. Brown '49 summed up the vets' attitude this way: "We were not to be slighted. We were going to make it through, and we weren't going to be looked down upon, academically or otherwise."

Brown was a 24-year-old sophomore in 1946, fresh from a tour of duty in North Africa and Italy. He arrived in Ithaca wearing pieces of his Army uniform because he was too tall for civilian clothes. He struggled through the Hotel program and passed one especially difficult course with the aid of Muriel Welch *47, a Home Economics student whom he later married. Brown's career led to the executive offices of Banfi Vintners (*see page* 136) and a major fund-raising role for the Hotel school in the 1980s and 1990s.

In the spring of 1946, three out of four Hotel students were returning veterans. "We were primarily interested in studying and graduating as soon as possible," says Roy Watson Jr. '48. This serious attitude helped produce some of the school's most distinguished alumni. Watson, for example, went on to become a president of the American Hotel and Motel Association, the first of eight Cornellians to hold the post (*see page 130*).

The new, larger Hotel program was not as intimate as the prewar program had been. In a July 1949 letter to J. Knight Willy, Meek lamented the loss: "It used to be that I could not only name every graduate, but tell you

he Hotel school's library is one of its greatest assets. At one time, the library was also one of the school's most unusual restaurants.

The first Statler librarian was Blanche Fickle, a native of Indiana, who began her Cornell career as a librarian for the College of Home Economics. When Statler Hall opened, Meek asked her to become the first librarian of the Hotel school. Fickle's lasting contribution was the creation and management of the world's largest collection of literature on hospitality.

Fickle's colleague and later director of the library was Kay Spinney, a soft-spoken woman who was the image of an old-fashioned librarian. But there was something adventurous behind Spinney's conservative exterior. Students saw a hint of it when, to their surprise, she allowed the seniors to turn the library into a Polynesian restaurant during one Parents' Weekend. "She pitched right in, and seemed proud that the library was to be the center of attention," said Frank Stover '65. "We emptied the library of all furniture, covered up the bookshelves, set up banquet tables and chairs, and grilled our Polynesian fare over open coals at the library's atrium entrance.

"Miss Spinney was such a good sport that she not only attended but also invited guests of her own. To reward her, we had the entire library set up and running on Monday morning, when our 'Island Embers' restaurant was just a smoldering memory."

where he came from, in exactly what hotels he had worked while on supervised practice, and the place he had worked following his graduation. I can no longer begin to do this."

Veterans brought along new challenges for campus administrators in the persons of 1,300 wives and 1,000 babies. "The wife is neither a student nor a townswoman," said President Day in 1948. "She affiliates herself with the other 'vet's wives' in a world of their own." That world, in an agglomeration of temporary barracks on Tower Road, had the local nickname "Fertile Valley." It soon included a cooperative grocery, a nursery school, a newsletter, a radio program, a charm school, and a chapter of the League of Women Voters.

Hotelies joined in the national baby boom. The November 1949 issue of *The Cornell Innkeeper,* a student newsletter of the Hotel program, listed five alumni marriages and four births between June and

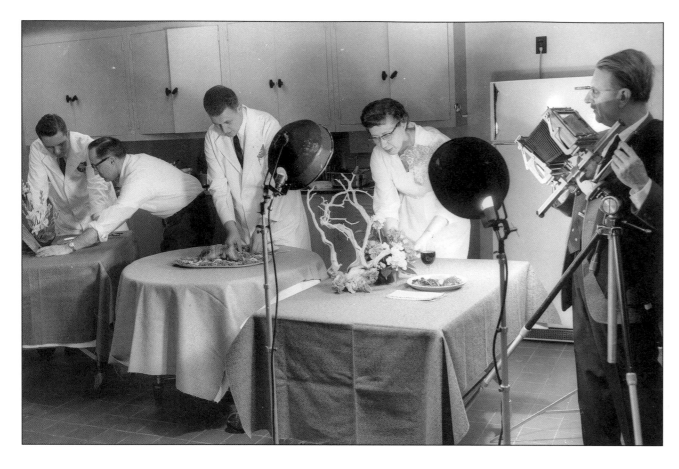

*Above:* Students learn from faculty and staff how to prepare to photograph food for a menu. *See Sources for names.*

*Right:* Visiting chef Joseph Faussone, executive chef of the Hotels Statler, speaks to a class.

September. The April 1950 issue announced the formation of a social organization for the sixty wives of Hotel students, and gave the address of a contact person "if any of you are bringing a new wife to the campus." With one in six Hotel students a married man, the parties of the late 1940s may have lacked something in youthful exuberance. But the students made up for it in other ways. Cornell historian Morris G. Bishop *14 recalls that students' wives held baby shows in Willard Straight Hall, "to the consternation of returning alumni in search of the Cornell of their youth."

As the 1950s wore on, the veterans and their families graduated and moved away. But the construction of Statler Hall and other successes had forever changed the nature of the school. By the late 1940s, the Hotel program had nearly 1,000 alumni, some of whom were in high positions at the peak of their careers. Alumni included Henry B. Williams '30, manager of the Waldorf-Astoria in New York City; Georges St. Laurent '33, a leading hotel engineer who also owned a chain of hotels; Joseph P. Binns '28, vice president of Hilton Hotels; and Ralph J. Barell '34, senior executive in the treasurer's office of Hotels Statler.

Hotel students found it far easier to meet industry leaders after 1950, because they often interacted with them while doing their jobs and spending informal time in Statler Hall. Students didn't always pick up their

The new Statler's main kitchen, preparing for its first Hotel Ezra Cornell, in 1950. Student directors include, from left, Kenneth Short '50, Martin Horn Jr. '50, and Walter Herrmann '52, chef.

When he got the call from Prof Meek, J. William Conner '40 was a young executive in Cleveland. "We arrived in Ithaca in mid-April, 1950," remembers his wife, Margaret. "Bill had less than three weeks to hire all employees, set up the organization and train before the opening of Statler Inn on the weekend of Hotel Ezra Cornell." Conner, the Inn's first manager, barely made it through. "Everything was ready by the Friday night of HEC, except Bill. He had passed out from exhaustion."

For the next twelve years, the Statler Inn was run by Conner, a staff that included many Hotel alumni, and paid student workers. Margaret Conner remembers that "Meek made one stipulation. The club had to be a success. There had to be great activity, and activity there was. Prominent Ithacans were invited to become members so that there would be no conflicts between town and gown."

Conner saw that the Inn took care of the service details befitting the Statler tradition. "The printed menus were changed every day, and every morning the son of the local printer would run up with the two menus of the day," says Mrs. Conner. Cornell faculty and alumni often held wedding receptions at the Inn. Many couples made reservations for the New Year's Eve party a year in advance.

Because it was the hotel of record for Cornell, the Statler Inn hosted more than its share of prominent guests. Nelson Rockefeller stayed there when he was governor of New York, and Eleanor Roosevelt was a guest several times. Mrs. Conner remembers the day her husband was proudly showing the hotel to Frank Lloyd Wright, who "put his arm around Bill and said, 'Son, we don't build corridors any more.'"

William V. Eaton '61 literally gave up a career in rocket science because of the Statler Inn. "I was not a happy camper [at the engineering school]," he remembers. In the summer after his first year, Eaton got a job as a bellman at the Statler—and that job changed his life. He fell in with a tightly-knit group that included Conner, Henry Langknecht '53 as controller, Robert Powell '53 as food and beverage manager, and Don Tarbutton '58, dining room manager. He also became friends with Prof. Ernest Bangs, who persuaded him to switch to a new course of study in food facilities engineering.

Working in the Statler was exciting, says Eaton, and at times terrifying. "Those who worked in the dining room will remember a great round table in the Sun Room, the favorite dining location of Cornell President and Mrs. Deane W. Malott. She was a stickler for protocol, and one day she was entertaining some incredible dignitary. She worked out the seating plan with great care and had the place cards delivered to my mailbox at the Statler desk, and I forgot about them. She accosted me as the guests were having cocktails; we ran to the desk and put the cards out together. I offered my resignation to Bill Conner the next day, but President Malott graciously said that I would have another chance.

"The chance came quickly, with another great entertaining occasion. Flowers were ordered by the president's office, and the florist missed the delivery completely. Again I was accosted by Mrs. Malott as guests were arriving. A quick phone call identified the florist as the source of the problem. I quickly raced to the hotel's flower cooler, grabbed everything I could, and chose two of my most delicate banquet waiters to climb out onto the fully set table to arrange loose flowers in the center, while Bill Conner pacified the president. In the end, we all got thank-you notes."

cues, however. Shirley Axtmayer Rodriguez '57 writes, "During my first Hotel Ezra Cornell in 1954, as a *very, very* green freshman, I was nervously serving a big hors d'oeuvre platter in a crowded function room to a group of VIPs (I had been told beforehand) during the traditional 'smoker.' Dean Meek, in animated conversation with a group of gentlemen, called me aside. He proceeded to introduce me: 'Shirley is the first freshman at the Hotel school from Puerto Rico. This gentleman has business down your way.'

"For the next few minutes, I chatted with the man very cordially. Before taking my leave, I asked the man with whom I was talking: 'Sir, what exactly is your business in Puerto Rico?' Dean Meek answered with a big grin: 'Shirley, this is Mr. Conrad Hilton!' I smiled sheepishly, turned around, and highly embarassed, went on serving my hors d'oeuvre."

Conrad Hilton and other powerful men were the exceptions in the Hotel school, however. In a 1948 interview with the *Southern Hotel Journal*, Meek said that the goal of an average Hotel student at Cornell was to manage a hotel of 100 to 300 rooms in a city of 20,000 to 100,000 people. "He hopes to take an active part in the life of such a community," Meek added. Many alumni had already fulfilled that ambition. When the *Journal* published a study of smaller hotels in 1946, it chose six leading operators of such hotels to edit the special issue. Four of them were Cornellians.

The Hotel department also got a major publicity boost from the opening of Statler Hall, which brought it a wave of international attention. Typical of these articles was the pronouncement in *Future* magazine, later reprinted in *Reader's Digest,* that "Statler Hall is the West Point of the hotel world." Meek himself shared in much of the praise. In 1949, for example, he received an honorary doctorate in education from his alma mater, Boston University. During the ceremony, Meek was lionized as the Cornell program's "informing genius" and "the world's foremost authority not only in training men to make a living in the hotel business, but also in training them to live rewardingly by making the hotel business an instrument of service to others."

Meek was also a success among the deans on his own campus, if success is measured by pleasing one's students. In a June 1951 poll, 52 percent of all Cornell students surveyed said that their vocational training was satisfactory. Sixty-nine percent of Hotel Administration students held this view, compared with just 42 percent of students at the College of Arts and Sciences.

### Meek's Boys and Girls

The 1950s were Meek's fourth and final decade at the Hotel school, and in some respects they were a time for him to enjoy the fruits of his labors. With a handsome facility, administrative independence, widespread praise, and ample funding, Meek could have rested on his laurels. But he never did. As soon as Statler Hall opened, he began a campaign to make it bigger by adding the auditorium he had originally requested. While he was campaigning, he expanded the curriculum, enlarged executive education programs, and led a major drive for scholarship funds.

The main lounge of the Statler Inn within Statler Hall, originally designated as the Men's Lounge. A separate Women's Lounge was on the other side of the Inn's entrance foyer.

Hotel faculty of the newly separate School of Hotel Administration in 1952. Dean Meek is at the center of the first row. *See Sources for names.*

The Hotel school, like the hospitality industry it serves, has always been a home for those with an overdose of the entrepreneurial spirit. In a 1951 student body survey, for example, 41 percent of Hotel students felt that big businesses should not be encumbered by regulations. Only 8 percent of students in Home Economics agreed. With irreconcilable differences like those, a split between the two schools was inevitable—and so was a promotion. In 1950, the Department of Hotel Administration became a separate school within the College of Home Economics. In 1954, the trustees separated it from Home Economics and the state programs and gave it the status of a separate college, with Meek as dean.

The restless energy of Hotelies brings accomplishments and accolades to many alumni and to the school. But Hotel alumni remain passionately loyal to their school for highly personal reasons. "Hotel people are itinerants," explains Mary R. Wright '45. "That's always been the personal difficulty with the industry. It's wrecked marriages. We work seven days a week and we work while other people play, on the weekends. It also involves lots of moves. Properties will change hands, and managers will go out with their clothing." In many cases, alumni who lead chaotic lives rely on their Cornell Hotel connections for a secure source of friendship and affection. In a real sense, their alumni connections serve as replacements for a family.

In the late 1940s and 1950s, the alumni—who called themselves "Meek's boys," even when they were referring to girls—led a revolution in hospitality and travel industries that were ripe for change. During the war, demand for hotel rooms exceeded supply. Managers were almost sure of a full house regardless of their service quality, and industry standards suffered as a result. Occupancy rates reached an all-time high of 93 percent in 1946, then began sliding downward. After the war, hotel and restaurant managers rediscovered the fact that high-quality services gave them a competitive edge, and they looked to Cornell to set the standards.

Mergers and the growth of hotel chains defined the 1950s. When Conrad Hilton bought out Hotels Statler for $111 million in 1954, Hilton faced just one other full-service chain of comparable size—the Sheraton Hotels. But in the mid-1950s, full-service hotels like Hilton and Sheraton were becoming the mature segment of an emerging multitiered industry. The construction of interstate highways and metropolitan airports took a quaint concept of the 1930s, the motor court, and turned it into the industry's focus of growth, the mid-range and budget motel. These newer, less expensive inns and restaurants were not designed to impress their patrons with architectural grace or culinary excellence, but with affordable rates and consistently high standards of cleanliness and service.

Financial imperatives also shaped the hospitality industry in the 1950s. In 1955, the average occupancy rate at a U.S. hotel was 75 percent. Profits were still possible at this level, but they were not as easy to achieve as they had been a decade earlier. Consequently, the newer hotels were also designed to wring as much revenue as possible from every square foot of space.

In 1952, the first Holiday Inn opened in Memphis, Tennessee. It offered two double beds per room, a restaurant, and a pool; free television, ice, and a telephone in every room; and best of all, rooms with parking places at the front door. The chain expanded at a torrid pace. Franchisees enjoyed an average of 80 percent occupancy until the mid-1960s. Overall, the number of motels grew from about 18,000 in 1940 to 60,000 in 1960.

## JOE BINNS HELPS HILTON BUY STATLER

Conrad Hilton said that the acquisition of Hotels Statler was easy. Hilton, founder of that great hotel chain, told an associate, "one day we'll get it." Sure enough, they did. And a Cornell Hotelie helped make it happen.

The Statler-Hilton merger on October 27, 1954, was the largest real estate and hotel deal to date, with a then-impressive value of $111 million. One of Hilton's chief negotiators was Joseph P. Binns '28, who served as vice president of Hilton Hotels and general manager of the Waldorf-Astoria in New York City. But in a 1961 account, Binns made it clear that the deal wasn't easy.

Statler had originally agreed to sell to another company. While Hilton raced up from Texas to meet with Alice Statler, Binns visited her apartment in the Waldorf-Astoria and kept her from consummating the deal. Once that crisis passed and Alice Statler agreed to sell to Hilton, Binns had to ensure

three things to make the deal work: favorable tax exposure, minimum debt against the properties, and, most important, a small group of shareholders "in absolute control of enough stock to make possible a majority control."

In 1954, almost 49 percent of the shares of Hotels Statler were controlled by the Statler Foundation and Alice Statler. Binns helped craft a complicated deal that required Hilton to raise $77.5 million in cash by a certain date or forfeit $8 million, a hefty sum at that time.

The deal almost fell through after the sellers were ready, because Binns could not get Hilton's board of directors to agree to the terms. "I was broken-hearted," he wrote. But additional backing from three banks sealed the deal. The result for Hilton and Statler, after consolidation, was a sizable saving in operational costs. Meanwhile, the Statler Foundation and its chief project, the Cornell Hotel school, reaped a financial windfall.

Conrad Hilton is inducted as an honorary member of the Cornell Society of Hotelmen in May 1954, the year he bought the Statler hotels. Wallace Lee Jr. '36 makes the presentation.

The initial reaction of hotel owners to their new competitors was alarm. But eventually most of them followed the shift in travelers' preferences and began opening motels of their own. In 1962, their common interests were accepted when the American Hotel Association changed its name to the American Hotel and Motel Association.

Parallel developments were taking place in the restaurant industry, as entrepreneurs developed restaurant concepts and made fortunes by mass-producing them.

## EDGERTON, McLAMORE, AND BURGER KING

In 1954, two Hotel school graduates, James W. McLamore '47 and David R. Edgerton '48, bought a struggling Miami-based chain of restaurants. With their schooling and professional experience, they hoped to make their mark in the new and growing field of fast food. They pinned their hopes on the Insta-Burger cooking machine.

Unfortunately, it was a lemon. Recalls Edgerton: "What can I say? The guy who sold us the machine drove a pink Cadillac." The burger patties would stick to the machine's conveyor belt, causing frequent backups. But the duo had an inspiration. "A company called Whataburger had this big burger," Edgerton remembers. "We looked at it, and we had this little burger like everybody else had at the time. We said, 'We can do this!'" Using mechanical know-how from his Hotel school training, Edgerton redesigned the Insta-Burger machine to hold a bigger burger. "We made it more flexible,

faster, and bigger," he says. "When you looked down at the burger, it looked big. And no one else had it."

They called the burger The Whopper and priced it at 29 cents, just slightly less than twice the price of a hamburger at McDonald's. The public loved it. Edgerton and McLamore changed the name of their struggling chain to Burger King and proceeded to make a fortune.

In 1967, the two Hotelies sold their 274 restaurants to Pillsbury for $18 million. By the 1990s, three alumni were among the major Burger King franchisees: Richard D. Fors '59, Manuel A. Garcia '65, and Charles J. Mund '51. In 1995, Burger King was a global restaurant chain owned by Grand Metropolitan PLC, with nearly 7,700 units and estimated annual revenues of $7.5 billion. Edgerton owned various restaurants and restaurant chains and McLamore was chairman emeritus of Burger King. Both agree that the training they received at the Hotel school was invaluable.

An early restaurant chain, Howard Johnson's, began in the late 1920s and grew steadily; by 1967, it was the largest restaurant chain in the U.S. But Howard Johnson's faced increasing competition after the war ended. In 1941, Carl Karcher bought a hot dog cart and hit the streets of Los Angeles; fifty years later, the 640 Carl's Jr. restaurants had sales of $620 million. In 1946 an Ohio hog farmer named Bob Evans opened a restaurant to serve breakfasts featuring his own brand of sausage. Harry Snyder pioneered drive-through fast-food in 1948, when he opened the first In-N-Out Burger stand in Baldwin Park, California. In nearby San Bernadino, the most popular restaurant at that time was a hamburger stand owned by Mo and Dick McDonald.

The phenomenal success of McDonald's is a well-known story. Less well known is that the driving force behind Burger King, America's second-largest fast-food hamburger chain, was a pair of Hotel alumni—James W. McLamore '47 and David R. Edgerton '48 (*see left*).

### Restless Energy

Like his students, Prof Meek had an entrepreneur's restless energy and a chronic dissatisfaction with the status quo. He may have enjoyed the praise and honors that surrounded the opening of Statler Hall, but he also seemed to distrust it. Even as he was leading the school to a position of undisputed dominance in its field, he continued to entertain offers from other employers. In November 1945, after Meek told him of one such offer, President Day increased Meek's salary to $9,000 a year, with a promise of $10,000 within three years.

Meek's private response to the Boston University honor is particularly revealing. In a September 1949 letter to W. I. Hamilton—the man who had observed him at the Ocean House in York Beach, Maine, in 1922—Meek said that the degree "represents just another case where one man gets the credit for what a lot of others have done." Hamilton had suggested that Meek cultivate an understudy to prepare for his eventual retirement. Meek replied that he was already surrounded by "a corps of young men, any of whom would be well qualified to carry the banner forward." He even admitted, "I am beginning to wonder if I ought not seriously consider stepping down and giving one of them the helm."

When Meek wrote those words, he was less than nine months away from the realization of his lifelong goal—the opening of Statler Hall. Yet he had recently visited Day's office to tell the Cornell president that he was seriously considering yet another offer. Clearly, Meek was a complex character. His personal identity, goals, and ambitions went beyond the boundaries of his job at Cornell.

Of course, Meek may have used the outside offers simply to gain leverage in discussions with his boss. Three decades on the Cornell campus had made him a consummate university politician. His letters to university officials asking that the Hotel department be made into a separate school within the College of Home Economics date back to at least 1936. But in a 1964 interview, Meek says he never suggested that the school be made independent of Home Economics.

Meek claimed that the separation of the two schools was the idea of Arthur Peterson, a professor of agricultural economics who later became university controller. Peterson felt that the Hotel school should be indepen-

A lecture on hotel modernization ends with H. L. Toombs, chief engineer of Chicago's Conrad Hilton, passing out pictures to students and Dean Meek.

dent of the State University system because it was the only state unit that charged tuition to New York State residents. This was not a new idea, but Meek had resisted it for years because he was concerned that Hotel faculty and staff might lose their state pensions if the split occurred.

Meek says that when the university agreed to switch his employees to the private TIAA-CREF pension system, the separation idea became "a very logical step. The Hotel school had established itself sufficiently academically so that for it to be an independent faculty was perfectly logical and consistent. But this was nothing that I had a share in." If Meek ever did seek power for its own sake, he was careful not to show it.

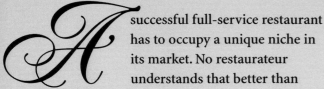successful full-service restaurant has to occupy a unique niche in its market. No restaurateur understands that better than Joseph H. Baum '43. Baum made his mark as president of Restaurant Associates, a company that created a new idea—theme restaurants. At its height in the late 1960s, Restaurant Associates operated over 130 restaurants and had annual sales exceeding $130 million.

Baum grew up in the hospitality industry. His parents owned a resort hotel, and by the age of 5 Joe was interested in cooking. He graduated from the Hotel program and gravitated toward restaurant management after a short time in an accounting firm. But managing existing restaurants was not Baum's forte. He began experimenting with new styles of service and new restaurant designs.

In 1953, Jerry Brody, owner of the fledgling Restaurant Associates, hired Baum to realize his idea of a "destination" restaurant at the Newark Airport. Experts predicted doom: the existing restaurant was up two flights of stairs, the airport had few travelers at the time, and Newark was not exactly a restaurant mecca. But Baum turned The Newarker into a stunning success that grossed $3 million a year. One typical touch: It offered seven oysters instead of six, with the seventh oyster on a separate plate.

Baum quickly capitalized on his success by opening other restaurants, each one organized around a bigger and flashier "theme." At the Forum of the Twelve Caesars, diners were reminded of the ancient world in not-so-subtle ways; in a typical touch, the wine buckets were upended Roman helmets. Critics called it tacky, but the restaurant packed them in for twenty years. Another restaurant, La Fonda del Sol, was described by a critic as "Cliff Notes on South American food," but it ran for fifteen years. The Four Seasons, still operating in the mid-1990s, was among the first luxury restaurants to feature California wines; its glassware designs are in the Museum of Modern Art.

Baum opened his own company in 1970. He attracted raves in the industry for restoring the Rainbow Room at Rockefeller Center. But his crowning achievement was Windows on the World, a world-famous restaurant on the 107th floor of the World Trade Center in New York City that was still going strong in the 1990s. It featured a three-tiered floor plan so all customers could enjoy the stunning views. According to Charles Bernstein's book, *Great Restaurant Innovators,* Windows has grossed as much as $22 million in a particularly good year.

Many of the products of Joe Baum's fertile imagination have now become standards throughout the restaurant industry. He invented the practice of "cupping" a dirty ashtray with a clean one as it is removed from the table. Colleagues claim that he was the first to order waiters to refold a diner's napkin whenever they went to the rest room. Even the practice of servers offering self-introductions—"Hi, my name is Adam, and I'll be your waiter tonight"—was supposedly started at the Tower Suite in the Time & Life Building, another Baum creation.

Joe Baum's legend grew when he was inducted into the Culinary Institute's Hall of Fame in 1995. He shared that honor with only seven others, including Julia Child, Paul Bocuse, and Craig Claiborne. After he threw his own induction party, Baum quickly got back to work on his latest show-stopping project—the renovation of Windows on the World.

## The Alice Statler Years

Meek's personal ambitions were masked, but his ambitions for the school were always public. And in the mid-1950s, his primary ambition was to expand the school to support 450 students, just as he had requested in 1942.

Almost before the paint was dry, Meek began arguing that Statler Hall was too small. It was built to serve 300 students, he pointed out, and enrollment was steady at 400. Fortunately he did not have to go far to find a sympathetic ear. In December 1951, when Statler Foundation trustee Edward Letchworth made the final $241,000 payment on Statler Hall, he added that the foundation "shall not lose our interest in the school in any way." The school's "success and progress" would be a continuing Statler concern.

Over the next six years, Meek courted the Statler Foundation like a persistent suitor, alternating expressions of gratitude with lists of new needs and wants. In June 1952, Meek made his first request for a new wing that would include a large auditorium. Statler trustees postponed that request. But in December, they announced $360,000 in gifts of cash and stock to support building maintenance, scholarships, and faculty research. Meek was pleased to report that the inn and restaurant operations of Statler Hall were showing a profit.

Mrs. Statler breaks ground in May 1956 for the Alice Statler Auditorium addition to Statler Hall. From left, Cornell President Deane Malott, Mrs. Statler, J.R. Williams, a university administrator; Dean H. B. Meek, Dan Silverberg '56, and Joseph Woods '56.

The money was sorely needed, because the Hotel faculty was in need of renewal in the 1950s. In his annual report written in July 1952, Meek announced that Prof. John Courtney was retiring after twenty-seven years of service. Worse were the unanticipated departures of five other Hotel faculty members and staff. Despite its expansion, the program was still small enough that the departure of six key people at once created real hardship.

"It is not easy to locate proper replacements for so highly specialized a field," wrote Meek, "and the worst is perhaps not yet." The departing staff members' salaries were under $10,000 a year. But "offers of $25,000 for work in the industry and of $15,000 for teaching hotel subjects elsewhere have been received by members of our staff," he wrote. By this time, a dozen other colleges were offering courses in hotel education. Meek concluded: "If we are going to hold our position of leadership, if we are going to use our great resources of building and of students, we must find ways to hold our staff."

While Meek was forced to rebuild the staff, he did not tamper with the school's core curriculum. Accord-

Although The Greenbrier Hotel always drew more than its fair share of affluent guests (*see page* 4), it never showed a healthy profit until a Hotel alumnus became its manager. One reason was the guests, who often were presidents, monarchs, and members of high society. They demanded the highest degree of creature comforts, and furnishing those appointments drove up the cost of doing business in remote West Virginia.

The Greenbrier's financial history makes it particularly impressive that E. Truman Wright '34 managed to turn a profit in just his first year as its resident manager. Wright joined the hotel in 1951 after working as executive assistant manager of the Waldorf-Astoria. The Greenbrier had fired four managers in four years. But Wright had spent his time at the Waldorf under the personal supervision of the great hotelman and Hotel program benefactor Lucius Boomer, and he was ready. "My experience at his elbow was equal to four years at Cornell," he says.

Wright coaxed a $17,000 operating profit out of The Greenbrier in 1951, and the hotel's board of directors made him general manager one year later. In 1962, he became vice president and managing director. Eight years later, he was president of the hotel. When he retired in 1974, Wright had served one of the longest tenures in The Greenbrier's history.

The hotel underwent enormous expansion under Wright. Tennis courts, an Olympic-size pool, corporate meeting rooms, and a mountain retreat were just a few of the major additions that Wright fought for and oversaw. "They called me The Builder," he says.

In the mid-1990s, Wright lived near his children in Sea Island, Georgia. One son, Edward T. Wright Jr. '58, is vice president and managing director of Sea Island's exclusive Cloister resort.

North entrance of The Greenbrier.

ing to the school's 1952 *Announcement,* the curriculum stressed instruction in accounting, administration, secretarial studies, economics and finance, engineering, food preparation, housekeeping, language, and expression.

Introductory courses in subjects like chemistry and mathematics still depended on examples from the hotel industry, as they had since the beginning. A substantial amount of hotel work outside of classes was still required of each student, although practice in the Statler Inn could now help satisfy the requirement. The curricular changes of the 1950s were gradual. One was the offering of a new bachelor's degree in Food Facilities Engineering, or the design of restaurants and institutional food operations. Another was a course on tourism developed in association with the American Express Company.

In his report on the 1956–57 year, Meek noted that applications and enrollment had been decreasing. He blamed competition from other hotel education programs that cost less than Cornell's, and expressed his wish for greater scholarship funds. But he also mentioned the success of the school's expanding programs in executive education.

The established summer "refresher" courses that began in 1928 attracted 179 executives in 1956 and over 205 for 1957. During the 1956–57 school year, short courses were also offered at the Statler Inn. Some 268 professionals came to learn about hotel, club, and restaurant management. In addition, the school trained food-service officers from the Navy and Air Force. All of this was accomplished by just six resident full-time professors.

Overcrowding, inflated tuition prices, and overtaxed professors—the problems must have seemed overwhelming. One can imagine Meek taking a break from writing his annual report, walking down to the other end of Statler Hall, and checking on the progress of his latest accomplishment. It was a new wing, another gift from the Statler Foundation. The $1.75 million project would include a 900-seat, air-conditioned auditorium named for Alice Statler; additional laboratories for food and engineering courses; offices, lecture rooms, test kitchens, and a 25,000-volume library.

The library, which was originally named for Meek, may have proven to be the most valuable part of the new wing. Although strong competition had arisen from hotel programs in other schools, no other place had a separate collection of books and resources devoted to the hospitality industry that could match the Cornell collection. In the 1960s and 1970s, the Hotel library staff began fielding so many research questions from hospitality executives that Dean Robert Beck began managing the library as an industry outreach program.

When the Alice Statler Auditorium and the new wing opened at the 1958 Hotel Ezra Cornell, the value of the Statler Foundation's total gifts to Cornell reached $5 million. In 1961, Statler gave another $1.5 million. One-third of it would endow a Statler Professorship, with Meek holding the first chair; one-third would enhance the building maintenance fund; and one-third would expand the school's research program.

When Alice Statler announced the gift in 1960, Meek was closing out four decades as chief of Cornell's hotel education efforts. He had accepted the retirement of his first employee, Prof. Frank Randolph. It was time to begin hiring a new generation of Hotel professors, and

Charles F. Feeney '56 once gave a talk to Hotel students about the entrepreneurial spirit. Feeney knows a little about the subject. With Robert W. Miller '55 he cofounded Duty-Free Shoppers, which grew to a major international business with outlets in airports across North America, the Pacific, and elsewhere.

"There are a lot of kindred spirits in the Hotel school," Feeney said. "The hospitality industry lends itself to a lot of small startup situations. The makeup and the personality of the students is probably the reason for that. A Hotel student has that self-starter attitude."

Feeney came to Cornell on the G.I. Bill and sold sandwiches and other goods to help pay his way. While at Cornell, he got as much out of classes as possible. For example, he prepared for a business career in Europe by taking extra credit hours of French and Russian. When he landed in France, he almost immediately embarked on his first business venture: a summer camp for children of sailors in the U.S. Sixth Fleet. After that camp, he noticed that people were selling "everything from soup to nuts" to U.S. naval ships. Feeney joined the business and sold mostly liquor. In 1963, he struck gold. He and another Hotelie, Peter S. Fithian '51, bid on 105 square feet of space at the Honolulu International Airport. In return, they had to pay $135,000.

How did the Hotel school help Feeney? "I got a lot out of Cornell," he told the students, "more than a simple diploma. It prepared me. When you come out of Cornell, you've got good baggage. When you say 'Cornell University,' everybody knows it's a damn good university and the Hotel school is the best in the world."

it was time to change the school yet again to meet the challenges of the 1960s. Meek was 67. He may have been tired. He was facing the university's mandatory retirement age. But the most important fact was that he was done. The school was finally close to the way he had planned it. It was a good time to go.

### Meek Takes His Leave

Before Meek retired from the Hotel school, he planted the first seeds of a major expansion of hotel industry research at Cornell. In 1960, he announced a study of vending machines funded by the Vendo Corporation. He also mentioned an initial Statler grant of $70,000 for the first phase of a new study, to be led by the venerable Professor Sayles, "of the possible application of

Today, restaurant diners think nothing of ordering wine with a meal. But forty years ago, Americans usually ignored wine in favor of martinis, manhattans, or other mixed drinks.

The acceptance of wine in the United States has been a long, uphill struggle. The problem was ignorance; few Americans, even in the hospitality industry, understood wine. "In the 1950s the cause of the ignorance was fourteen years of Prohibition," says Julius Wile, who taught in the first accredited wine appreciation course in American collegiate history at Cornell in 1953. "There is still ignorance about wine today, but at that time, it was abysmal. Wine was not a basic part of Americans' consumption, as it is daily in Europe."

The European example frustrated American winemakers and importers. Five of them—George Lawrence of Taylor Wines, John Longwell of Urbana Wine Company, Tony Doherty of Great Western Champagne, Julius Wile representing the wine importers, and Jim McNamara of the California Wine Institute— met with Prof Meek.

Doherty recalls he mentioned that the Finger Lakes have many nationally recognized vineyards, and suggested that Hotel students might find it useful to visit some of the vineyards and learn about wine-making. "Meek thought for a minute and then asked, 'Can you set up a fully rounded course on wine, [with] ten one-hour lectures and a final exam?'" Doherty recalls. "After I swallowed a couple of times I said, 'Yes, we could.'"

In the fall of 1953, seven leading vintners from New York and California visited the campus to lecture on such topics as the chemistry of wine, champagne and sparkling wine, foreign wine, and cooking with wine. The course was offered to juniors and seniors as an elective, and more than half of eligible students attended. The course was ridiculed outside of Statler Hall by those who felt that wine should not be the subject of academic study. Even within the industry, some vintners and restaurateurs said that such a course was unnecessary. But this was probably expected by Meek, who had faced the same kind of resistance when he founded the Hotel program three decades earlier.

Support for wine education grew through the 1950s and 1960s, as industry leaders recognized the value of Cornell's efforts directed by Prof. Matthew Bernatsky. In 1978, the first chair of wine education and management was established at Cornell by Banfi Vintners, with Vance Christian '61 as professor. Spirits were eventually included in the course, which was renamed Beverage Management. In the mid-1990s, Stephen A. Mutkoski, PhD '76 held the chair.

Wines are now a standard part of restaurant management courses, and hundreds of wine appreciation courses are offered to non-professionals every year. Americans appreciate wine much more now than they did at mid-century, due partly to the foresight of industry leaders and Cornell professors.

The Banfi-Cornell ties are many, based on the enthusiasm of John *54 and Harry Mariani, owners of Banfi, and of Richard W. Brown '49, assistant to John Mariani. The Marianis built their wine importing business on the belief Americans liked cold drinks, proven by the success of their Italian red wine, Riunité.

A Mariani gift (*see page* 127) was key to the school's capital campaign in the 1980s, and Brown is former president of the Cornell Society of Hotelmen and Cornell Alumni Association, and former executive VP of the National Restaurant Association.

data-processing equipment to the various aspects of hotel operation." Thus did the Hotel school's computer era begin.

Another step toward research was taken on May 1, 1960, with the first issue of the *Cornell Hotel and Restaurant Administration Quarterly.* This scholarly journal would quickly become the leading publication in its field, under the able editing of Prof. Helen Recknagel. *The Quarterly* filled a gaping hole in the hospitality industry and in hotel education. Before the second issue appeared, it had almost 3,000 subscribers. Within a year, it had added 1,000 more.

The 1960–61 academic year became Meek's victory lap. He attended over fifty testimonials and other farewell functions around the country, including the thirty-sixth Hotel Ezra Cornell, which was dedicated to "The Century's Greatest Hotel Educator." Roy Watson, who was then the president of the Cornell Society of Hotelmen, gave a speech in the form of a letter to the "Prof." "Immediately thereafter we presented him with a large scrapbook containing letters to him from almost all of the then graduates," Watson writes.

"The demonstrations of affection have been embarrassingly overwhelming, but abundantly appreciated," Meek wrote. His farewell report closed with his personal thanks to Cornell "for providing the opportunity, the framework within which to work, and to those many friends and supporters, fellow teachers, students, alumni, and hotel men generally without whose assistance the Department of Hotel Administration might still be a one-man affair in a basement office on the east campus."

In forty years, Meek had taken Cornell's hotel education program from obscurity to prominence, with support from a large network of powerful men and women. His influence was felt throughout the hotel industry. A few weeks before his retirement, he used that influence to solve a problem for Michael Z. Kay '61, who had six months to fill between graduation and a military commitment and no job offers. "In a matter of minutes, [Meek] determined that I wanted to work for a hotel chain," said Kay. "He picked up the phone and called Joe Binns, a graduate who was then senior vice president of Hilton's eastern region in the U.S. He arranged an appointment for me with Binns. His parting words were, 'Don't mess it up and you ought to land a job.' With a class of 100 it was easy to have this kind of relationship, even with the dean."

After his retirement, Meek continued to be an influence on hospitality education. He retained an office in Statler Hall and was a regular guest at Hotel Ezra Cornell. In 1964, he completed a report for the National Restaurant Association on the status of restaurant education in the United States. He served terms as president of the Tompkins County Hospital and of Ithaca's Reconstruction Home. He also made another major contribution to the hospitality industry.

Shortly after his retirement, Meek became the executive director of the Council on Hotel, Restaurant, and Institutional Education (CHRIE), a small association of hotel and restaurant educators that had existed since 1946. Meek brought many new initiatives to the organization just as a major expansion of college-level hospitality education began. In the mid-1990s, CHRIE had 2,200 members and was a thriving international organization.

Although Meek's retirement years were busy, he was able to enjoy more time with his wife Lois, their two children, and their home at 422 Highland Road. His summers were devoted to his most cherished pastime, sailing. "I insist on sailing in open water, not the ponds that you have [in Ithaca]," Meek said. He had sailed with his father and grandfather when he was a boy in Boston; later, he taught his children the skills his father had taught him. His daughter, Lois Jean Meek, became an architect in New Haven, Connecticut. Son Donald Meek, whom his father said "tipped his first boat over when he was 7," grew up to become a commander in the U.S. Navy.

John H. Sherry, who came to the school from New York City once a week for forty years, teaches a class in law. His son Prof. John E.H. Sherry continued the family tradition, joining the faculty to teach law in 1972.

*Top left:* Dean Meek, on a trip in 1959 near the end of his career, is instructed in how to eat poi by the wife of Howard Donnelly '47, manager of a Waikiki Beach hotel in Hawaii.

*Top right:* Dean Meek presents certificates to U.S. servicemen trained in Cornell Hotel school courses in Germany in January 1961, part of a program of off-campus training for the hospitality industry.

*Bottom:* Lois Meek, left, wife of the dean, at an alumni gathering in the Poconos. Dean Meek is at right.

On July 16, 1969—the day the Apollo 11 astronauts took off for the moon—Prof Meek set out from his Cape Cod summer home in a sailboat he had received as a retirement present from the Statler Foundation. He was 75. Meek had been born in a world that had no automobiles, refrigeration, or electric light, but now he was pondering the reality of space travel. During his life, he had mastered four academic disciplines—mathematics, astronomy, economics, and accounting—and created a fifth, hotel education. He guided the Cornell Hotel program through four decades of technological and social change, and he laid the foundation for an era of global expansion in the 1960s and 1970s. But through it all, he was happiest when sailing in the waters around Cape Cod.

At the end of that day, Meek's boat approached his dock and was spotted by Mary Cosgrave, a neighbor. Cosgrave later told Meek's daughter Lois Jean that he missed the mooring at the dock, ran aground, slipped, and fell in the boat. She came to the dock to help, but he angrily waved her off. "He was disgusted with himself," said Lois. Cosgrave went back toward her house.

Then she heard a sound that filled her with dread. "She heard the sail flapping, just loose and flapping," said Lois. "She got in her skiff and rowed out, and my father was collapsed in the boat." Meek was dead of a heart attack. When the police arrived, they wrapped him in one of his sails, and brought him in.

## FROM THE MEEKBAKE

n March 10, 1961, the New England chapter of the Cornell Society of Hotelmen held a "Meekbake" to say farewell to their beloved "Prof." One of the highlights of the evening was the following number, sung by a group of "Meek's Boys":

My name is Howard Bagnall Meek, I'm glad to be with you,
  I came to Cornell way back, in nineteen twenty-two;
I found a group of odd balls, who caused me grief and woe,
  Like Jim Smith, Jennings and Grohmann, and Thomas C. Deveau.

In forty years I've done my best by teaching at Cornell,
  To turn out men who'd be adept at running a hotel;
My hair has gotten thin and gray, don't think it's been fun,
  I never thought I'd make it, to nineteen sixty-one.

If I'd behaved like you did, I'd not be here to joke,
  While you all drank your way through school, I wisely stuck to Coke;
I never smoked a cigarette, I never even swore,
  Like Arthur Murray, I got my fun by dancing 'round the floor!

Albert E. Koehl '28 sings a tribute at a "Meekbake" in Boston in March 1961, at the end of H. B. Meek's tenure as founding dean of the Hotel program.

When asked for their most dominant memory of Meek, many Hotel alumni remember his gaze. "The stare he shoots at you is like a steel beam," recalled one alumnus in a 1961 appreciation in the *Cornell Alumni News*. "It has a shining quality, but is unwavering. It extends—uniting you to him. You know you couldn't bend it if you wished. It reassures you. For here is a man, you surmise, who can structure a relationship that will endure and make you more a man. But it weighs upon you. It frightens you a bit. For here is a man whose very attitude demands that you hold up your end of the structure."

# We Ought to Lead the Way

T ALL STARTED with a dead battery. A rural road on Cape Cod was

a bad place for a car to break down on a hot summer day in 1932, and

H. B. Meek was relieved when a passing motorist slowed down to lend a

hand. "I was 12 years old, driving along with my mother," says Robert A.

Beck '42. "She saw this great big old Buick that had stalled, and [Meek] had a

chain . . . she pulled him and got him started."

Meek became friends with the Becks, and he soon learned that young Robert

had something that interested them both. "I had a little sailboat, a fourteen-footer,

and he loved to sail but didn't have a sailboat," says Beck. "So we went sailing. And

Dean Robert Beck '42 and Paul Gaurnier '50, right, assistant dean, talk with undergraduates in 1973 in the Statler student lounge. The dean was generally available mid-mornings in the lounge.

then every summer they came down [to Cape Cod]." On long

summer days, the middle-age man and his teen-age friend

would hoist their sails and take a spin in Buzzards Bay.

Meek was "one of the most distinctive men I knew," remembers Beck, and at some point, "he brainwashed me." Soon the young man was convinced that the Cornell Hotel program was the only place to be.

When his time came, Meek's protégé sped through the ranks of the Hotel school like a skiff catching a fresh breeze. After graduating from public schools in his hometown of Milton, Massachusetts, Robert Beck enrolled in the Cornell Hotel program in 1938, graduated in 1942, returned as a graduate student in 1951, joined the Hotel faculty in 1954, was awarded tenure in 1957, and was made a full professor in 1960. A year later, at the age of 41, he succeeded Meek as dean. Over the next two decades, he proved to be a skilled fundraiser and inspiring leader during a period of extraordinary growth and challenge.

During Beck's twenty years as dean, student enrollment in the Hotel school doubled. When Beck arrived, the school's executive education program hadn't been fully developed; when he left, it was a program of global proportions. Before Beck, research was a minor part of the Hotel school; during his watch, Statler Hall became an internationally known research center.

## Becoming Dean Beck

The 1930s were relatively tranquil for Cornell. Students in the Hotel program were a small, tightly knit group in an obscure, poorly funded corner of a big university. They weren't often noticed by other students, and their classes were held in the rooms and offices no one else wanted. "I think I had a class in almost every building on the campus," says Beck. "I remember I used to have to go to Allan Treman's famous Business Law class in the morning in Rice Hall, the poultry building. All you could smell was hen droppings at eight o'clock in the morning."

Beck was an able though not a particularly distinguished Hotel student. He made his mark on campus in two other areas. The first was the track team. "We had a two-mile relay team that was supposed to be pretty hot stuff," he says. "We were invited to appear at Madison Square Garden at the top meet of the winter. So [track coach] Jack Moakley got us together, and he said that I was going to run the anchor leg, which is usually given to the best runner. I wasn't the best runner. And I said, 'Mr. Moakley, I'm very honored that you've given me this opportunity, and I'll do the best that I can.' And he said, 'Well, the reason I'm putting you in the last lap is because I think the other three will get you so far ahead that even you can't lose.'"

New, larger library is a feature of the Alice Statler wing added to Statler Hall.

The 1960s and 1970s were years of transition for the Hotel school faculty. When Dean Meek retired in 1961, many of the men he hired in the 1920s and 1930s were still teaching. By the time Dean Beck retired in 1980, none was. Beck oversaw the transition to a second generation of Hotel faculty.

**Thomas W. Silk**  Alumni of 1938 to 1968 have fond memories of Thomas W. Silk '38 (1904–1971). Silk taught basic accounting, but he is best remembered for his enthusiastic ability to counsel students. Jack Craver '52 remembers that Silk loved word play, and that students called him "Mot Klis," which is his name spelled backwards. Craver also faced Silk out of class, because Silk was head of the University Student Conduct Committee when Craver and other Hotelies got in trouble for raiding the campus radio station.

Richard D. Fors '59 is one of thousands of students who faced the blackboard of Silk's classroom and was told to enter their debits on the "window" side, to the left on a ledger. "[Silk] demonstrated a fantastic knowledge of the hospitality industry on opening day of his course," he says. "Each student was asked to stand and provide the name of his hometown, and no matter how remote, Silk would discuss the leading restaurant or hotel in that location."

Silk sometimes called his students "dummies" in class, but he would go to any length to assist their personal well-being. He was especially active as an advisor to international students. Hiroshi Kohda '64 was suffering through a cold Ithaca winter, "and with the lack of a hot daily bath and the change in diet, I suffered from very painful hemorrhoids," he says. "Professor Silk got a hint of my problem and diplomatically asked me if I had received an injury during judo practice, to which I timidly nodded yes. The next day he quietly gave me a doughnut-shaped rubber pillow to sit on."

"Silk really gave me a strong basis for accounting, and I view accounting as the cornerstone of every business transaction I have ever done," says Kenneth B. Hamlet '66. "To this date, I never use a red pen or pencil unless it is a negative number. And I always remember debits to the window, credits to the wall."

**O. Ernest Bangs**  Another strong influence on students in the Beck era was Prof. O. Ernest Bangs (1904–1995), who helped pioneer the first college courses in food facilities engineering. Bangs joined the Hotel faculty in 1958 and retired in 1971. He helped create hotel administration programs at colleges in Seoul, Korea and San Juan, Puerto Rico.

In the summer of 1958, "Ernie would come through the Statler lobby each day at lunch time," says William Eaton '61, who had a job at the Inn after his first year at the Engineering school. "We made friends by talking about engineering and his course in food facilities engineering. He piqued my interest in the Hotel school and in his courses to such an extent that I transferred to study with him." Eaton eventually became senior vice president of Cini·Little International, a restaurant design firm with headquarters in Rockville, Maryland. "Ernie really created our field," he says. "Fifteen Cini·Little employees came through his course."

Bangs also was an advisor to young faculty. "He sat in on my classes and corrected my many mistakes," says Prof. Richard H. Penner. "He insisted I refer not to 'cheap' equipment, but rather call it 'inexpensive.' I am still careful in my terminology 25 years later, and attribute it to Ernie's tutelage."

"He taught us to think, to plan," says Eaton. "And above all, he taught us ethics."

**Matthew Bernatsky** (1906–1981) served on the Hotel faculty from 1960 to 1972, and was a summer school instructor prior to 1960. He taught courses in restaurant management, and he may have been the first to expand wines instruction to include beverage management.

Bernatsky fascinated his students with his encyclopaedic knowledge of food and hospitality history, some of which he had seen firsthand. He was born in Budapest, Hungary, and at one time served as an apprentice chef on the fabled Orient Express passenger train. He worked as executive chef in many of the finest hotels in Europe and North America, and was the director of the Hotel Department at the University of Denver just before he came to Cornell. An obituary written by his colleagues Peter Rainsford, Laura Lee Smith, and Donal Dermody said, "Matt Bernatsky was more than a teacher of techniques. He was, more importantly, a food historian and, to a real degree, a philosopher in his field."

**Vance A. Christian**  "The closest thing we have to a legend at the school" was how one colleague characterized Vance A. Christian '61 (1928–1984), who taught foods courses and a popular wine and spirits course from 1961 until his death. "Decent, kind, and thoughtful, he was the emblem of a caring person," says Nami Thiyagaratnam MPS '85. "Who else would have thought of my family and driven to Hasbrouck Apartments, searched out my number, and collected my wife, two little children, and myself for our first American Thanksgiving dinner. When we reached his charming house, I found that Vance had collected twelve others for the same dinner who would also have been alone during this holiday."

Christian was a mentor to many students. He was also the school's first African-American professor, and although he did not seek recognition of his race—"I don't teach black management, I teach management," he once said—he eased the way for many African-American students who studied in Statler Hall in the 1960s, '70s, and '80s.

Vance Christian's down-home style endeared him to everyone he met. In one early meeting of the large lecture course called Introduction to Kitchen Equipment, he asked several students to tell about their summer work experiences. "I stood up and told the class that I had worked in the kitchen in an inn in New Hampshire, and that I was the 'Assistant Chef,'" writes Helaine Aronson Winer '84. "Then I sat down, feeling pretty good about my experience and that I got to tell my story. Well, Professor Christian started walking slowly up the aisle toward me with his rather formidable self. He came within about a foot of my seat, bent over, looked me straight in the eye and said, 'You was a cook, sugar.' Needless to say, I was humbled."

The other extracurricular activity wasn't entirely optional. "When I was at Cornell, every male American had to do two years of ROTC," says Beck. "If your grades were right and you wanted to, you could opt for two more years." Beck did, but not for patriotic reasons. "In those days, much of the field artillery was pulled by horses. I wanted to learn equitation—and besides, they paid 25 cents a day, including Saturdays and Sundays. So I signed up. Then, bingo!—Pearl Harbor."

Beck became an Army artillery officer immediately after graduating in 1942. In 1943, while at home on leave from the Army, he called a girl he had met in high school. Jan Murray was a stewardess on a train that ran from Boston to New York City, so she kept an apartment in both places. In January 1944, when Beck called on her in New York City, their friendship turned to love. In February, they were engaged. In March, he left for Europe.

Three months later—on D-Day, at 5:20 in the morning—Bob Beck landed on Utah Beach. "I was supposed to give commands to a Navy officer on the beach who was going to give commands to the battleship USS Texas. Unfortunately, the Navy guy got shot early on." Beck had been trained to use a howitzer that fired a thirty-pound shell, and he found himself giving orders to a twelve-inch gun that fired a shell weighing nearly 1,000 pounds. "The first time one came over, I thought I was going to kill everybody around," he says.

Beck came through his first day of combat unscathed, but he was severely wounded one week later while fighting about seven miles in from the coast. His right leg had to be amputated above the knee, and he spent the next eleven months in hospitals in England and Washington, D.C. "I was one of the lucky ones," he says. In his unit of 185 men, only eleven survived. While an outpatient at Walter Reed Hospital, he and Jan were married.

Back in Boston, Beck spent the next seven years working for the city's huge food center, the Quincy Market. Jan stayed home to care for their two young daughters. Beck was hired as a food technician, but because he was one of the few employees with a college degree, he began doing labor relations work. He liked that field and wanted further training in it, so in 1951 he returned to Cornell on a leave of absence to study at the new New York State School of Industrial and Labor

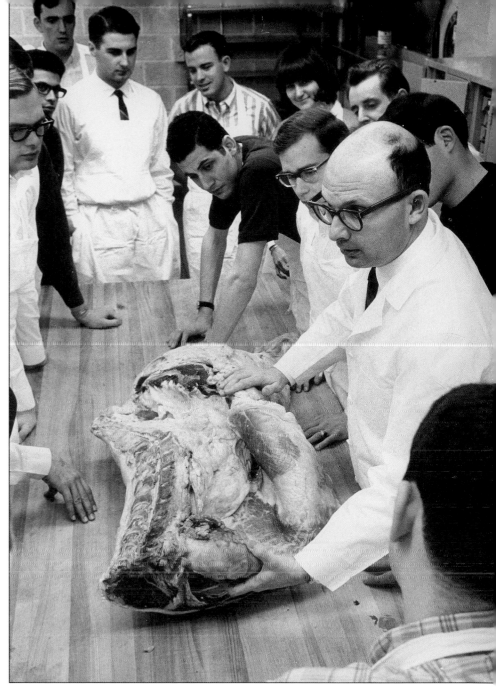

Professor Wanderstock lectures in a basic meats course in the mid-1960s.

Relations. Not long after he arrived, a position opened up at the Hotel school. Meek asked Beck if he wanted to teach basic accounting. "I wasn't all that affluent at the time, so I said sure," he remembers.

Once he discovered the pleasures of teaching, Beck never thought of returning to private business. He earned a master's degree in education, and at Meek's insistence went on to get a Ph.D. with a concentration in psychology. In February 1954 Meek hired him as an assistant professor. Beck's diverse academic background enabled him to teach labor relations classes to Hotel students in the morning, then teach accounting to students from Home Economics and the ILR school in the afternoon.

Looking back in a 1994 interview, Beck attributes much of his success at Cornell to being in the right place at the right time. "When you were born, the time you're living in, these things over which you have no control—they're extremely important," he says. But there was more. Although Beck may have been lucky, he also had a knack for making the right choices and knowing the right people. "When I became a professor, John Courtney was retiring. They needed someone to do *The Bulletin of the Cornell Society of Hotelmen,* and to take over from Courtney as secretary-treasurer of the society. They asked a lot of people to do it, and by default it came to me. That's how I got to know the old boys very well. And of course I knew the group from

my own classes, 1938 to 1942. And then I began to pick up the younger alumni from teaching them. So I had a great expanse of people that I knew."

In 1957, granting tenure to a university professor was much simpler than it is now. Beck simply got the nod from Meek and President Deane W. Malott, and a guarantee of lifetime employment came with that nod. Beck soon learned that even the appointing of a dean could be done without much paperwork.

Through a friend, university Athletic Director Robert Kane *34, Bob and Jan Beck were introduced to Deane Malott and his wife Eleanor. Malott was an agricultural economist from Kansas who had become president of Cornell in 1951. The couples became friends, and Malott appointed Beck to the search committee for Meek's successor. "We'd meet every two weeks to cull all the people out, and the only ones we didn't cull out were the people on our own committee," Beck says. "So we submitted a group of names, among which was mine, to President Malott. There weren't all the layers of committees we have today. There was the search committee, we gave the names to Malott, and he made the decision.

"One February day I got a call from his office, so I went over and he said he would like me to be dean. I said that I liked things the way they were, and was there any possibility that Meek's tenure could be extended? He said no, it couldn't be extended. Then he said to me, 'There's a saying that goes, change for change itself. And I think it's about time for the Hotel school, because Meek has been in there for thirty-nine years.'

"He said, 'Let me tell you this. If you don't take the job, you'll never forgive yourself.' If he hadn't said that, I might not have taken the job because I really didn't covet it. After all, the life of a university professor is fairly satisfying.

"So I talked it over with my wife, and I decided maybe I never would forgive myself. I also did it in self-defense, because I didn't know who else was being considered. So on July 1, 1961, I became the second dean of the School of Hotel Administration.

"I was probably the youngest member of the faculty, or close to it, and all of a sudden I was the boss. These were the people who had taught me as a student. They had been my mentors, and now I was their mentor. But by and large, I got marvelous cooperation from them all."

### Seizing the Opportunity

While Meek had been a life-long academic and small hotel operator, the new dean was a former military officer. It was an abrupt change in leadership style. Robert Beck was an executive who liked military precision and statistics. Beginning in 1961–62, for example, the dean's annual reports list the number of books in the library and the number of research requests received during the year.

Beck also liked giving orders, and he liked to see obedience in the people who reported to him. "Meek was a benevolent dictator," he says. "I was a dictator, period."

People who worked with Beck say that his self-assessment is too harsh. "He was a gentleman in every sense of the word," says Cheryl Farrell, his administrative assistant from 1973 to 1977. "His military background came through in some ways; the women who worked in his office did have a strict dress code. But it was all done with great respect. He respected us, and we showed respect for him."

Beck's by-the-rules style was also tempered by a great deal of personal warmth. He made himself approachable by keeping an "open-door" policy in his office that applied to everyone. He also poked fun at his own authority with self-deprecating humor. One

Prof. Stanley Davis *47, director of the school's new master of professional studies program, talks with students in his office in 1977. Dean Beck credits Davis with being largely responsible for establishing the graduate program and for its ultimate success.

day in 1959, then-professor Beck confronted a growling campus dog that wandered into his classroom in the middle of his lecture. According to Richard D. Fors '59, Beck turned to the dog and said, "take a bite out of my leg and you'll get the biggest mouthful of splinters you've ever had!"

For many years, this style of leadership worked well. Veterans of Beck's early years remember that many faculty members kept an informal dress code of dark suits, white shirts, and conservative ties. Every day at lunch, Beck would sit in Statler Hall's Rathskeller dining room, and many of the faculty would sit with him. It was the style and tone of the Organization Man, and in 1961 it was the mainstream approach.

A disciplined staff was only one of the many advantages Beck enjoyed. Again, his timing was important. He arrived in the dean's office as the school and the industry it served were poised for rapid growth. Moreover, the school was in a good position to capitalize on the many opportunities of the era.

Ironically, the Hotel school's low profile within the university turned out to give Beck a powerful advantage. The school had to be self-supporting, because Cornell would not support it with university funds. "There was a certain amount of feeling among some of our scholarly colleagues," says Beck. "They were fond of saying, 'What the hell is a hotel school doing on the campus of a great American university?'

"I remember one time we had a meeting with a faculty committee that was examining each school. The chairman was a professor of philosophy named Max Black, and he was very British. He asked us about our program, and we described it, and finally he concluded, 'Well, I suppose it's all well and good to know the physical properties of water, but the world does need its plumbers, doesn't it?' And that sort of set the stance for the way much of the university saw the school."

A by-product of the Hotel school's low status was that university administrators usually let Beck do as he pleased. "In my twenty years, I don't think I was ever told I did a good job or a poor job," he says. "I never sat down with the president to review anything. The only thing was the budget—and since the university wasn't kicking in any money, we went over it ourselves."

As a self-supporting unit that operated its own hotel, restaurant, and "franchise" education operations, the Hotel school's existence depended on maintaining a businesslike attitude toward revenue and expenses. Revenue, in Beck's case, was dominated by one source. "It is through tuition income primarily that the School of Hotel Administration must make its way," he wrote in 1968. "This calls for considerable planning and constant attention to the day-to-day problems of operation." In other words, Hotel students were not viewed as the least privileged members of the academy. Rather, they were customers who must be satisfied with their educational experience.

Like any educational institution, the Hotel school had a seemingly limitless need for equipment and staff. The needs were especially acute when Beck arrived on the scene, because all the equipment in Statler Hall was at least ten years old. The dean's office telephone, for example, was a constant source of frustration to Beck. It had two lines, and the dean's secretary had a buzzer to tell the dean which line to pick up. "The buzzer rang once, you picked up line one. It rang twice, you picked up line two. And I didn't know if it would be my wife, or someone calling from Hong Kong." Other deans had intercoms. But if Beck wanted one of those, he had to find the money for it himself.

The Hotel school receives a check for $410,000 in April 1972 from the Statler Foundation to expand its research work significantly. Peter Crotty, left, foundation chairman, makes the presentation to Thomas Mackesey, a Cornell vice president. Mrs. Lois Meek, widow of the school's founder, looks on.

The presence of the Statler Inn also forced the Hotel dean to deal with mundane management problems, because the Inn was both a business and a model for other hotels. Small thefts by employees, for example, would have a small but direct effect on the Statler Inn's profitability. This would affect the money available for other things.

In the mid-1960s, the Statler Inn kitchens were experimenting with boil-in-bag meals called "ready food" that could be stored in a freezer. "It didn't work all that smoothly," remembers Beck. "We had a maintenance man who would go around checking temperatures. When he saw these things, we began to lose our inventory. So one day we got suspicious because the guy was walking around with a big overcoat on. We made him open up the coat, and he had all these packages of frozen food strapped all around. The poor bastard must have been frozen himself!"

Bob Beck was a man of high standards and definite opinions. "He was a stickler for proper use of the English language," remembers Cheryl Farrell, his administrative assistant in the 1970s. "Split infinitives would drive him up the wall." Beck also had his quirks. One was his disdain for Manhattan clam chowder: "He was a proper Boston gentleman, and New England cream-style chowder was the only proper variety," Farrell says. Another was his hatred of maraschino cherries. He banished them from the Statler Inn and attacked them whenever the subject came up. The reason? "They were artificial," she says.

One day, a mysterious message appeared in the glass display case outside the dean's office.

The case was for very important notices, and it was kept under lock and key. Although the dean never learned who broke into his case, Farrell says he was delighted to read the following poem:

REFLECTION ON THE
DECORATION DETESTABLE

I execrate in the drink I quaff

A maraschino, whole or half,

And heaven knows what pains I take

To scrape it off ice cream or cake.

This cloying artificial sweet

Is sickly to look at, worse to eat.

Thus, when at table I orate

The maraskeynote is one of hate.

versity's School of Hospitality Management, founded by Gerald W. Lattin, PhD '49 in 1972, and the Harrah School of Hotel Administration at the University of Nevada–Las Vegas (UNLV), founded by Jerome J. Vallen '50. Vallen went on to become founding dean of the Australian International Hotel School in Canberra, which was affiliated with Cornell in the mid-1990s.

The explosive growth in hotel education during the 1960s and 1970s reflected a great boom in the hospitality industries. Between 1960 and 1980, the number of passenger-miles Americans traveled on airlines quadrupled. Between 1967 and 1982, sales at eating and drinking places also quadrupled. Hotel revenues per available room quadrupled between 1963 and 1982, while hotel income per room (after taxes and insurance) increased from $1,000 to about $4,000. And the number of franchised restaurants doubled between 1960 and 1970, then doubled again to reach 60,000 by 1980.

Cornell Hotel school alumni were central players in this expansion, and for many the school served as a kind of professional refuge. "The bonding between people says a lot to me," says Beck. "Maybe [the alumni] don't see each other often, yet they feel that [Cornell] is always there for them." For some, the school even took on a family role as the children and grandchildren of alumni began enrolling in the 1960s. These powerful emotional connections made Statler Hall hallowed ground to a growing list of industry executives around the world.

Competition also kept the Hotel school on its toes. In 1968, the annual report noted that about twelve other schools offered instruction in mass housing and feeding. By 1981, about eighty hotel schools were offering training in direct competition with Cornell. They ranged greatly in size and scope. A few were independent four-year programs, such as the Conrad Hilton School at the University of Houston. Others were two- and four-year courses of study within other schools. All of them drained potential applicants away from Cornell.

In fact, many of the newer hotel education programs were founded by Cornell alumni, staffed by Cornell graduates, and supplied with Cornell-produced teaching materials. They included Florida International Uni-

A meeting of the European Chapter of the Cornell Society of Hotelmen, alumni of the Hotel school and associate members, in October 1967 in Berlin. *See Sources for names.*

## Going International

In July 1962, after one year on the job, Beck wrote a short statement that would guide his activities for the next decade. While he acknowledged that the prime objective of the school was "the education of young men and women to assume the responsibilities and leadership of the mass housing and feeding industries," he added that "there are peripheral areas which, in the past, have not been sufficiently developed.

"The most critical areas where considerable development is necessary are, in the writer's opinion, research, adult education (extension education), the utilization of Statler Inn for training purposes, and an evaluation of the existing curriculum."

Beck believed that reaching out beyond Statler Hall was the key to increasing the stature of the Hotel school, and increasing the school's stature was the key to preserving the thing he valued most—independence. "Malott had proposed that we fall under the wing of the Business school. But Business was strictly for graduate study, and its dean didn't want any part of undergraduate education. The Business dean and Alice Statler discouraged Malott, and he backed off."

The school's future depended on finding a way to expand rapidly, stay profitable, and cultivate sources of

Students in Prof. Matthew Bernatsky's summer course in teacher training for chefs in the 1960s inspect a product of their work. They are Sister Fabien of the Mother House of Sisters and Eric Lafond-Favières, chef instructor at the Hotel Training School in Port-au-Prince, Haiti.

support strong enough to outflank detractors. The solution was provided, indirectly, by the Boeing Corporation.

Before 1959, air travel across the Atlantic required at least fourteen hours in a loud, piston-driven, cramped airplane. But when Boeing put the jet-powered 707 transatlantic airliner into regular service, the world shrank. Transit time was cut in half, and the quieter, larger jets made travel infinitely more comfortable. The cost of jet travel was too high for middle-class Americans until the 1970s. But for affluent travelers and inter-national hotel executives, the dawn of the jet age brought revolutionary changes.

"I was very international-minded," Beck said in 1991. "I figured that was the way tourism was going, and we ought to lead the way."

Cornell was already leading the way. The Hotel school had been training students from all over the world for forty years, and these alumni served as the school's ambassadors. The program's first international student was a Canadian, H. Alexander MacLennan '26, who was instrumental in the founding of Hotel Ezra Cornell. Another early alumnus was Kakumaro Kemmotsu '28 from Japan. In fact, overseas students have accounted for an average of 10 to 15 percent of the Hotel program's student body since the beginning. In contrast, foreign students were only 2 to 3 percent of Cornell undergraduates until the 1980s.

Why would students from Europe, Asia, and elsewhere travel all the way to Ithaca to study? There were already several hotel training programs in Europe. But according to Beck, even the best European programs, such as the great Lausanne, were more concerned with cooking and the details of providing service. "There was nothing in Europe that allowed for the managerial level" of hotel training, he says.

Another reason was that many deserving and affluent students were shut out of the European university system. Tests given in European secondary schools determine whether a student can get into a university; those who fail to make the cut are shunted into trade schools, and hotel training is considered a trade. Cornell did not allow European students to transfer any credits, but it did offer them an education in hotel management with the added prestige of an American Ivy League university.

The constant presence of a foreign contingent gave Hotelies firsthand experiences in diplomacy at a time when most Americans had little contact with other countries. A 1961 article in the student newsletter, *The Cornell Innkeeper*, describes the plight of foreign students as they struggle to understand American slang and rapidly spoken English. The article advises Hotelies not to "feel sorry for your neighbor and fellow student from far across the seven oceans. Instead, try to understand his problems. Give him a hand without being asked for it. Our Hotel school is a relatively small community on this campus. Making the newly arrived and perhaps bewildered foreign student feel part of *all* phases of our school should be an easy task."

Many of the international students have fond memories of professors, staff, and fellow students who invited them into their homes when their own families were far away. In many cases, American-born Hotelies made great efforts to boost the morale and grades of their foreign friends. "I remember once being invited to one of the professor's homes the night before an exam," says Hiroshi Kohda '64, who in the mid-1990s was general

A meeting of the Japan Chapter of the Cornell Society of Hotelmen in Tokyo in July 1972. Dean Robert Beck, who emphasized the international reputation of the school, and Mrs. Beck were present, and stand in the back row. *See Sources for other names.*

Alumni gather in New Delhi in July 1972 for a Southeast Asia Chapter meeting of the Cornell Society of Hotelmen. *See Sources for names.*

Grace Brigham conducts a summer course in hotel housekeeping at Statler Hall. She was head of the National Executive Housekeepers Association.

manager of the Hotel New Otani Osaka. "Subtle and not-so-subtle hints of exam questions were lightly included in the conversation. Not to worry—it didn't make a dent in my test results."

International students contributed greatly to the school, sometimes in unexpected ways. For example, Prof. Thomas Silk and his accounting students were impressed by Yuji Yamaguchi '61 and his abacus; in the days before calculators, the ancient Chinese device was much faster than paper-and-pencil calculations. "Professor Silk was very severe and strict in his class, but very warm when I was invited to his home," says Yamaguchi, who became executive vice-president and general manager of Fujiya Hotels Co., Ltd.

In the 1950s, the number of alumni in other countries grew large enough to form social organizations. In 1953,

Ichiro Inumaru completed the program and returned to his family's business, the Imperial Hotel in Tokyo, as managing director. Soon after, he joined with Kemmotsu and Frank A. Ready Jr. '35 to form the first overseas chapter of the Cornell Society of Hotelmen. The chapter grew rapidly to accommodate returning Japanese alumni, American servicemen, and executives who were helping build the Japanese hotel industry. In 1959 the chapter was instrumental in arranging seminars for U.S. Armed Forces club managers at the Imperial Hotel, with Meek and other professors teaching. Members also interviewed and recommended prospective students, thereby maintaining the flow of people from Japan to Ithaca.

In 1959 a Caribbean chapter was formed, and in November 1961 a chapter formed to serve alumni in Central America. But these events were dwarfed by the

1961 founding of a European chapter. That chapter's annual meetings in Frankfurt quickly became a focus of Hotel activity, with Beck and others flying over to meet alumni, solicit donations, and make deals. By July 1966 the Cornell Society of Hotelmen could report that "the sun never sets on a Cornell Hotelman."

Beck moved quickly to develop the international market for American-style hotel education. In 1961 he appointed Prof. Gerald W. Lattin as the school's first assistant dean, an administrative expansion that gave both men the time to develop seminars and short courses all over the world. The few efforts made during the Meek years convinced both men that the field was ripe for expansion. In 1959 the Hawaii chapter of the Society of Hotelmen sponsored a "Cornell Summer School of the Pacific." Two years later, this program included eleven courses and enrolled 340 students, with additional courses on the cruise ship that ferried students to and from the Islands.

The next seven years were boom times for international seminars. During the 1965–66 academic year, for example, Hotel faculty and graduate students taught a six-week management course in Manila for the Philippine government, with 120 executives attending. Additional seminars were offered on every continent except Antarctica. Hotel faculty taught in major cities like Vienna, Austria; Hannover, Germany; Caracas, Venezuela; Bangkok, Thailand; Djakarta, Indonesia;

Alumni harmonize at a gathering of the Western International Hotel Association in Carefree, Arizona, in January 1961. *See Sources for names.*

Melbourne, Australia; and Kingston, Jamaica. In addition, management seminars for U.S. armed forces were offered in Rotterdam, Holland; the Azores Islands; Greenland; and other areas. The school even sponsored seminars in Moscow and Leningrad for Intourist, the Soviet tourist agency.

The international influences on Statler Hall sometimes took on humorous or bizarre aspects, as students from small-town or provincial upbringings created elaborate celebrations of cultures they barely understood. Lalit Nirula '66 was managing director of Nirula's chain of restaurants and hotels in India in the mid 1990s. But one evening in the mid-1960s, he was a confused Indian boy a long, long way from home. "At the Hotel Ezra Cornell, the formal banquet was called 'The Egyptian,'" he writes. "Hence the waiters had to dress in Egyptian

Prof. Robert Chase *59 speaks to guests at the 1970 Hotel Ezra Cornell in the new Statler Hall research center. *See Sources for other names.*

pharaoh-style headdresses. Initially, it was decided that men would not wear anything above the waist. However, someone pointed out that it would be rather embarrassing to have the guest smell sweaty waiters when food was being placed in front of them!

"We also had to wear a short skirt to complete the Egyptian look. I, unfortunately, was given a table in front of the Head Table, next to the center aisle. It was a disconcerting experience to carry ten dinners on a tray (using both hands as the tray was very heavy and I was not that experienced) after the headdress had slipped to one side (so that I could only see with one eye) and also being very worried about what I would do if my skirt fell down!"

In the late 1960s the pace of international seminars slowed as the focus turned to the expansion of Statler Hall operations and seminars offered in Ithaca. But a major effort returned in 1971 when the Tourism Development Company of Puerto Rico proposed that the Cornell Hotel school cooperate in a joint educational venture. Beck agreed for several reasons, chief among them the need for funds.

"At that time, there was a moratorium on the number of students we could take, and we were up to our maximum. Dale Corson was president then, and he said 'go out and see if you can enhance your income—but not through more students.'"

Beck was approached by Lloyd Carswell, an old friend who was running the Sheraton in Puerto Rico. "I went down and met with all the elite Puerto Rican businessmen, and Lloyd put on a marvelous spread—cocktails, caviar, the whole works. We set up a deal to establish a two-year community college. We would send two people from the Hotel school down to teach, and I or somebody else would go down twice a year. They paid us $65,000 a year."

In the same year, the Puerto Rico Commission donated $400,000 to build a hotel school on the campus of Inter-American University. By the 1979–80 academic year, all of the staff and students of the school were residents of Puerto Rico.

Beck found another moneymaker in courses that were taught by Hotel faculty for students throughout the university. The system of "accessory instruction" provides that one Cornell school shall reimburse other schools for any courses its students take at those other schools. Beck assigned Prof. Vance Christian '61, who taught the school's wine course, to teach a two-credit-hour course on wines to students from other schools. The sold-out course was eventually held in the 961-seat Alice Statler Auditorium, with waiters stationed in the aisles to dispense wines for tasting while Christian and visiting lecturers explained each wine's variety and source.

The course was so successful and lucrative that Beck set up a similar course on tourism in 1966. And in 1974 he invited Graham Kerr to teach a cooking class. Kerr, the host of a hit television show called "The Galloping Gourmet," attracted more than 1,000 students to Bailey Hall.

Kerr's class and other Hotel-sponsored courses became famous throughout the university as "gut" courses—in other words, they offered a way for students to amass credit hours while having fun and not working too hard. Professors in the Arts college and elsewhere claimed that these courses were cheapening

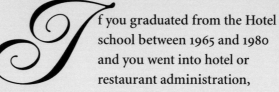

## THE MARRIOTT–CORNELL CONNECTION

*I*f you graduated from the Hotel school between 1965 and 1980 and you went into hotel or restaurant administration, chances are you were hired by the Marriott Corporation.

Hotelies hold positions in every major hotel chain, but nowhere has their presence been more evident than at Marriott. The relationship started in the mid-50s, just as J. Willard Marriott Sr., the owner of a successful chain of restaurants called Hot Shoppes, opened his first two "motor hotels" in Washington, D.C. One of Marriott's first decisions was to hire Hilton's Winthrop W. ("Bud") Grice '53 as general sales manager for its new hotel division. Grice soon hired another Hilton employee and a fellow Cornell grad, Maurice O. ("Bus") Ryan Jr. '54, as his assistant.

For Marriott, hiring Cornell Hotel graduates made sense for two reasons. First, they were the best young talent on the job market. "We felt the program was the best in terms of getting young people ready for the business," says Ryan, who was a senior vice president for Marriott in the mid-1990s. "We also hired people from other schools, but Cornell grads were the best."

The second reason was Marriott's explosive growth in the 1960s and 1970s. The chain grew steadily to its mid-1990s size of 903 hotels while much of the industry went through cycles of boom and bust. The stage was set for a symbiotic relationship, as Hotelies were attracted to a "hot" company that needed smart young managers.

Ryan and Grice, guest lecturers at the Hotel school, had their pick of students. "Bud was a profound salesman, and he did a good job of getting the kids excited," says Ryan. "Dean Beck once told us that we were sweeping up his whole field."

Later, the Marriott Corporation funded a new executive education center at the Hotel school.

the quality of a Cornell education. But the courses were no more than Hotel instruction made approachable to a general audience. And to Beck, they were an indispensable source of income.

**An Overseas Study Center** The influence of international students and alumni peaked in the 1966–67 academic year, when one-fifth of the student body came from outside the United States. "There is little doubt that the school's quota could be filled entirely by qualified students from foreign nations," wrote Beck. Moreover, the international influence was even stronger in the summer.

Prof. Laura Lee Smith, Grad '30–37 conducts a class in food chemistry in 1963.

work all night to record the lectures and give the students a bound book to carry home with them."

These courses were the origin of executive education at the Hotel school. In the 1960s, Beck expanded the summer courses to seven weeks and opened them to all hospitality executives, and the programs continued to grow. In the summer of 1961, 234 students came to Ithaca. In 1962 there were 250 students, including those from sixteen countries on four continents. "They represented every phase of the business," wrote Beck. "In coming to Cornell, they had in common a shared desire to apply modern methods to their businesses, to find improved ways of caring for the traveler and making him happy and comfortable away from home." Another reason, according to Amalani Nizarali of Uganda, who attended in 1970, was "to learn the American way of hotel-keeping . . . as most of our guests come from the U.S." By 1968 nearly half of the 350 summer students were from overseas. In 1969 the majority of 500 students were from overseas.

In the meantime, many other short courses for executives were being held at Statler Hall during the school

Dean Meek originated summer programs of one to three weeks in 1928. In the mid-1950s, at the suggestion of Statler Inn manager William Conner, he also began offering refresher courses to club managers. Conner initially taught these courses, but they quickly grew into major undertakings.

Margaret Conner remembers that some of the club managers' meetings were so large that telephones were installed by each participant, "so that questions could be heard by the speaker. Girls in typing pools would year, including three seminars for the "Yugoslavian Hotel and Restaurant Team." In fact, demand for adult education courses on and off the campus consistently outran Beck's supply of teachers. International students who attended these seminars are now recognized by the Cornell Society of Hotelmen as a special category of alumni, and their participation has become a major addition to alumni activities.

In September 1971, Assistant Dean Gerald Lattin left Cornell to begin a hotel school at Florida International University. He was replaced by Prof. Jeremiah J. ("Jerry") Wanderstock *41, a popular foods instructor who had taught Meat Science to nearly two decades of Hotel students. Wanderstock was a beloved figure in the school; "he was absolutely brilliant," says Kenneth B. Hamlet '66, CEO of Holiday Inns in the late 1980s. "He made school fun, and his course was a great experience." Tragically, Wanderstock died only a year after he was appointed assistant dean.

In July 1972, Prof. Donal Dermody was made director of workshops with responsibility for executive education. A full slate of seminars continued through the 1970s, and the summer school was renamed the Center for Professional Development. Another highlight came in 1979, when representatives of the Cornell Hotel school made contact with hotel operators in China.

Perhaps the most audacious move of Beck's tenure came in 1980, when Cornell entered into an agreement with the Paris-based IMHI, the Institut de Management Hôtelier International. The agreement

Prof. O. Ernest Bangs addresses students at lab tables in 1966.

Prof. Vance Christian '61 teaches a class in Foods 101 in 1966.

was similar to the one Cornell had with Puerto Rico, but the French reaction was less friendly. At a press conference in Paris announcing the agreement, Beck—who was far from fluent in French—found himself facing 350 angry French journalists. "They were saying, 'Why does France need Americans to come over and teach them about hotels?' One man got up, and he had a Vandyke beard that was twitching, he was so mad. And he said, 'This means the burgerization of France!'"

Beck and the French program survived that day, and the program prospered. In fact, Beck took over direction of the IMHI the day after he resigned as dean in 1981.

### Research Grows Rapidly

Industry leaders who supported Cornell's Hotel program in the early days often claimed that campus-based research would benefit the entire industry. During Prof Meek's tenure, this promise went largely unfulfilled. Before 1962, research was a minor part of the Hotel school. But Beck's aggressive pursuit of this opportunity included a stepped-up schedule of research projects by the faculty. The results were impressive, although the new initiatives sometimes met the more relaxed personalities of the veteran faculty members.

From 1944, when she arrived from the University of South Dakota, until her retirement in 1975, Myrtle H. Ericson taught quantity cooking techniques to Cornell Hotel students. But to everyone concerned, the course was called "Fancy Foods."

"No one told me what I could or couldn't do," Ericson says. "The sky was the limit. I didn't have a favorite part, but my students always liked cake decorating the best.

"I gave one lecture a week and taught two or three sections of twenty students or so. I didn't have a teaching assistant until 1973. I knew most of the students, and I liked them all. They were from all over the world. I remember in my first lecture of the semester, I would tell them, 'I'll be learning things from you just as much as you learn things from me.' And I did. I made several trips to visit my foreign students. If they weren't around to receive me, their parents would."

About the opening of Statler in 1950, Ericson recalls, "In the first half of the year, a lot of pots and pans and other equipment weren't there. [Florence] ("Tossie") George had to go to New York City to buy all the stoves for the new labs. She bought twenty-four stoves at Macy's!"

Ericson remembers that women Hotel instructors did not receive equal pay unless they demanded it. "Helen Recknagel, Laura Lee Smith, and I were the lowest-paid faculty on campus. We complained, and in 1955 we got an increase." Ericson retired in 1975 and didn't look back. "It was good to get out of there and get new ideas," she said in 1995. "I had a lot to do."

Prof. Myrtle Ericson, who teaches the course in Intermediate Foods in 1971.

Beck remembers telling Prof. Charles Sayles, who had been appointed director of research by Meek, to create a proposal to design a kitchen for Boeing's new transatlantic jet, the 747, for Pan American Airways. "We had a big long talk about it, and then he went away. A couple of months later, [the client] called and said, 'We don't have a proposal from you people, what's the matter?' So I went up to see Chuck. And he had a board on the table, and he had two wooden round disks with holes in them. And he was turning them.

Professor Sayles oversees early work on data processing boards. *See Sources for other names.*

"I said, 'What are you doing, Chuck?' and he said, 'I think I've solved it.' 'What have you solved?' 'Well, I like to play cribbage, but I don't like to take the pegs out and put them on the board. Now I've invented a board that turns.' And I said, 'What about the Pan Am contract?' And he said, 'Oh.'"

Despite his fondness for cribbage, Sayles was a leader in the school's early research program. His major effort involved the school's pioneering work in data processing. This remained a major focus of research in the mid-1990s. But the industry had a real need for new ideas in a wide variety of areas. In 1962, the industry's average occupancy rate was languishing at just 62 percent. Luxury hotels were struggling against new competition from budget and mid-scale motels, just as full-service restaurants were faced with mounting losses from fast-food competition. And in Washington, D.C., the pressure was mounting to pass minimum wage legislation that could dramatically increase the industry's labor costs.

In September 1962, seventeen industry leaders met with Beck and others from Cornell, along with trustees of the Statler Foundation, to discuss a new center for hotel industry research at Cornell. The foundation was prepared to make an annual grant of $100,000 for five years to support research efforts. Beck formed a research committee to screen proposals from the faculty, industry, and suppliers. President

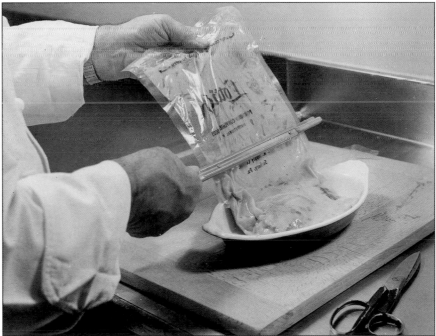

*Above:* Faculty from several schools at Cornell discuss a Hotel school research project in 1962 for the American Gas Association on the speed of thawing frozen foods. Professor Sayles is at right. *See Sources for other names.*

*Left:* Emptying a Ready Food packet in a school lab in 1964, part of an early study of packaged prepared food.

Hotel School's well publicized mattress testing research gets close attention.

Malott appointed a fifteen-member Research Advisory Council to make funding decisions. The chairman of the Advisory Council was Ernest Henderson, president of the Sheraton Corporation of America.

Six months later, the Advisory Council referred eight projects to the research center. The total estimated cost of these was $186,000; one-third of that would be taken by the data processing study, and one-third by a study of "ready food." Other studies concerned the economics of hotel room construction, the effect of fringe benefits on profit-sharing plans, studies of carpet padding materials, mattresses, and the motivations of personnel and guests. Another $57,000 was spent during the academic year on other research projects, including $40,000 from the U.S. Office of Civilian Defense to study "food service for fallout shelters."

The school's two biggest research projects of the 1960s, "ready food" and data processing, were well ahead of their time. Ready food was directed by H. A. MacLennan '26, who joined the research program staff in 1963, after retiring from his job as vice president of Hilton Hotels. MacLennan defined "ready food" as "menu items which are partially or totally prepared and need only one production operation for serving." He was determined to show that modern technology "will not deal the death blow to gourmet cooking, but will be the reason for its renaissance."

The promise of MacLennan's research was restaurant food that was cheaper to serve and required less labor, and fewer cooks, to prepare. Early experiments in hotel kitchens seemed to confirm that some prepared-in-advance items could be served to guests, thereby lowering kitchen costs.

"We had these meals in a bag, and one package would hold a meal," says Beck. "They were flash-frozen. The idea was that a diner would come in and say, 'I want chicken à la king,' and the waitress would go to the freezer, where the bags were stacked like records, and then put it in a big tub of boiling water with a timer. Twelve minutes later, she'd come back with a pair of scissors, snip open the bag over a plate, and there would be his dinner."

The main problem was that only foods drenched in sauces would heat quickly enough in boiling water or a conventional oven. Ready food research continued at Cornell through the 1960s, but the concept did not find its way into mainstream restaurant kitchens until microwave ovens made it feasible in the 1980s.

Data processing research faced similar obstacles. In the early 1960s, Sayles and others tried to use punch-card and keytape technology to create a centralized data processing system for hotels. In 1964 IBM and Cornell published a list of functions that such a system could do faster, better, and cheaper than the old ledger systems. Accounting, reservations, inventory, and other aspects of hotel operations were all considered. But little progress was made in creating a practical system until 1966, when the National Cash Register Corporation (NCR) began supplying Cornell with the latest versions of its mainframe computers.

"We brought one computer up to the third floor, and it was so heavy that someone noticed the floor was starting to sink," Beck remembers.

In 1967, NCR donated another computer in exchange for Cornell's assistance in developing a complete on-line accounting package for hotels. Eventually NCR marketed an accounting program for hotels that was developed at Cornell, along with programs for registration and guest services.

A more mundane, less expensive, probably more useful, and certainly more humorous research project of the mid-1960s was Statler Hall's famous mattress-testing machine. Supported by grants from the National Association of Bedding Manufacturers and the American Hotel and Motel Association, researchers developed "bowling ball buttocks" to measure spring reaction in different mattress types. They also placed test mattresses in an area near the school library, where they asked students to evaluate three different mattress-and-spring types. The jokes flew thick and fast, but bedding manufacturers had adopted the mattress-testing machine for their own use by 1968.

The research center achieved a much higher profile when its new home on the brand-new fifth floor addition to Statler Hall opened in 1969. That summer, more than a thousand people toured the center. The follow-

A guest at the 1969 Hotel Ezra Cornell at the craps table, part of the luxury liner theme, "Inn of the Seven Seas."

The Hotel school has produced more than its fair share of entrepreneurs. One of the most successful is Michael S. Egan '62, chairman of Alamo Rent-A-Car.

Egan joined Alamo in 1976 when it was just a regional company with three outlets. Before that, he managed another car rental company and spent eleven years in academe. In 1979, Egan and others bought Alamo and he was named president. Under Egan's leadership, Alamo became the third-largest car rental company in the country. Egan also gained a reputation as an industry innovator, introducing unlimited free mileage and off-site rental plazas for better service.

Egan believes his success at Alamo was not part of a grand design. "Necessity was the mother of invention," he says. "We had to do [innovative] things to survive. We couldn't get spaces in the airports, for example, but we ended up better off for being off the airport grounds. That gave us a price advantage."

Like many Hotelies, Egan grew up in the hospitality industry. His parents owned Storybook Gardens, a family theme park in Wisconsin. Managing Storybook as a teenager, part of his responsibilities included driving around the countryside and stopping at roadside diners, stores, and gas stations. There, he would offer free passes to the park in exchange for promoting Storybook's brochures.

Years later, when Alamo was a struggling 400-car firm, Egan trained all the people who were "just sitting around," drove them to New York City, then had them drive south to Alamo's Florida headquarters and stop at every travel agency along the way to sell them on Alamo. "It sounds corny, but it worked," he says. "We had to find ways to attract business."

About Cornell, he says, "The Hotel school made me into a working man. It was a no-excuses environment. You got the idea that there were deadlines that had to be met come hell or high water."

of microcomputers. Industry interest was keen. In 1973–74, an article in the *Cornell Hotel and Restaurant Administration Quarterly* on hotel uses of computers sold 9,500 reprints between November and June. Researchers were working on an integrated computer system for the Statler Inn that would handle accounting, billing, payroll, and personnel reporting.

In 1974, Prof. Robert M. Chase headed a committee effort to find ways to get more faculty and student participation in the research center. But when the Statler Foundation grant ran out in 1977, little enthusiasm for the research center remained. The following year, it was disbanded—although individual professors continued to do research throughout the school.

ing year, Sayles retired. The center's new director, Prof. Paul R. Broten *47, vowed to make his operation self-supporting through research grants and revenue within three years. Yet he also pledged to make research projects more relevant to the current faculty and staff. These two goals were often in conflict, and the search for new grants had to come first.

In 1972, the Statler Foundation again committed to make a five-year series of donations to research, for a total of $410,000. Computer applications were once again a main focus of research, and this time the faculty were able to work with the first generation

### Mortar and Money

Robert Beck's entrepreneurial spirit bolstered the school's financial strength. In 1964, the school had $300,000 in reserves and the Statler Inn showed its fourth straight profitable year. When Beck resigned in 1981, the school's reserves totaled $2 million. He had four main reasons for his good financial record: more students, a lean faculty, the ever-generous Statler Foundation, and his outside programs.

In 1961, the Statler Foundation donated $500,000 to endow a faculty position for Hotel Administration.

In 1965, it agreed to fund a fifth-floor addition to Statler Hall that would include space for the research center, additional rooms at the Statler Inn, and an expanded kitchen and main dining room. Construction began in April 1968, and the new facilities were dedicated nineteen months later. For the first time in decades, Alice Statler did not join the celebration. She died on October 16, 1969, at age 87, at her home in the Waldorf Towers.

Alice Seidler Statler had been Ellsworth Statler's widow for forty-one years. For more than twenty years, her arrival in Ithaca marked the unofficial beginning of the annual Hotel Ezra Cornell. As a trustee of the Statler Foundation, she arranged for donations of more than $10 million to the Hotel school. Her death occurred just three months after that of her friend and colleague H. B. Meek. Their passing marked the end of an era for the school.

Alice Statler's wit and grace are still remembered by those who knew her. When she arrived for the 1962 Hotel Ezra Cornell, she was met at the airport by a freshman whose job was to roll out a red carpet for her as she stepped from the airplane. As the boy strode toward the plane, he tripped, dropped the carpet, and sent it rolling in the wrong direction. Humiliated, he picked himself up to see Mrs. Statler detour to where the carpet had stopped rolling. She walked down the red pathway toward him. When she reached him, she said, "That's

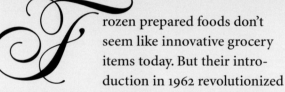

Frozen prepared foods don't seem like innovative grocery items today. But their introduction in 1962 revolutionized the way Americans live. By helping women prepare quick meals for their families, they encouraged more women to join the workplace.

A Hotel graduate was a key player in the development of frozen prepared foods. C. Alan MacDonald '55, was vice president of manufacturing of Stouffer Foods when the firm first brought frozen prepared foods to market. The idea came from one of Stouffer's restaurants. "Customers started asking the manager for spinach soufflé to take home," he says. "So they started preparing that and other specialties."

Stouffer technicians started researching frozen foods in 1953. "The technology was there," MacDonald says. "But we had to develop different recipes, and that took some time. You can't take a normal recipe and freeze it." Skeptics said the public wouldn't buy frozen foods at a premium price. It took time, but in time they were accepted. The first items ranged from common (macaroni and cheese) to complicated (lobster Newburg). MacDonald became president of Stouffer's frozen foods division in 1971. Sales that year totaled $32 million; in 1995 they were $1.4 billion.

MacDonald gives Cornell a great deal of credit for his success. "Because of the practical, hands-on education, it's the single best undergraduate business school in the country," he says. But MacDonald almost attended the University of Denver. "My father, an electrical engineer, said I was 'out of my mind' to study hospitality," MacDonald says. "He made me take a job at the Drake Hotel to learn more about the business. But the Drake was run by Cornellians. They liked me and put in a good word for me at the school, and I headed to Ithaca. Now I wouldn't trade my Cornell degree for anything."

okay, son. You'll get it right next time." In her will, Mrs. Statler left $125,000 to endow student scholarships.

Beck had to spend $200,000 from reserves to complete the fifth floor of Statler Hall, and the addition, although impressive, was not helpful to the financial condition of the Statler Inn. Starting in 1969, the Inn lost money for eight years in a row. Many factors contributed to the loss, including rising labor and energy costs, perpetual money problems with the faculty club, and lack of convenient parking. By 1973 Beck seemed resigned to the fact that the Inn would not be self-supporting, and he began concentrating on ways to improve its value as an educational tool.

*Above, left:* Prithipal Lamba '56 carries a giant champagne bottle through a Hotel Ezra Cornell ballroom in the mid 1950s.

*Above, right:* Hotel Ezra Cornell directors prepare to issue stock in their 1969 venture, a tradition that went back to early HECs.

The Inn's financial troubles were not a reflection on the quality of its service. After Bill Conner retired, its general manager for thirteen years was Walter Herrmann '52, who had been trained as a chef at the Waldorf-Astoria before coming to Cornell as an undergraduate. Herrmann was executive chef of the

1950 Hotel Ezra Cornell that opened Statler Hall, and he returned in 1963 after a decade with Richmond Hotels and Holiday Inns. One of his trademarks at the Statler was a Sunday smorgasbord, where students in foods courses taught by Herrmann and Vance Christian got to show their stuff to a hungry campus.

German-born, Herrmann and his family had fled from Nazi Germany when he was a teenager. "He was a gentle man, dedicated to the 'mine host' principles of hotel management and fairness for all who worked for and with him," says George Bantuvanis '51. Herrmann died in 1977, while on a teaching assignment in Pakistan.

Beck was not troubled by the Statler Inn's red ink. He knew that the efforts led by Herrmann were a source of great pride for the school. He could also afford to subsidize the Inn because his primary source of funds was expanding at a steady pace, while one of his major costs was not. In 1961, enrollment stood at about 400. In 1969, enrollment was 495 and tuition was $2,350, for a gross of more than $1.1 million. By 1979, total enrollment was 744 and tuition was $5,256, for an annual gross of more than $3.9 million.

Meanwhile, Beck kept the cost of faculty lean by hiring young professors and not replacing those who retired. In 1971–72, for example, two professors retired, one died, and two left to take jobs elsewhere. This amounted to the turnover of one-sixth of Beck's full-time faculty. He responded by hiring two new faculty members, Stanley W. Davis *47 and John J. ("Jack") Clark, Ph.D. *69; by bringing in more visiting lecturers; and by adding to the workload of the remaining members.

The school's cash reserves allowed Beck to make some bold moves in the late stages of his career at Cornell. In 1980, he took $950,000 out of reserves— "cash on the barrelhead," as he put it—to buy a complex of twelve buildings on 150 acres, including three Gothic stone buildings, on the west side of Cayuga Lake, just south of the Tompkins Community Hospital. The former retirement home of the International Order of Odd Fellows (IOOF) had been vacant, and Beck felt that it would make a good conference center. This dream was never realized. In fact, Jack Clark sold the building—which became known as Statler West—soon after he became dean.

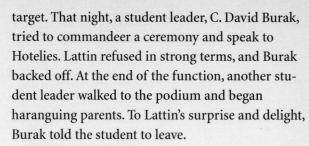

In the 1960s, protests were a big part of life at American universities. Radical student leaders occupied buildings, shut down campuses, and forced schools to deal with divisive issues like Vietnam and civil rights. But as Cornell was nearly consumed by protests, the Hotel school hardly noticed.

In 1969, Cornell's student union, Willard Straight Hall, was occupied by black students. The Straight takeover was a wrenching experience that forever changed the nature of Cornell. But the Hotel school managed to celebrate Parents Weekend while the takeover occurred, followed one weekend later by the forty-third Hotel Ezra Cornell. Campus radicals tried to disrupt these events, even issuing a bomb threat at Statler Hall. But a combination of strong leadership and a pervasive Hotelie dislike for the radicals kept the conflict away.

The bomb threat came during Parents Weekend. Assistant Dean Gerald Lattin, who was in charge while Dean Beck was in Mexico, didn't know if he should evacuate Statler Auditorium or ignore the warning. Because previous bomb threats at Cornell had been hoaxes, Lattin crossed his fingers and ignored this one. Nothing happened. "I must admit that once the function was over and the last parent had left the auditorium, I breathed a very happy sigh of relief," he says.

A group of African-American students occupied the Straight early the next morning. Rumor had it that Statler Hall was also a

target. That night, a student leader, C. David Burak, tried to commandeer a ceremony and speak to Hotelies. Lattin refused in strong terms, and Burak backed off. At the end of the function, another student leader walked to the podium and began haranguing parents. To Lattin's surprise and delight, Burak told the student to leave.

The next weekend, Lattin wasn't sure about playing host to hundreds of industry VIPs at Hotel Ezra Cornell. But he managed to get assurances that there would be no trouble. Hotelies who were on the football team guarded all doors to keep trespassers out, and things went ahead as planned. "The Hotel students weren't involved with the radicals," explains Lattin. "They were basically conservative."

"Graduation day 1970 was strange," writes William J. Caruso '70. "As the processional marched through campus, the Hotelies were like an undefeated visiting team arriving at the arch-rival's doorstep. We endured taunting on our way to Barton Hall—some of it was good-humored, but it was directed to make sure we knew we were different from most graduates. I realized that we were looked on as the group most out of the norm that day—the conservative, business-trained executives of tomorrow. Suddenly I knew why I was at Cornell, and I knew in my heart that I had made the right decision!"

A waiter at the 1969 Hotel Ezra Cornell, which went on despite unrest on the campus, including a large student gathering next door in Barton Hall.

Dean Beck speaks at the opening of a refurbished main kitchen in Statler in 1979.

changed the schedule of Hotel Ezra Cornell so that students would have more time to socialize with the executives who were their guests and potential employers. In 1971, he expanded the school's long-standing work study requirement to allow twelve undergraduates to spend a year working in a hotel as interns. And in 1973, he inaugurated the nation's first Master of Professional Studies program in Hotel Administration.

The MPS program was created by a group of faculty, under the direction of Stanley Davis, to serve as a training ground for mid-level hotel executives who already had a college degree. Before that time, 25 to 30 percent of Hotel undergraduates already had a bachelor's degree from somewhere else, so they would do the Hotel program in two years and get a second bachelor's degree. "Some of them were unhappy," Beck says. "They were older and wanted to study, and they felt that some of our courses were not up to a graduate level." The new program catered to their higher standards, and it was an immediate success. In 1974, it received 250 applications for 85 slots. By 1979, the Hotel school enrolled 643 undergraduates, 95 MPS students, and 8 Ph.D. candidates.

In 1969, Beck authorized changes in the curriculum to reflect changes in the hospitality industry. The growing importance of tourism and other businesses serving leisure activities made it necessary to train

## Students As Customers

Beck never forgot that his first duty was to the students who were the school's main reason for existence. He knew that students came to the Hotel school for one reason only—to become successful hospitality executives—and made several moves that increased the value of their education. In the 1970s, for example, he future hospitality executives in new ways. "Operations research, industrial engineering, systems analysis, market research, value analysis—these are some of the areas which must be considered as part of an educational program if the graduates of the school are to continue as leaders of the industry," he wrote in July 1970.

The new curriculum included "core" courses in such areas as accounting, foods, and physical properties management for first-year students and sophomores. Upper-class members could continue to take a range of courses, or they could choose one of the three core areas as their major. New courses were also added in marketing, managerial economics, computer science, and franchising. In 1975, more new courses were added in environmental control, property development, and taxation. And in 1977, an ad hoc committee led by Prof. Jack Clark reviewed the curriculum and made another round of changes.

In 1978–79, the operations of the entire school were reviewed by a newly created "Triad Committee." Representatives of the students, faculty, and alumni got together to suggest areas for improvement, and Beck was purposely not involved. "I tried to stay out of it as much as I could, so that the information would flow," he says. "What I hoped to get was feedback from faculty to alumni, and from students to alumni, who perhaps would not vent their unhappiness with me directly. And I did get a lot of input about a lot of things."

## BOB JAMES, MULTI-BRAND MANAGEMENT

In the 1960s, new hotels were opening like wildfire. Some investors, sensing opportunity, plunged in without any knowledge of the business. These neophyte owners soon discovered they needed someone with experience to manage their hotels. That's where Robert M. James '54 came in.

James had opened the Pittsburgh Hilton in 1959 as resident manager. Later, as vice president of operations for Howard Johnson Motor Lodges, he saw "a window of opportunity." In 1971 he founded the Hotel Management Company, the industry's first third-party or independent management company. The idea was radical: one entity could own a hotel, another could franchise it, and a third company could run it.

Management companies would need a spotless reputation for honesty, because opportunities to cheat owners abounded. They also needed to stress quality in order to thrive. Hotel Management Company and James's next management company, Motor Hotel Management, delivered on both counts. It grew to be the biggest independent management company in the business, operating 170 hotels under seventeen flags.

James was born to be successful in some aspect of the hotel industry. His father, Ward B. James, managed the St. Louis, Detroit, and Buffalo Statler hotels. Ward James named him Robert Milton after Ellsworth Milton Statler, the industry giant who died a week before he was born. James met his wife, Constance '54, at the Hotel school. His daughter Susan and son Robert '71 also entered the hotel business.

In semi-retirement, James served as executive-in-residence and teacher at the Hotel school. He also was president of the Cornell Society of Hotelmen. "It's good to give something back," he says. "At Cornell, you learned how to work with and meet people. The word 'Cornell' opens a lot of doors. It gives you self-assurance."

## Friction with the Faculty

When Beck began as dean, the Hotel faculty was dominated by men and women who had been appointed by Meek in the 1930s and 1940s.

When the Meek-era faculty retired, Beck tended to replace them with recent Hotel graduates such as Vance Christian '61, William P. Fisher '60, and Warren M. Cole '63. The 1970s brought a new round of faculty hiring. Four faculty members left in 1970–71, and five more, including Charles Cladel '29, left in 1971–72.

When Beck filled these and subsequent slots, he looked to a new source of faculty talent—non-Hotel

*L*ike his brothers David and Nelson, Laurance S. Rockefeller was a businessman whose success enhanced his family's fortune. But he was also an ardent conservationist at a time when conservation was not fashionable. In 1955, he combined his two interests and opened Caneel Bay on the Caribbean island of St. John. This resort, and others that followed, became known as Rockresorts. They were pioneers in the burgeoning field of luxury ecotourism, and a Cornell Hotel graduate led their way.

Rockefeller hired Richard E. Holtzman '41, the president of Sheraton Hawaii, to manage the business in 1965. Holtzman ran Rockresorts until 1986, expanding it to a chain of nearly a dozen properties in locations such as Puerto Rico, the mainland U.S., British Virgin Islands, and Hawaii.

Rockresorts were unique for their understated, even austere design. They offered no television or phones and few catered activities, but they did feature secluded surroundings and excellent food and service. Caneel Bay, for example, has just 171 guest cottages spread over 171 acres, and is located within the 5,000-acre Virgin Islands National Park. The formula worked: Rockresorts had 90 percent annual occupancy and earned the highest revenue per room of any hotels in the world for nearly thirty years.

Today, Holtzman's son Richard Jr. '76 is partner in a Rockresorts-type chain for the 1990s called Carefree Resorts. Ironically, the original Rockresorts concept of ecotourism is one of the fastest-growing segments of the travel industry. The Rockresorts properties themselves continue to operate as part of a larger enterprise.

---

alumni with impressive academic credentials. Stanley Davis, for example, was a former vice president of Ithaca College. Jack Clark was a former associate professor at Northeastern University. In July 1976, with the retirement of Helen Recknagel and appointment of Paul Beals as her successor, Beck had been dean through a complete turnover of the Hotel faculty. More importantly, he had shifted the focus of faculty hiring away from alumni and toward teachers of the highest caliber, regardless of background.

The new generation of faculty members were young, energetic, and ready to take an active role in school policy decisions. This caused problems for Beck, who was accustomed to being the undisputed leader. In 1972,

Beck had negotiated the agreement with Puerto Rico on his own, and no one complained. In 1979, negotiations with the French school, IMHI, proceeded in much the same way—but by this time, the faculty had changed. "I made the deal on my own and bypassed all the committees, and [the faculty] were really unhappy. The first time they heard about it was a brochure we had printed in color, 'Cornell in France.' They were so unhappy that they didn't want the program to go through, although they've been very supportive of it ever since."

The truth was that Beck was constitutionally unsuited to the new, committee-oriented style of college administration. "I reminded the faculty that you could walk the length and breadth of this nation, visit every park, and you'll never see a statue of a committee. They didn't laugh, though. They wanted more and more committees, and they wanted to have a faculty meeting every ten days. And I began to think, 'Life is too short to put up with this.'

"Part of it was the fact that the faculty wanted to play a larger part in the administration. What bothered me was that the faculty wanted it both ways. They wanted to be in on things, but if they were on sabbatical, they weren't in on things. Still, they would criticize what would happen when they were away. They might make committee meetings, they might not, and there might not be a meeting. And that led me to think that this might be a time to leave.

"Twenty years is a long time. And after fifteen years, I thought I owned the bloody place. Anyone who interfered with the school was interfering with my place. It was just as Meek told me once. He said he couldn't bring himself to share this place with anybody else. And after twenty years, that was how I had come to feel, too."

Beck announced his resignation in 1980, and Jack Clark assumed the job on July 1, 1981. But at 61 years of age, Beck was not ready to retire. He spent the next three years in France as director of the IMHI, an experiment in international hospitality education.

At the outset, between twenty-five and forty bilingual graduate students took courses in accounting, hotel and restaurant administration, food and beverage management, and marketing at the Hotel school affiliate in France.

They then worked six months in hotels and kitchens, and took elective courses at École Supérieure des Sciences Économiques near Paris.

After IMHI, Beck went on to teach in Athens, Greece, and in Switzerland. He served on the Board of Directors of the Penn Central Railroad while it was in bankruptcy proceedings. In 1995, he was serving as a member of the corporation of the Culinary Institute of America in Hyde Park, New York, and as a trustee of Ithaca College.

*Above:* Hotel Ezra Cornell guests applaud chefs who come into the banquet room during the 1970 event.

*Left:* A guest at the 1970 Hotel Ezra Cornell answers student questions at a reception.

Jan Beck at a school event in 1979

One of the most lasting memories alumni have of Beck is the kindness and attention he and his wife Jan showed them as students. This was particularly true of international students. "Foreign students used to regard [Jan Beck] as a mother figure," says Michael W. N. Chiu '66. Born in Canton (Quanzhou) China and raised in Hong Kong, Chiu did not know any English until he was 12. But he made the most of his time in Ithaca, working full-time as a banquet waiter while studying for his Hotel degree.

Such was her contribution to their lives that Hotel students of the 1960s and '70s dubbed the dean's wife, Jan Beck, "the First Lady of Statler Hall," and the Becks' 150-year-old home east of campus the "Slaterville Hilton."

The Becks had entertained students at home ever since Bob Beck joined the faculty, but the pace picked up dramatically during his deanship. While raising three daughters, Mrs. Beck put on at least two functions a month during the school year and was a regular presence at Statler Hall itself. The events at home ranged from coffees for international students and seniors and the Sunday after Hotel Ezra Cornell, to Christmas parties for faculty and administrators, Christmas dinners for international students, and parties for retiring faculty.

On campus, Jan Beck was on hand for all key Hotel school events; she played a key role in redecorating the Statler's main ballroom, main dining room, faculty lounge, and west lounge; and she was active with the Campus Club in seeing that students who were confined to the university infirmary had visitors.

With her husband, she traveled each year to six major industry trade shows for 500–1,500-person receptions given by the Cornell Society of Hotelmen, and visited at least twenty-five chapters of the society.

Daughters Susan, Janyce, and Robin were caught up in the whirl of events at the Slaterville Hilton. They admit in retrospect that "the duties required at the social functions weren't always what we as teenagers wanted. But we learned how to make people feel welcome in our home. As a result of our travels and the people who visited our home, we learned there were many cultures different from the average American way of life we experienced in rural Upstate New York."

Chiu remembers the kindness of Prof. Charles Cladel, who tutored him after class several times to improve his grasp of food and beverage control. He remembers a reception at Beck's house for international students where he struck up a friendship with Hiroshi Kohda '64. Thirty years later, Chiu and Kohda met again at the inaugural reception for the Kansai Chapter of the Cornell Society of Hotelmen in Osaka, Japan; Kohda was chapter president, and Chiu was to be president of the society. But Chiu says he is most grateful for the day Dean Beck introduced him to Shirley Tung, who was applying from Hong Kong to the Hotel school. They married, and their daughter Jennie C. Chiu graduated from the Hotel school in 1991.

Beck's colleagues remember that he had a deep and abiding interest in the welfare of students. George Bantuvanis '51, who taught executive education in the 1980s, says that the dean was always aware of students' class schedules. Beck would stand in the doorway of his office as classes changed, so he could joke with students or say a few encouraging words to them as they hurried to the next class.

One day, Beck called Peter Rainsford '68, PhD '74 into his office. Rainsford had recently been hired to teach at the school, and Beck had heard through the grapevine that the young faculty member was developing a bad habit. Apparently Rainsford had told a student that he was too busy to talk that day. When Rainsford arrived in Beck's office, Beck told him never to forget that the students were the clients of the school, and they should never be put off if they wanted to see a teacher. Rainsford then put a permanent sign on his office door which reads, "Walk In."

"The students were my first priority," said Beck in 1994. "That might not have set well with a lot of people, but I feel very strongly about it and I'd do it again. The students are the heart and soul of the whole program."

Dean Robert Beck waves goodbye in 1980 to the last meeting of "Brownies with Beck," a series of guest lectures held each Friday afternoon in Statler Auditorium during the fall semester. At right is the dean's assistant, Michael Rawson '81.

# A Bridge Between the Generations

*J*ACK CLARK PUT THE FOLDED NOTE into his shirt pocket and hurried out the door. He had just finished presenting the latest plans for the expansion of the Statler Inn to a group of high-level alumni, and he had to get to another meeting. It was 1983. He was trying to raise $25 million, and he had about $24 million to go. There was so much to do, and so little time to do it.

The note to Clark was from John F. Mariani Jr. *54, the chairman of Banfi Vintners. Mariani was a major figure in the global beverage industry and a major supporter of the school. Clark forgot about his note as he scurried through his day. Hours later, as he was changing his shirt for dinner, he took the note out of his pocket. It read: "Jack, I loved the presentation. How about $3 million."

A newly expanded and renovated Statler Hall under construction in 1987, culmination of a drive to improve the School of Hotel Administration.

Chairman of the campaign to expand the school and its facilities, Richard Holtzman '41, left, and a key contributor, John Mariani *54, chairman of Banfi Vintners, in 1986.

"That was a very important single gift," says Clark. "I had no fundraising credibility before that gift came. I had done nothing." But with Mariani's support, the campaign got rolling.

John J. ("Jack") Clark was a man in a hurry. In eight and one-half years at the helm of the Hotel school, he oversaw the biggest curriculum revision in the school's history. He planned and executed the school's first capital campaign outside the Statler family, exceeding his original goal by more than $18 million. He demolished Statler Inn and rebuilt it to three times its original size. He gutted and then renovated Statler Hall, packing it with high-tech teaching aids, a full-service conference center for executive education and conferences, new faculty and staff offices, and more support space.

Nearly everything about the Hotel school changed under Clark. But institutions that hurry tend to make mistakes, and the costs of the school's haste were considerable. By the end of his tenure, Clark was in conflict with some of his tenured faculty and with the university administration. The final cost of the 150-room hotel was almost double its original 100-room estimate, due to large-scale additions and design changes made relatively late in the process. An accelerated construction schedule, chosen to cut the time Statler Inn and Statler Club users were displaced, added at least $500,000 to the project's cost.

Clark had a full-speed-ahead style that never let up. He likes to say that being a leader is like being a gambler with a stack of poker chips. Every time you make a difficult decision, you hand over a chip. When the chips are gone, you're out of the game. "I believe that change agents pay a price. The price is that you're fairly short-lived," he says. "But I would not ever have taken the job if I thought it was a steady-state proposition. My criterion for success was not how many years you spend on a job, but what you can do. The thrill of being dean was to look at the school and say, what is it that needs changing?"

Despite Clark's distinctive management style, the changes he wrought were timely and essential, and the results speak for themselves. He put his stamp on almost every aspect of the school, from the luxury

guest suites in the hotel to the first-class computer center and food labs in Statler Hall. He overhauled the Hotel school, and his vision ensured that it will remain a leader in a new era of hospitality.

| **Getting to the Dean's Office** | Jack Clark has an advanced degree in a non-hospitality field, just as H. B. Meek did. He somewhat admires the |

military style of decision-making embodied in Bob Beck. He also hails from Boston, has a one-syllable name that ends with the letter "k," and deplores the politics he finds in universities. There his similarities to previous deans end.

"I was like a bridge between the generations," says Clark. "I came to the school during the Bob Beck years, when war veterans were revered and the dean's word was law. By the time I left the dean's job, everything was being done by committee and figures of authority weren't being shown the same respect. It was a generational shift. It all happened in fifteen years."

Clark joined the Hotel faculty in 1972 as an outsider to the school, but not to the university. After earning his B.A. from Boston College and M.S. in physics from the University of Buffalo, he came to Ithaca in the early 1960s with his wife Pat, two young sons, and a daughter. Clark studied for a Ph.D. in Electrical Engineering while Pat taught at a local elementary school. He was

employed briefly by Sperry Gyroscope and the now-defunct Cornell Aeronautical Laboratory in Buffalo. After he earned his doctorate in 1969, an offer came from Northeastern University. He eagerly returned to Boston and his favorite job, teaching. He had few thoughts of ever returning to Ithaca to live.

*Above:* James McLamore '47, co-founder of Burger King and major supporter of the school's campaign, is serenaded by a student musical group after he was named the 1989 Entrepreneur of the Year at Cornell.

*Left:* Dean Jack Clark and Christopher Hemmeter '62, a major hotel developer in Hawaii, after he was honored at Entrepreneur of the Year ceremonies at Cornell in 1985.

The Hotel school's success is reflected in the hundreds of alumni who have risen to prominence in the hospitality industry. In the school's first seventy-five years, nineteen alumni have become president of the national associations for hotels, restaurants, and club managers. And three others have served as chief of staff of these organizations.

Nine alumni became president of the American Hotel and Motel Association: J. Frank Birdsall '35, John A. Brooke '57, Paul R. Handley '43, Richard E. Holtzman '41, Howard P. James '46, Richard C. Nelson '57, Philip Pistilli '54, Maurice O. Ryan '54, and Roy Watson '48.

Six became president ot the National Restaurant Association (NRA): Henry W. Bolling '43, Robert D. Flickinger '47, Robert E. Heilman '45, Martin L. Horn Jr. '50, James W. McLamore '47, and Henry A. Montague '34.

And four served as president of The Club Managers Association of America: Whitney Travis '42, Raymond D. Watts '56, James E. Petzing '55, and James D. Pearce '52.

In addition, two alumni held the post of executive vice president of the NRA, Richard W. Brown '49 from 1968–72, and William P. Fisher '60, PhD *68 from 1972–77, and again beginning in 1984. Edward W. Lyon '38 served as executive director of the Club Managers association from 1958 to 1972. Brown's career is traced elsewhere in this book, particularly on pages 73, 86, and 136. Fisher taught accounting, finance, and general management at the Hotel school and was a hospitality industry consultant before heading up the staff of the restaurant association.

The Clarks did have a slim connection to the Hotel school, although they hardly knew it. One of Pat Clark's teaching colleagues was Catherine ("Cay") Dermody, wife of Donal Dermody, a Hotel professor. The wives kept in touch after the Clarks went back to Boston. In 1970, at the wives' urging, the couples took a summer trip to Europe with a mutual friend and, in Clark's recollection, "had a marvelous time. Out of that, and without telling me, Don had decided that if the engineering properties management group was ever going to do any faculty additions, that I would be a candidate."

When the job offer arranged by Dermody came in 1972, Clark was skeptical. "I said, 'I just don't know how I could. I don't know a hotel from a steamship.'" Dermody says he asked because he felt Clark "had the personality that would fit in with a hotel school. Jack was very personable. He would work well with Hotel students who weren't engineers." After several conversations and a visit to Ithaca, Clark accepted the offer. "I loved Cornell as a university," he says.

Clark's talent and enthusiasm soon made a difference. He immediately suggested changes in the properties courses that would make them more useful to future hotel managers. Instead of teaching purely technical aspects of engineering, he tried to teach students how to ask the right questions when dealing with engineers, architects, and interior designers. He also stressed to his colleagues the importance of keeping up with technological change. During the 1974 energy crisis, for example, he experimented with ways to make hotels and restaurants more energy efficient and conducted an extended series of seminars for Holiday Inns, Hilton International, and others. Soon after, he was installing solar energy demonstration projects in hotels in the Caribbean.

It didn't take long for Bob Beck to see the potential in his new faculty member. One year after Clark arrived, Beck promoted him to coordinator, or head, of the school's properties area. Promotions were done informally in the 1970s because Beck's word was law. "Bob called me on the telephone and said, 'Starting next week, I'd like you to be coordinator,'" says Clark. "I didn't have any better sense, so I said, 'Gulp, well, okay. Go for it.'"

In 1977, Clark had another new job. He was appointed chairman of a schoolwide curriculum review committee at the urging of faculty members who shared his views. From this platform, Clark unwittingly became a thorn in Beck's side. "Bob and [assistant dean] Paul Gaurnier '50 really didn't think these changes were necessary," he says. "I didn't realize I was making Bob's life more difficult by suggesting them. But every time someone stands up and says, 'This is what we need,' someone has to come up with the money. That would be the dean. So it makes the dean's life miserable."

The 1977 curriculum revisions were relatively minor, easily done, and, in Clark's view, insufficient. But they were a political milestone for dean-faculty relations in the school. They elevated the status of Clark and other faculty members, and they demonstrated a measure of faculty independence from Beck.

When Beck announced his resignation three years later, Clark was contacted by, and discussed the position with, several faculty members. "It never occurred to me that I might be the right person," he says. "I was one of 1,600 Cornell faculty members, and I don't think [university President Frank H.T.] Rhodes knew me from a hole in the wall." Clark had few relationships with Hotel alumni or key industry figures. Moreover, there were several other candidates who seemed more suitable. But Clark's work on the curriculum committee had made a strong impression on the faculty, and that fact made an impression on the administrators in Day Hall.

Eventually a letter arrived from university Provost W. Keith Kennedy inviting Clark to become a candidate. He was soon interviewed in New York City by Kennedy and an alumni committee of Leslie W. Stern '60, Fred J. Eydt '52, and Burton M. ("Skip") Sack '61. More informal dinners and meetings followed in Ithaca. Much to his surprise, Clark was recommended for the dean's job by President Rhodes and received a 95 percent vote of confidence from the faculty. He says he never lobbied for the job.

*Above:* Dean and Mrs. Clark with Aaron *25 and Marion Binenkorb, in 1984, contributors of the computer lab for the school.

*Left:* Cornell President Frank Rhodes and Marica Taylor, widow of Charles Taylor, whose family contributed to the school over several decades.

## DREW NIEPORENT'S MONTRACHET

New York City's restaurant scene was once dominated by classic, old-school establishments like Delmonico's and 21. Exclusive, expensive French restaurants like La Côte Basque and La Caravelle usually drew the most critical raves. Drew A. Nieporent '77 helped change that.

In April 1985, Nieporent scraped together $150,000 from a friend, the Small Business Administration, and his own savings. He opened a 1,500-square-foot restaurant called Montrachet in the Tribeca section of New York. The idea was simple: to serve good food at a reasonable price in a contemporary setting. "We served the most pared-down menu at $16, including the coffee," Nieporent told *Crain's New York Business*. "A few months later, we got a three-star restaurant review from *The New York Times*. Suddenly it was like the storming of the Bastille. We could have filled Shea Stadium." Nieporent has never looked back. Montrachet con-

tinued to maintain its three-star rating. A few years later, he started Tribeca Grill with actor Robert DeNiro; Nobu, a Japanese restaurant; and Rubicon in San Francisco, co-owned with actor Robin Williams and director Francis Ford Coppola.

Nieporent dreamed of owning a restaurant since he was 8. "I grew up during the period when Joe Baum '43 and Warner Le Roy were opening up restaurants all over New York City, and I admired them," he told *Crain's*. Food service jobs, a stint as teacher's assistant in the Hotel school's Quantity Food Preparation course, and studies in France followed. His latest venture in the mid-1990s was a cooking show on the fledgling TV Food Network.

Nieporent's restaurant philosophy is a simple one. "The restaurants are like children," he told *Nation's Restaurant News*. "You teach values and principles when they are new—they need your attention then. When they are older, it is really like the grown child that you just have to check in on."

## Changes for the 1980s

In the 1960s and 1970s, Bob Beck led the Hotel school into international markets just as American hotel companies were expanding overseas. Beck also supported research in computer applications for hotels when computers were in their earliest stages. He began graduate programs and expanded executive education programs to supply trained managers to an industry that sorely needed them. As employment in hotels, restaurants, travel, and other hospitality services surged, he expanded the student body from 400 to more than 700.

These changes were "the right things to do at the time," says Clark. "I think Bob did them effectively and very well." At the same time, Clark was convinced that the hospitality industry would expand and change much more rapidly in the 1980s than it had in the past. Hotel managers would need to know less about plumbing and furnaces than they used to, and they would need to know more about energy management systems, automated baggage handling, and satellite telecommunications. Mergers and acquisitions were sweeping the industry, making it important for top managers to have a sophisticated understanding of corporate law, finance, marketing, and accounting.

Computer technology, which had been a focus of Hotel school research since 1964, finally came into its

During the interview process, Clark was asked to write a short statement outlining his goals for the school. They included a complete revision of the school curriculum, an active fundraising program, and the need for dramatic improvements in the Statler Inn. These goals, all of which he accomplished, became his legacy. Yet he says that when he took over on July 1, 1981, "I was incredibly naive about university politics, and I didn't know many key alumni."

One thing Clark did know was that the school needed to change fundamentally and quickly. During the 1977 curriculum review, he had realized "there was a dissonance between where the [hospitality] industry was and where we were. We were falling behind."

own as a hotel management tool in the 1980s. Desktop computers surpassing the speed and power of the old mainframes made it possible for every small hotel—indeed, every small business—to computerize its operations. At the same time, newer mainframe computers with unheard-of speed were extending the possibilities for computers in design, publishing, marketing, and other areas. As the capability of computers to process vast amounts of information grew, managers needed to develop a whole new set of skills in information management and analysis.

A few months after Clark became dean, the school's faculty and staff turned in a preliminary assessment of the curriculum. They concluded that the purely technical aspects of Hotel education—what some alumni refer to as "flush and gush" or "sticks and bricks"—were becoming less important to managerial training, while interpersonal and analytical skills were becoming more important. A year later, the faculty agreed to revise the curriculum from start to finish.

One of Clark's cherished beliefs was that the new curriculum had to include foreign languages to prepare graduates for a global economy. "We were too Americanized in 1980," he says. "Americans dominated the hotel industry then, and a very high percentage of the senior managers of the largest hotel companies were Cornell graduates. But you could see in 1981 that the industry was going to globalize.

"I can remember when foreign students would come to our courses, and say, 'That's not the way we do it in Asia.' The professor would say, 'But that's the way we do it in the United States. And you're going to learn the U.S. way because this is an American school.'" That approach wouldn't work any more. "To turn out the leaders of multinational companies, we had to turn out people who had a multicultural, globalized attitude."

**Finding New Donors**

It soon became apparent that if the school was going to modernize and think big, it needed to try something new—a big, modern fundraising campaign. "Bob Beck did get a few sizable contributions, but there was no organized, focused undertaking," says Clark. "And the gifts were mostly small. The twenty largest hotel companies were all American. Their average gift was $2,500 a year—to the scholarship account. That was crazy. The scale of corporate and alumni giving had to change drastically. Our school could no longer remain as tuition-driven as it had been."

Decades of generous contributions from the Statler Foundation allowed the Hotel school to expand steadily without the need for organized fundraising. But by 1970, the Statler Foundation was donating to other programs in San Francisco and New York. By 1980, their gifts were even more diversified, reflecting rapid growth in the field of hospitality education. But while the foundation's interests were expanding beyond Cornell, their assets remained at about $25 million. To grow and remain in the lead, Cornell's Hotel school had to find new sources of income.

Shortly after getting the dean's job, Clark shocked the school and angered some faculty members by closing some international programs for lower-level industry employees. While Bob Beck was leading a master's level hotel education program he had created in France, Clark phased out lower-level programs in Brazil, Venezuela, and Mexico. He also discontinued a federally funded CETA hotel training program and sold "Statler West," the complex of Gothic stone buildings Beck had purchased two years before. Clark felt the complex was not suitable in location or structure for the higher-level executive programs that were to come.

"I thought we had to redefine our market niche," he says. "Our competitive advantage was to be the best, not the biggest, program. The federal and overseas programs that I ended were training mid-level or maybe even entry-level people." Statler West sold for close to the price Beck had paid for it, and the school donated two acres on West Hill for a new city fire station.

"We had to get going on research again," Clark says. "We had to prove to the industry that research was a good and useful thing, so they would support us. And research is expensive."

Clark needed to spend much of his time fundraising and making industry connections, so he promoted three faculty members to be assistant deans so they could handle the day-to-day management of the school. James J. Eyster Jr. '69, PhD '77, a finance specialist, would handle academic affairs. Peter Rainsford '69, PhD '74, for external affairs, was an expert in management. The third post went to Normand L. Peckenpaugh '72, who had been a non-tenured faculty member, had worked at the Statler Inn since his student days, and served under Beck. Peckenpaugh remained as assistant dean for business administration.

Clark had two more overarching concerns. The first was computers, which were rapidly becoming essential to research and teaching. Although the school's computer research was well established, relatively few of the faculty knew how to use computers in 1981. Clark began to seek funding for a computer laboratory for the students, and he bought PCs for the administration. "Then I made the faculty an offer," he says. "The school would pay for two-thirds of a computer, and the faculty member would pay the rest. I might have just given them computers, and some of them thought I was a cheapskate because I didn't. But I wanted to make them literally buy into their computers so they would fully use them."

In 1983, the school received a generous donation from Aaron Binenkorb *25 and his wife Marion. Binenkorb had made a fortune as a paper distributor and then had a successful second career making non-fiction travel movies. The Binenkorbs donated their extensive selection of movies and video equipment, plus enough IBM and Apple computers for general use in classrooms. Once the faculty and students had adequate access to computers, their own interests and creativity ensured that the school made good use of them.

Clark's final problem was his status as the school's first dean without alumni connections. "I didn't know the alumni as a group, so I didn't know where I stood with them," he says. David Thomas, who was then acting dean of Cornell's Business school, suggested to Clark that the Hotel school form a small advisory board of successful, highly motivated alumni. "Most of the other colleges had been doing this, but the Hotel school had never had one," says Clark.

The Dean's Advisory Council included both alumni and friends of the school, and this group greatly influenced his decisions as dean. It included John Mariani *54; Charles F. Feeney '56, co-founder of Duty-Free Shoppers; G. Michael Hostage *54, the chief executive of Howard Johnson's; Jon Canas '65, chief operating officer of Aer Lingus / Dunfey Hotels (later Omni International Hotels); Lilyan H. Affinito '53, CEO of Murray Corporation; Frederick Malek, executive V.P. of Marriott Corporation; C. Alan MacDonald '55, president of Nestlé Foods; Robert Burns, CEO of Regent Hotels; and Jonathan Tisch, president of Loews Hotels.

The "Meek Tree," in 1986 before start of building, left standing despite 1940s and 1980s Statler construction. Statler Inn managing director Howard Kaler '78 wears a Cornell mascot's garb for the occasion, assisted by Fleet Morse, an employee since the Statler opened in 1950.

"I wanted bright, imaginative people who were strong enough to tell me when I was going down the wrong road. And boy, what a spectacular group I got! They had intellectual power, financial power, and a strong commitment to the school. Getting all three together is absolutely amazing. They understood the industry because they were our customers. I'll always be immensely grateful for their outstanding efforts on behalf of the school."

These early moves laid the foundation for the revolutionary changes Clark made. "The game plan for the new building began when the pieces started coming together," he says. "We needed personal computers. To do that right, we needed a large computer lab." To improve teaching, the classrooms had to be updated technologically. To become profitable, Statler Inn had to get bigger. "It was the encouragement of people like John Mariani and his executive assistant, Richard W. ("Dick") Brown '49, Chuck Feeney '56, and other members of the Dean's Council, that led me to believe we could do all of these things," says Clark. "Go for it."

### Changing the Curriculum

For nearly sixty years, curriculum changes at the Hotel school had been happening more or less constantly—but there was no apparent strategy for those changes. The courses largely emphasized technical proficiency in food preparation, hotel design, accounting, and other essential skills. In the 1970s, Dean Beck began introducing courses on the theory and practice of business management. But years of incremental changes had created a curriculum that packed each student's first two years with classes specific to hotel and restaurant administration skills, instead of the broader concepts of business management.

In the 1980s, Clark and the faculty turned the curriculum on its head. Skilled top-level managers, they felt, needed to learn management skills first and technical proficiencies second. In their 1981 study, the faculty told Clark that the existing system was like an "inverted funnel." An ideal course of study would impart the big ideas and then move on to specific applications, but the 1981 curriculum did the reverse.

The faculty report said that the school's mission should be to encourage skills in communication, human relations, analysis and problem solving, creativity, and leadership. The new graduates might choose to learn how to design a walk-in freezer or make an acceptable hollandaise sauce, but they should be required to learn the workings of airlines, car-rental companies, vacation lease-management firms, and dozens of other businesses that were joining hotels and restaurants under the general term "hospitality." Many participants were fond of saying that the school's goal was not to prepare students for their first job out of college, but for their third, fourth, or fifth.

In December 1982, the faculty approved a thorough review of the curriculum. The new effort would go much further than the 1977 effort Clark led under Beck; for one thing, it began by soliciting comments from a wide variety of alumni, industry figures, and hospitality educators from other schools. Prof. Michael H. Redlin *67 was asked to lead the Curriculum Review Task Force. "I gave him carte blanche in expenses and time," said Clark. "It probably cost us $200,000 or $250,000 to do this, which was unheard-of in those days."

Redlin's task force included industry representatives such as Michael Z. Kay '61, president of Omni International Hotels, and K. Shelly Porges *74, director of consumer card marketing for American Express. Outside academic views came from Lawrence K. Williams of the Cornell School of Industrial and Labor Relations, and Eddystone C. Nebel III from the hotel school at the University of New Orleans. The Cornell Hotel faculty was represented by Professors Leo M. Renaghan, who came to the school in 1982 from Penn State, and Eyster, who had returned to teaching.

The group took polls of industry leaders and solicited their views through an exhaustive series of interviews. "We brought deans in from other schools and gave them the run of the place," says Clark. "They could get any information they wanted and ask any question they wanted." Consulting firms were hired, alumni polled, and the faculty and staff organized into small groups for intensive study of different subject areas. Faculty were also assigned to write individual reports with the request that they ignore the constraints of time and money when visualizing their goals. Later, small groups with light-hearted names—Team Marinara, Team Bernaise, Group Teriyaki—considered heavyweight questions such as the number of credit hours and required courses.

Meanwhile, Clark was making a deal that would help flip the inverted-tunnel structure of the curriculum.

One of the reasons Hotel school students took so few classes outside the school was financial; the school had to pay a fee whenever a Hotel student took a course at another college at Cornell. This had the potential to create a significant burden on a school that was totally self-supporting and funded by tuition. After some discussion with Clark, university Provost W. Keith Kennedy agreed to reduce or eliminate some of these extra charges. In return, Clark agreed to actively pursue funding for something Kennedy wanted dearly—a conference center for executives on the Cornell campus.

The task force issued its recommendations in January 1985. The general idea was to turn the inverted funnel into a cylinder. Undergraduates would be encouraged to take courses outside the Hotel school throughout their four years on campus, with a roughly equivalent mix of courses in liberal arts and sciences, general business, and hospitality, while a greater emphasis on electives and faculty advising would allow specialization according to the students' interests. Says Leo Renaghan, "We basically kicked the kids out the door and said, 'Go find Cornell.'"

## TYPICAL COURSE SEQUENCE, 1989

The following was a typical course sequence of a Hotel student after the major curriculum revision of the 1980s.

**Freshman Year**

Rooms-Division Management
Organizational Behavior/Interpersonal Skills
Financial Accounting
Food and Beverage Management
Managerial Communication 1
Microcomputing
Quantitative Methods
Microeconomics for the Service Industries
Macroeconomics
Three credits of distributive or free electives

**Sophomore Year**

Human-Resources Management
Managerial Accounting
Finance
Culinary Theory and Practice
Principles of Marketing
Hotel Development and Planning
Three to six credits of distributive electives
Three to six credits of free electives

**Junior Year**

Strategic Management
Hospitality Financial Management
Restaurant Management
Hospitality Facilities Operations
Managerial Communication 2
Business and Hospitality Law
Six credits in chosen area of concentration
Three to six credits of free electives

**Senior Year**

Three credits in marketing elective
Six credits in concentration
Fifteen to 23 credits in free electives

Summer program students work with computers under Lecturer Roy Alvarez *72 in the Binenkorb Center in 1989 after reconstruction of the Statler is completed.

The faculty attended a retreat to hammer out the final revisions, then approved the new curriculum by an overwhelming margin in the spring of 1985. It required 67 credit hours in core courses, down from 78 in the previous curriculum, in such areas as marketing; management and organizations; and food and beverage, human resources, financial, and properties management; and the new curriculum called for a capstone course that integrated all fields of hospitality education. Also, students were required to take 12 credit hours in a declared area of concentration; 18 hours of electives in language, humanities, fine and performing arts, social sciences, and physical and natural sciences; and 23 hours of free electives; for a total of 120 credit hours.

One important component of the curriculum did not change. Hotelies were still required to put in the equivalent of 800 hours of work in the hospitality industry before they could register for their final semester at Cornell. The balance between theory and practice that was so important to Meek was preserved, although students could now fulfill the requirement by working over the summer, the winter intersession break, or even during semesters. Hotel students of the 1980s, like those of five decades earlier, often said that their jobs were crucial in shaping their career choices. Felix Laboy '86 says that his turning point came while "operating the Statler dining room with Brian Hale '85 and Dawn Young '85 for a semester and realizing that,

## THIRD-GENERATION FACULTY INNOVATORS

In the 1980s, an increasing proportion of Hotel faculty was hired from the ranks of non-Cornell alumni, and research became a more prominent part of the school's academic atmosphere. In 1989, the Hotel school had 41 assistant, associate, and full professors, 16 of whom had received their graduate degrees from Cornell. The four faculty members profiled below were chosen to represent the diversity of academic pursuits found in Statler Hall in the 1980s.

**Stephen A. Mutkoski** PhD '76 succeeded Vance Christian as Banfi Vintners Professor of Wine Education and Management. In 1994, he and his wife Patricia Mutkoski *66 brought wine education into the computer age with The Wine Professor, a series of interactive CD-ROM discs packed with text, color photos, and recipes.

The Wine Professor was a huge hit at the 1994 New York Hotel Show. "You'd think we were pouring wine," says Mutkoski. "I'd start about 9:30 every morning and go nonstop until the show closed." The first four discs described wines from Bordeaux, Germany, Napa / Sonoma, and New York. Mutkoski loves to show the program to people, he says, "just to watch the expressions on their faces."

**Avner Arbel,** a professor of financial management, used a stock-picking formula that he developed to accurately predict the 1987 stock market crash. He also wrote books and more than one hundred articles on finance and its relation to the hospitality industry. In the 1980s and 1990s, Arbel appeared frequently in national media.

**Robert M. Chase** is perhaps best known for his two computer simulation programs about restaurant and hotel operations: CHASE & CRASE (Cornell Hotel & Restaurant Administration Simulation Exercises). Yet Chase also received a BME and MBA from Cornell and had teaching experience in a variety of subjects, including property management, finance, accounting, hotel operations, and information systems.

**James J. Eyster,** with a B.S. and Ph.D. from Cornell, inaugurated the study of hotel management contracts. He developed the first hospitality management course about housing and feeding the homeless, and taught at the Centre International de Glion and IMHI-ESSEC.

**Thomas John Kelly** '71, MS '78 developed a restaurant rating system for the American Automobile Association and for DiRoNa, which was controversial because it gave low marks to some famous fancy establishments. He taught restaurant management, both at Statler and IMHI-ESSEC. In addition, he was chairman of the American Institute of Wine & Food in the mid-1990s.

even though it was a great experience, I didn't want to own or operate a restaurant upon graduation as I had originally intended." Ten years after graduation, Laboy was director of marketing for ANA Westin Hotels and Resorts.

Not all Hotel school graduates end up holding jobs in the hospitality industry. The school's hands-on business experience is strong preparation for practically any profession. Just ask Richard J. Ferris '62, former CEO of United Airlines.

Ferris, who ran United from 1983 until 1987, owned an aviation company and was co-chairman of Doubletree Inns in the mid-1990s. Before he joined United, Ferris managed a chain of coffee shops and worked as general manager of an Inter-Continental Hotel. He spent ten years managing various properties for Westin Hotels and Resorts before he moved to United Airlines as vice president of food services. Then, he moved away from the hospitality end and became vice president of marketing, eventually rising to CEO.

Ferris first became interested in the hospitality industry while running an officer's club in Japan during the late 1950s. "Frank Ready Jr. was impressed by my work and invited me to attend a Cornell Society of Hotelmen meeting in Japan," Ferris recalls. "I liked what I saw. I took the college boards in Japan . . . and that's how I got into Cornell." While he was a student, Ferris was a sommelier at Statler Inn. In 1962, he was managing director of HEC.

"What you get at Cornell are basic tools," Ferris says. "You begin your real learning after you leave. But Cornell opens your mind to many possibilities. It broadens your thinking. It allows you to really learn. And for that, I'm forever grateful."

Finding jobs for new Hotel graduates was not a problem, thanks to the extraordinary devotion of more than 5,000 alumni. In 1985, more than 400 summer jobs were posted, and over 1,000 managerial and executive positions were listed in a weekly alumni job bulletin.

New courses for the school's 650 undergraduates and 100 graduate students quickly evolved. By the end of Clark's tenure, the courses included such topics as the analysis of financial markets, management of centers for the homeless, and interpersonal communication. Prof. David C. Dunn, PhD '70, who succeeded Eyster as the school's associate dean for academic affairs, put it this way: "We prepare students for all fields in the hospitality industry, including airline catering; marketing; and club, hotel and restaurant, casino, property, and financial management. Today, the avenues open to [Hotel students] have multiplied and diversified considerably."

The curriculum review had taken an intense three years, but the payoff was enormous. "The way we did it built a strong consensus and belief in the curriculum among the faculty," said Michael Redlin, leader of the review. Shortly after the vote, he said that the faculty "has been filled with an enthusiasm so thick it could be cut and served with Crème Anglaise."

The curriculum changes also energized students, although some alumni from that era remember that their attentions were often diverted from their studies. "Friends were the center of my experience," writes Elizabeth A. Harlow '85, the first woman to be managing director of Hotel Ezra Cornell (see page 50). "When I think of studying, I think of sitting with my best friends and roommates in the living room of our apartment, trying to decipher engineering formulas or how to make a balance sheet balance. Amidst the discussion of the topic at hand would be varying non-related conversations on what happened at a party, clothing, or guys. We also inevitably found an opportunity to take a 'study break,' which usually involved a hot fudge sundae or a trip to the 'hot truck' for a PMP [sandwich]. When I think about it, I don't know how we ever passed our classes!

"The in-class antics were equally memorable. Courses which involved any sort of food preparation were teaching skills that were foreign to many of us. On one occasion, our prep team attempted to make an angel food cake. It turned out to be like a Styrofoam disc, rather like a Frisbee. It only seemed natural to see if it would fly like one. That cake put Frisbee to shame."

"My fondest memories of Cornell involve humor," says Michele Chandler '86. "Cornell Hotelies are an elite group of extroverts who have opinions on everything. Our class was responsible for producing a farcical 'Coarse Supplement' that included great courses like 'Napkin Folding in the 18th Century.' We also formed the Yo-Hos, the tasty society of underachievers. All of these things involved learning how to work as a team. These lessons in human nature were more important than anything else I learned."

## Learning How to Ask

Early in the curriculum revision, a glaring problem had become apparent to Clark. "We were bursting at the seams," he says. The original Statler Hall was built to serve about 400 students, but total enrollment had swelled to about 750. "And every time you add students, you add faculty. With the new rules, we were also talking about adding technology and staff to support it. Things were really growing, and we were simply running out of space." This led to a major new phase in his deanship.

Although he did not know many Hotel alumni in the beginning, Clark knew of the intense loyalty and camaraderie alumni felt toward each other, their school, and its first two deans. These powerful emotions would be an advantage to his fundraising campaign, but Clark was also aware of the dangers. Every night in the early years, he said, he would think of the alumni loyalty and say, "Please, God, don't let me mess that up."

The money began to flow early in 1983, after Clark and others drafted a preliminary statement of need for classroom improvements, hiring and training faculty, integrating new technology into the school, and increasing the size of Statler Inn. The Binenkorbs' $200,000 gift was one of the earliest responses. Another $275,000 came from an anonymous foundation to support new staff, foreign language instruction, and—most important—a complete architectural study of Statler Hall that would specify the needs for various physical improvements.

Consultants recommended that a massive fundraising campaign would have more success if a significant amount of support from the wealthiest and most powerful prospects was secured before the campaign was formally announced. Clark immediately set about to do just that.

The 1986 Hotel Ezra Cornell banquet is transplanted to Barton Hall, university drill hall, when it became too large to stage in Statler Hall. Two years later Barton housed the HEC banquet again during the Statler reconstruction.

Vintners as vice chairman. Holtzman counted many of Clark's top prospects as personal friends, which made the initial contacts easier and more productive. Clark said that because of Holtzman, he received a one million-dollar pledge after a single meeting with the donor. And if Holtzman couldn't provide an introduction, it was likely that someone else on the Dean's Council could.

Some of the faculty also proved to be skilled fundraisers. One notable example was Stephen A. Mutkoski '67, PhD '76, the Banfi Vintners professor of wine education and management, who raised a substantial amount for a new beverage management center.

At the center of the fundraising team was a dynamo named Shelley Semmler, whom Clark hired as the school's first development director. Semmler helped Clark tailor proposals to individual donors and companies. She also built a database of alumni that showed prospects how successful the school had been in training hospitality leaders, and supervised and coordinated all fundraising and public affairs events.

Another behind the scenes leader was Richard E. Holtzman '41, president of Rockresorts and chairman of the campaign committee, with Dick Brown of Banfi

John Mariani's $3 million gift came late in 1983. The next two years were probably the most exhilarating of Clark's tenure, as he flew to dozens of meetings all over the world to solicit support—and usually got it. "It got to be a chess game," he says. "We needed to get the big bucks to motivate everyone else, and the heavyweights were the most fun to deal with. Planning out their support, and then putting the pieces together, was really fun. And in a few cases, we didn't even ask for money. It just came in because they liked the plan."

In November 1985, Clark spoke at a meeting for 200 Hotel school supporters at the Waldorf-Astoria Hotel. He announced that the school was embarking on a $25 million capital campaign for the improvement of Statler Hall, and that $11.6 million had already been pledged by major donors. The strategy worked. Momentum built as each alumni class sought to outgive the other. The pace for these medium- and small-size donations was set by the Class of '56, which alone donated $1 million to the campaign.

Two things added more fuel to the fundraising engine. The first was Clark's increasing emphasis on building a sizable conference center and executive education facility in the new Statler Hotel. The venerable summer programs and seminars for hotel executives were still going strong when Beck turned the reins over to Clark. In 1983, for example, more than 1,500 adult students took part in sixteen Cornell-led seminars away from Ithaca, and another 600 attended the on-campus summer session. These non-matriculating alumni formed another pool of potential donors who were especially interested in executive education. The key occasion in this effort was the early 1988 announcement of a major gift from the Marriott Corporation and the J. Willard Marriott Foundation, which funded the Marriott Executive Education Center.

More help for fundraising came from improvements to Hotel publications. *The Bulletin of the Cornell Society of Hotelmen* was redesigned by Fred Conner *78 and given a larger budget. In addition to notices of society meetings and alumni milestones, it began running more information on fundraising progress and later the rebuilding of Statler Hall, illustrated with photographs. No less important was the *Cornell Hotel and Restaurant Administration Quarterly*, which had a circulation of more than 7,000 by the mid-1980s. The *Quarterly*'s mission was to distribute hospitality research to academic and business readers—but talented editors like Joan Livingston *75 and Glenn R. Withiam *74 made it a much livelier publication than most scholarly journals. Nearly every issue reported the results of basic and applied hospitality research done at Cornell, which gave fundraisers more and more examples to use when seeking support for research.

In 1985, Jack Clark seemed to be riding high. The Hotel school had money in the bank, and more was coming in all the time. He had a large and growing circle of friends in the industry. He had discussed a five-year reappointment as dean and had the strong support of President Rhodes. Most of all, he had big plans to give the school he loved the building and programs it deserved. What Clark didn't know was that his ride was about to get a lot rougher.

## The Big Decision

The decision to demolish Statler Inn, gut Statler Hall, build a new Statler Hotel, and completely renovate the teaching spaces did not come easily or quickly. "I thought I was going to be an academic dean who was going to change the programs," says Clark. "That's where my real interest was. I slowly realized that in order to have that happen, the other stuff had to come first."

Clark knew that the Statler Inn had been struggling financially. After taking a close look at the numbers, Clark, Norm Peckenpaugh, and others concluded that the Inn would have to expand from 50 to 100 rooms to make money. A 1983 architectural study, conducted by Warren Platner Associates, included a list of essential improvements to the structure and an estimate of their costs. The report came back loaded with ideas for minor expansion projects and cosmetic changes to the teaching spaces in Statler Hall. For Statler Inn, the firm suggested building a "slipcover" around the existing building that would contain fifty additional rooms and a new facade.

The plans for classroom improvements were solid. But "as we began to look into [the Statler Inn] and where the column spacings were and so on, we realized that we just couldn't do it," says Clark. "We went through three architects, and every scheme we came up with didn't look right and cost too much money. As we dug further into this, the five or six key people involved began to have thoughts that maybe we should tear it down and start over again.

"Then one day I had a conversation with one of the major donors. He said, 'If you were really going to do this right, is 100 rooms enough? If you looked at the needs of the campus and your own needs, what would you do?' I told him that if I had the money, I'd go for 150 rooms. And he said, 'Let's discuss it.'"

The anonymous donor's pledge was a death warrant for Prof Meek's Inn. After a few encouraging discussions with Marriott officials, Clark decided to tear down the old Inn, rebuild it as a 150-room, four-star hotel, add a large Marriott-funded executive education center, and boost the campaign goal to $35 million. Several Hotel administrators immediately began working out the details of the new plan; for example, much of the groundwork for the new Statler Hotel was done by Howard M. Kaler '78, the last general manager of the old Inn. But the decision to raze and rebuild was withheld from the public, alumni, and the Hotel faculty for over a year, until the architectural plans were complete and the financing was in place. Clark sensed how unpopular the decision might be.

The Statler Inn closed for "renovations" on August 17, 1986. The decision to demolish it was announced publicly a week later; the reaction from some faculty, staff, and alumni ranged from disbelief to rage. "The building was only about thirty-five years old," says Clark. "All the alumni who graduated between 1950 and 1965 thought of it as brand-new."

The Inn staff was already stung by the closing, which laid off more than 100 workers. Project Manager Allan Lentini and the university's personnel office placed them elsewhere in the university, but many staffers did not understand why the building that represented their careers had to go. Students were facing up to two years of disloca-

tion, noise, and inconvenience. Many people in the neighboring School of Industrial and Labor Relations were opposed to Clark's plans for a nine-story hotel building that might dominate the campus, and some university officials felt the same way. Provost Keith Kennedy, Clark's ally in Day Hall, had retired, and the dean would not enjoy such good relations with the central administration again. More damaging in the long run, though, was the fraying of goodwill with some tenured members of his faculty. "I came in as

dean with the academic credentials," says Clark. "I became an external dean in their minds."

The decision to tear down the Inn made sense to those who were most closely involved with it. "It was cheaper to tear it down than to refurbish it," says Norm Peckenpaugh. "When the plan was presented to me, I saw that it made sense as a business decision."

Clark continued to have strong support from the Dean's Council, many of his largest donors, and those in the Hotel community who either agreed with his plans

*Left:* Executive in residence Robert Perry, lecturer on management in 1988.

*Right:* Wally ("Famous") Amos of Amos Cookies speaks at the 1989 Hotel Ezra Cornell.

The new Statler Hotel, completed in 1989.

or were willing to follow the leader. But he cashed in a lot of chips in August 1986. In this difficult atmosphere, he began the arduous job of supervising a major construction project.

**Construction and Conflict**

On November 4, 1986, about sixty Hotelies gathered behind a chain link fence that separated Statler Inn from Ives Hall. Wearing party hats and grasping pink and white balloons and noisemakers, they huddled in the cold air to await the first swing of the wrecking ball. As glass shattered and bricks fell, some applauded. But others were disappointed with the slow pace of destruction. Said one student, "Why don't they just dynamite it?"

Demolition of the Inn was completed in December, and the foundation for the new hotel was poured in February 1987. Statler Hall itself closed at the end of classes in May 1987; the faculty and staff relocated to offices in Sage Hall across the street, and Brown Road several miles away.

"Topping out" for the hotel took place in January 1988. By August 1988, the staff and faculty moved back into a renovated Statler Hall, in time for the 1988–89 academic year. Grand opening of the new Statler Hotel would wait until April 10, 1989 at Hotel Ezra Cornell 64.

The road to the reopening of Statler Hall and the grand opening of the hotel was a bumpy one. "I didn't understand how hard it would be to make the physical changes in the plant so we could have the programs we needed," says Clark. For two years the community endured inconveniences and discomforts that frayed nerves and shortened tempers.

Students and staff labored mightily to keep school traditions alive during construction. For Hotel Ezra Cornell in the spring of 1988, for example, with Statler Inn gone, students with walkie-talkies shuttled HEC guests among several campus locations and the Sheraton Inn off campus. The weekend began with a Roaring Twenties cocktail party at a fraternity house, as students dressed as flappers and gangsters distributed peacock feathers at the door. Later, other students dressed as police officers "busted" the party and drove guests off in "paddy wagons" to dinner. Other events were held in the Big Red Barn, Sheraton Inn, and Teagle Hall. The Saturday gala dinner was held in Barton Hall, with food prepared in kitchens around campus and stored in refrigerated trucks.

During the 1987–88 academic year, the Hotel school's community experienced its own version of the scattered, chaotic conditions that pre-1950 Hotelies took for granted. Staff members who had direct contact with students were housed in the cramped, stuffy offices of Sage Hall. Others were housed in offices near

A new food lab in the reconstructed Statler Hall in 1989.

was brutally hot over there," says Clark. "We had our own version of the long, hot summer."

Parking for professors was a sore point that summer. But the petty conflicts between Clark and faculty members were symptoms of a more fundamental disagreement. As the building went up, and in spite of the undergraduate curriculum revisions and new executive education programs, more and more senior faculty questioned Clark's commitment to academic leadership of the school. Two-thirds of the capital campaign goal was now committed to the new hotel, and only one-third to Statler Hall. With a good deal of the dean's time spent raising funds, the faculty asserted a greater voice in setting academic policy for the school.

the Tompkins County airport. Classes were held in ten buildings spread all over campus, in a food lab at Ithaca College, and at the Sheraton Inn north of campus. The library kept a selection of heavily used books in trailers outside Statler Hall; most of the books were kept on the stage of Alice Statler Auditorium, and users had to wait hours or even days to retrieve them.

Sage Hall had no air conditioning, and the summer of 1987 was one of the hottest on record. "Getting Sage Hall was a real blessing, because its proximity made the move much easier than it would have been anywhere else. But it

In April 1988, as the skeleton of the new Statler Hotel was being closed and filled in, Clark submitted his resignation. He intended it to become effective in July 1989, after the hotel's grand opening at HEC in April 1989 and the conclusion of the fundraising campaign. He cited a "destructive environment" that he said made it impossible for him to continue. President Rhodes refused to accept the resignation; instead, he confronted the Hotel faculty at a tense meeting, demanded that power struggles be resolved, and appealed for more tolerance on both sides. In a statement released at the time, Rhodes said it was "essential to the long-term future well-being of the school" that Clark stay until the project and campaign were completed. Clark agreed to stay until January 1990, but with the feeling that his authority had been compromised.

Clark's old friend Don Dermody left the Hotel school in 1988 to become dean of the International Center for Tourism and Hospitality Management at Nova Southeastern University in Fort Lauderdale, Florida. "The Hotel school was always accustomed to being an institution that taught financial management and lived according to its teachings," he says. "[Prof] Meek was always proud of how the school raised money and didn't have to beg. It became part of the school's culture. Clark changed that, and it shocked people. When the numbers went higher and higher, people lost confidence in his ability to lead."

Jim Eyster, Clark's first assistant dean for academic affairs, probably put it best. "I thought he was a visionary because he tackled major projects which hadn't been addressed for years. But there was a high level of expectation when Jack moved in that he would govern in a democratic way. The faculty's expectations were so high that it was easy for them to feel let down."

## Sagging Fortunes

Any large-scale building project, particularly when fast-tracked, will face unexpected costs. Several architects and consultants were hired and fired by the university before the final plans were approved. A semifinal plan for a nine-story building was all but rejected by university officials, and a new design team had to make several more changes late in the design process to gain the approval of Day Hall. Providing adequate parking for the hotel took two years of negotiations with the university, and the small lot Clark finally secured near Barton Hall cost the school $1.1 million. In February 1988 the school's business officer and Project Director Lentini announced the cost of the building had grown from $35 to $39 million because builders had discovered a number of problems: Some walls and ceilings in the original building were packed with asbestos that had to be removed, while others failed to meet fire codes.

Then in May 1988 builders discovered cracks in some of the newly poured concrete beams. A careful inspection revealed they were only cosmetic flaws, and the structure was sound. Shortly after, they discovered a more serious problem. Several of the poured concrete floors weren't level. The university brought in a structural engineering firm that specialized in stresses in concrete. "We were absolutely guar-

A marketing class in Statler Hall taught by Prof. Chekitan S. Dev in 1990.

anteed that although it looked terrible, it was structurally sound," Clark said. Fixing the problem would cost more money. Clark says he suspects use of a "fast-track" mode of construction meant not enough time was allowed for the concrete to cure. But seven years after the fact, questions still remained on how the problem occurred.

## A Modern Home for the School

The work proceeded more smoothly in Statler Hall. And on Friday, August 26, 1988, Clark welcomed faculty and staff back into the renovated building at a jubilant reception in the new, sunlit atrium and foyer. Michelle Langas '89 told the *Daily Sun* that she was "excited" to return to Statler Hall for her senior year. Langas said that she was especially pleased to have a chance to build more school spirit. During the year out of the building, "Students lost the sense of being in the Hotel school," she said.

Eight months later, Langas managed the sixty-fourth Hotel Ezra Cornell, a celebration of the grand opening of the new Statler Hotel. Hundreds of industry leaders and several dozen reporters marveled at the new building's cherry paneling, polished granite floors and tabletops, and warm interior decor. Upstairs, the guest rooms offered cutting-edge technology and guest conveniences in the Statler tradition. Outside, the architects linked the new building visually to Statler Hall by giving it a limestone facade trimmed with granite. Between the hotel and the school, the J. Willard Marriott Executive Education Center boasted seven meeting rooms and a ninety-seat amphitheater. Each seat had a computer port and a microphone, and the room was equipped so that presentations could be videotaped and rebroadcast in the guest rooms.

The centerpiece of the hotel's Loews lobby is the "Wall of Honor," a permanent collection of twelve-inch lead crystal plates. Each plate was engraved with an appropriate symbol of the donors who gave $1 million or more to the capital campaign: Banfi Vintners, Marjorie Blanchard *62 and Kenneth H. Blanchard *61, the Joseph Drown Foundation, Duty-Free Shoppers, Christopher Hemmeter '62, Hilton Hotels, HVS (Hospitality Valuation Services) Stephen Rushmore '67 and Judith Kellner Rushmore, International Business Machines, Ichiro Inumaru '53 and Imperial Hotels, Loews Hotels, the Marriott Corporation, the J. Willard Marriott Foundation, Search America Foundation, the Ellsworth Statler Foundation, Stouffer Hotels and Resorts, the Taylor Foundation, and United Airline Foundation / Westin Hotels.

Eleven other donors gave betwen $250,000 and $1 million: Marion and Aaron Binenkorb *25, Burger King Corporation, CSX / Rockresorts, Carrier Corporation, the Coors Foundation, Hilda Longyear

Gifford '26 and John P. Gifford '29, Dorothy and Hubert R. Heilman *39, Hilton International, Regent International Hotels, Laurance S. Rockefeller, and Hubert E. Westfall '34. Altogether, more than 1,600 individuals, companies, and foundations gave to the Hotel school's capital fund campaign.

One of the busiest and most honored guests at the grand opening was Hans P. Weishaupt '64, the Robert A. Beck Professor of Applied Hotel Management, a position that included the title of managing director of the new Statler Hotel. He had been managing director of the thirty-ninth Hotel Ezra Cornell, and for the next quarter-century he managed some of the world's finest luxury hotels. Weishaupt was a guest that weekend because he had turned over the keys to the building to Michelle Langas and her crew. After the weekend was over, he returned to his Statler Hotel duties.

Weishaupt's dual status as a faculty member and hotel manager was part of Clark's master plan for the new building. The new Statler was officially designated as a "teaching hotel." As in the teaching hospitals affiliated with medical schools, Hotel faculty members were to function as heads of the hotel's functions and facilities in their classes. Assisting Weishaupt were David D'Aprix '84, a food and beverage instructor who was named director of food and beverage services, and A. Neal Geller '64, an accounting professor who would serve as the hotel's first director of accounting and finance while on a one-year leave from the school.

When the 1989–90 academic year began, Clark had accomplished almost all the things he had set out to do. The new hotel and renovated classrooms were open and running. The faculty was using them to teach a revised curriculum that was outstanding among hospitality education programs. Cornell was the top hotel school in the world, but Clark had spent his chips.

On January 1, 1990, he left Ithaca for a three-semester teaching appointment as the first holder of the Matson Navigation Company distinguished professorship at the University of Hawaii. While there he was chosen by the students as the outstanding teacher. A year and a half later he returned to rejoin the Cornell Hotel faculty as a professor of properties management. After nearly a decade of change, he had come full circle.

Why did Clark return as a teacher to the Hotel school after being the dean? Why didn't he stay in Hawaii or accept one of the other industry / academic positions offered him? "There was never any doubt in my mind that I would return to Cornell to enjoy our new facilities and programs," he says. "If you're teaching hotel students, there's no other game in town. You're either at Cornell, or hoping to get there."

Dean Jack Clark stands on the stairway of the dramatic new entrance atrium to the school in 1989.

# Global Leaders
# in Hospitality

THE FOURTH DEAN of the School of Hotel Administration,

David A. Dittman, might seem an odd choice for the job.

The son of a Cincinnati tobacco wholesaler, he had not traveled

extensively outside the Midwest before he arrived at Cornell in 1990.

He was known as a world-class accountant with a talent for academic adminis-

tration, but he knew next to nothing about the hotel business.

He may not have had experience running a hotel, but Dittman had grown up

helping his father run a service business, so he understood the importance of

satisfying the customer. He proved to be a consummate facilitator who could

Graduate students prepare to
make thesis presentations in
the amphitheater of the new
J. Willard Marriott Executive
Education Center in 1991.

lead an energetic and sometimes divergent faculty. He also got

results. The Statler Hotel was losing money when Dittman

arrived; three years later, it was generating a respectable surplus.

Dean Dittman greets students at a freshman convocation.

of properties management who had led the successful curriculum review of 1983–85. Norm Peckenpaugh continued as assistant dean for business and administration, and William Chernish was assistant dean for executive education.

The most pressing job in 1990 was to ensure the school's long-term financial health. The new Statler Hotel was beautiful and essential to the school's mission, but it was also expensive. Its construction budget had been exceeded by 36 percent, and many pledges to the previous capital campaign were still outstanding. A resulting debt had to be serviced regularly without cutting the programs and facilities of the hotel and school, which together ensured Cornell's position as a leading program in hospitality education.

And he may not have been well traveled, but by 1995 he was moving the Cornell Hotel school forward as a global player in the hospitality industry.

## Between Deans

Between January and July 1990, an administration team managed the Hotel school while a search committee looked for the next dean. The interim dean during this period was J. William Keithan Jr. '50, former senior vice president of Westin Hotels, a past president of the Cornell Society of Hotelmen, and a consultant during the Statler renovation. Academic affairs were handled by Associate Dean Michael Redlin, a professor

## From Minneapolis to Ithaca

In 1989, David Dittman was one of the country's leading educators in the field of accounting. He had an undergraduate degree from Notre Dame and a Ph.D. in accounting from Ohio State, had taught the subject at Duke University and Northwestern, and was enjoying a successful tenure as chair of the accounting department at the University of Minnesota. He had no connection whatsoever with Cornell.

"I was sitting in my office at the University of Minnesota when a man from an executive search firm

New entryway for the hotel.

The new food preparation lab, in use.

called to say my name had been placed in nomination for dean of the Cornell Hotel school. I said I understood the school was a very prestigious place, but obviously he had the wrong Dave Dittman: I was Dave Dittman, the accountant at Minnesota. So I politely said good-bye."

The recruiter called back and convinced Dittman he was a candidate. After an initial meeting, Dittman gave the offer some thought. "It became apparent to me that I was quite familiar with a lot of the things that go on at a hotel school. And there were quite a few things that I was not familiar with, which made that kind of intriguing."

The search team tapped Dittman because his skills matched the Hotel school's needs for the 1990s. "I think they wanted somebody that had been in academic management. I think that I had the right pedigree," he says. "I had been at some major universities, and I had the opportunity to deal with a divergent faculty at Minnesota in a fairly successful manner. And I think that given the time and the mood of the Cornell Hotel faculty, the search team needed somebody to come in here and provide leadership and direction. I think that's probably why I got the call."

When an offer from Cornell eventually came, Dittman still doubted he was the right man for the job. "I had a close friend at San Diego State, Bob Cabotini, who had heard I was looking at this position. Bob called one day and said, 'What are you going to do?' I

said, 'I'm trying to make up my mind.' And Bob said, 'Well, let me ask you this, Dave, has the Harvard Business School called you?' I said, 'No, Bob, they haven't been on the phone this week.' And he said, 'I don't think you're going to get a better offer.' So he kind of solidified my thinking."

Five years later, Dittman was glad he took a job that he describes as second to none.

Student servers poised moments before the Carrier Ballroom doors open and a banquet—"¡Mambo Caliente!"—begins.

Merv Griffin and Dean David Dittman at a visit to the Hotel school and talk by Griffin, 1991.

Restaurant, and Institutional Education (CHRIE). He also attended Cornell Society of Hotelmen functions in Montreal, Toronto, and several U.S. cities.

"I spent a lot of time in the first six months listening and putting together groups of advisors," Dittman recalls. "At the same time, I realized we had to do some things fast. In financial terms, we had to be moving in the right direction by the time we came out of the first year. So we asked a lot of people for their advice. We broke the faculty into strategic planning groups."

Before Dittman even arrived, he had made an interesting discovery. "I knew the new [Statler] hotel was not doing well, because I had done some analysis back in Minnesota. I knew that no matter how much occupancy it had at the then current room rate, there was no way it was going to make money."

While Dittman learned, he was also working on a financial plan. One of his first actions as dean was to ask several prominent hotel managers to study the Statler Hotel. The group included Stephen P. Weisz '72, senior vice president for sales and marketing at

### Dittman's Debut

Dittman started slowly when he took on the dean's job July 1, 1990. "I spent a lot of time getting to know people and hotel operations," he says. He visited companies in all facets of the hospitality industry to learn the details of managing in those businesses. He went to hotel schools in Europe to find out how other countries trained their hoteliers. In April, as dean-elect, he met alumni at the 1990 Hotel Ezra Cornell. In May, he met more alumni at the National Restaurant Association annual convention. In August, he went to the annual conference of the Council on Hotel,

Marriott; Michael ("Mickey") Silberstein '74, from the Holiday Inn Crowne Plaza in New York City; Michael W. Sansbury '74, from Disney's Swan hotel in Orlando; Nick Mutton, a friend of the school and executive at Four Seasons Hotels; and the retiring Statler Hotel general manager, Hans Weishaupt.

The team decided to pare hotel services. To explain the cuts to the faculty, the team made financial information available to all concerned.

Students bid to make the world's largest lasagna in October 1991 on the university's main quadrangle. They took six hours to create a 63 x 7-foot lasagna, that weighed 3,600 pounds. Four thousand people from town and campus paid $1 a plate, earning funds for community charities. Leftover food went to a community center Weekend Meals program, founded by students in the Hotel course, Housing and Feeding the Homeless.

### Building Teams to Solve Problems

"I knew there were several challenges like this when I came on board," Dittman says. "But I'm not sure I realized the depth of the challenges."

The 1990–91 operating budget for the entire school, drafted by Keithan before Dittman's arrival, projected a $400,000 operating deficit, in addition to $2.9 million in debt service that had to be paid. During the 1989–90 fiscal year, the new Statler Hotel had lost $1.1 million. Clearly, this performance had to improve.

Dittman asked faculty and staff planning groups to suggest ways for both the school and the hotel to save money. The teams came up with about 250 ideas, a number of which were implemented without delay. By pulling together, the school finished the 1990–91 fiscal year with a surplus of $800,000 before debt service. The hotel cut its budgeted losses by two-thirds.

Some of the cost-cutting ideas were small and symbolic, such as eliminating the dean's car. Others were larger and more controversial. In 1990, for example, full-time hotel employees outnumbered student employees by three to one. By 1995, there were three student employees for every regular worker. "The shift to student labor was a natural outgrowth of our teaching mission," Dittman says. "Students who are eager to learn the hotel business is what a Cornell Hotel school education is all about."

Students eating in the new McLamore student cafeteria in 1992. *See Sources for names.*

To increase the hotel's revenues, Dittman put greater emphasis on marketing. When Hans Weishaupt retired in 1991 and returned to his native Switzerland, Dittman chose James E. Hisle '68 as the next managing director of the Statler Hotel. Then he contacted John L. Sharpe '65, who was executive vice president of operations at Four Seasons Hotels, and asked for his help. "We needed first-class marketing executives, but Ithaca is an isolated market," he says. "I asked John to loan us a marketing executive to help us position the Statler."

Sharpe and Nick Mutton convinced Peggy Foster to become the Statler's new director of marketing, and she worked with Hisle to increase sales and improve profitability. Hisle and Foster saw that the hotel had an unusual problem: it was such an impressive building that outsiders commonly assumed that it was too expensive and always sold out. So they adopted more flexible room rates; cut the lunch prices at the hotel's signature restaurant, Banfi's; developed promotional events; and ran an advertising campaign aimed at Cornellians both on campus and around the world. Room occupancy at the Statler increased 5 percentage points after their first year, to 68.5 percent.

The Hotel school itself added a new team member in 1990, when Norm Peckenpaugh retired (for the third time). Replacing him as assistant dean for business and administration was Susanne Gurda DeGraba '76. She came to the position with an MBA from Cornell's Johnson Graduate School of Management, ten years' experience as a property manager, and a stint as a CPA with Price Waterhouse.

## The Need to Ask

Dittman had assembled a team of efficiency experts and revenue-builders, but they alone would not be enough. Fundraising had to be part of the plan. Cornell President Frank Rhodes had announced a $1.25 billion capital campaign in the summer of 1990, and the Hotel school was assigned $55 million as its share. This was a tall order, as the school had just finished raising $22.1 million in cash, with $9 million pledged over the next five years. In addition, the early 1990s brought the worst recession to the hotel industry since the Great Depression.

The campaign's goal was to build an endowment big enough to support the faculty, student scholarships, and research. Dittman argued that a bigger endowment was necessary to provide financial support to the "best and the brightest" students regardless of their socioeconomic background. He also saw that adequate support for faculty positions and for research was essential to maintaining a leading-edge position.

In the 1980s, Jack Clark had focused on corporate gifts. But the early 1990s recession prevented many hospitality firms from donating to the school. Instead, Dittman concentrated on alumni support, and the alumni gave as never before. After a slow start, the campaign hit its stride in 1993 and 1994. Halfway through 1995, the team had raised $22 million, mostly from alumni gifts that ranged from a few dollars to a single gift of $2 million. "If we can do that in a depressed market," says Dittman, "think of what we can do when the market is good."

### Six Guiding Principles

In the early weeks of his administration, Dittman organized a retreat away from Ithaca. Joining him were Mike Redlin, Bill Chernish, and Norm Peckenpaugh. The "host" and facilitator was Kenneth H. Blanchard *61, a loyal friend of the school and author of a best-selling business book, *The One-Minute Manager*. Blanchard asked the group to agree on six simple words and

*Above:* Members of the Student Committee for Continuous Improvement, fall of 1995. *See Sources for names.*

*Left:* Students at an HEC event in 1995.

phrases that would best describe the guiding principles of the Hotel school. The six proved to be: ethics, excellence, caring and sharing, personal growth, financial independence, and fun.

Backlighting allows closer inspection of fluids in the building's new winetasting facility.

Ethics was chosen because the school is committed to training responsible leaders as well as successful businesspeople; excellence for teaching, research, and service; caring and sharing, because caring and dedication to service are what define a hospitality professional; personal growth, because acquiring professional skills must balance with achieving one's full potential as a human being; financial independence, because the school must remain free and strong if it is to serve its other ideals faithfully; and fun, because it is important to enjoy work for its own sake.

This definition of the school's guiding principles was the basis for a detailed strategic plan. In the next year, all faculty and staff members played roles in drafting the document which was reaffirmed independently by the faculty a year later when they voted unanimously to accept the plan, which began with this mission statement:

"The goal of the School of Hotel Administration is to achieve excellence in creating and sharing knowledge in the field of hospitality management. This goal imposes on the school a three-part mission of excellence and creativity in teaching, research and scholarly activity, and service. In all three of these activities, the School of Hotel Administration must respond to the changing environments in which the hospitality industry operates, particularly the global economy, the internationalization of business, and the diverse nature of the merging work force."

The plan signaled the school's intent to broaden its educational focus. It defined the term "hospitality industry" as a collection of businesses that extends far beyond traditional lodging and food service firms to also include those in travel, tourism, and other related lodging, feeding, and leisure industries. Hospitality also includes many supporting enterprises that depend on these core businesses, including professional services, educational services, associations, food and beverage vendors, equipment and hardware vendors, and business development firms.

The strategic plan also announced the school's intent to create a new center that would conduct sponsored research in conjunction with hospitality firms. But the bulk of it was a detailed set of goals and action plans for service to all of the groups that make up the "Hotel community." The term was defined broadly to include full-

Stephen A. Mutkoski, the Banfi Vintners professor of beverage management, in the new Christian Beverage Management Center, named for the late Prof. Vance Christian.

time undergraduate and graduate students; part-time students in seminars and executive education programs; alumni, faculty and staff; other academic institutions; the entire hospitality industry; and "the larger community," which reflects the belief that the school should promote positive social change.

One of the most valuable aspects of the strategic planning process was that the dean and faculty agreed on specific standards of behavior. The six key princi-

*Above:* Lecturer Giuseppe Pezzotti '84 demonstrates a cooking technique to a student.

*Right:* A table of exotic desserts in a Statler Hall lab.

ples "guide the way we interact with each other," says Dittman. "If someone is determined not to live in a sharing and caring environment, it becomes very easy to say that they're out of bounds."

The prodigious energy and talents of the Hotel faculty pose a significant management challenge for the dean. "Managing personalities is half the job of being dean," he says. "Trying to figure out what motivates people, what their ultimate goals are, and how to align their goals with those of the school is—interesting."

## Building a Hotel Boot Camp

One of Dittman's major goals for undergraduate education is to put basic hotel skills back in the curriculum. "We do a wonderful job of teaching management. We got away from teaching the basic hospitality skills that an entry-level student needs to know. That is what differentiates our undergraduate students from business students, after all."

Proposals for change, in discussion stages in 1995, might restore the teaching of basic hospitality skills such as operating the equipment in a restaurant kitchen, maintaining housekeeping standards in a hotel, or waiting on tables. "What do we bring to the party? We bring a better understanding of the hospitality industry," says Dittman. "What does that mean? It means our students can go into a hotel and be able to train people how to run it. I think that the best way to teach these skills is on the job, not in a classroom.

"That's why we have the Statler Hotel. That's why over 250 students were working in the Statler in 1995, compared to 59 in 1990. We have the largest job-sharing program of any hotel right here on campus."

In 1993, alumni and friends of the Hotel school welcomed undergraduates in a new way. That was the year all students automatically became members of the student chapter of the Cornell Society of Hotelmen. In 1994, the student chapter replaced the school's Student Activities Committee, which had distributed funds to other student organizations such as Ye Hosts and the Minority Hoteliers Association. The student chapter now serves a dual purpose: it is the Hotel school's student government organization, and it ensures that all Hotelies are seasoned members of the CSH even before they graduate.

### A Teaching Edge

Cornell's position as a top school of hospitality management meant much more in 1990 than it had in Meek's day, because many more schools were in the field. In some cases, Cornell encouraged the growth, as with another of the top hotel schools in the U.S., the University of Nevada–Las Vegas (UNLV), a school founded by Jerome J. Vallen '50 in 1967, with advice from H. B. Meek himself.

Lecturer Rupert Spies instructs Wendy H. Starkman '95 during a cooking class in 1992 in new Statler Hotel teaching facilities.

Noted television chef Julia Child and Brian Halloran, executive chef of the Statler Hotel, prepare food in 1990. She was on campus to stir interest in a student chapter of the American Institute of Wine & Food.

In the 1990s, Cornell's strategy for hiring new faculty was the same strategy that brought Dittman to the school. The goal was to get the best people from individual academic disciplines, regardless of hotel experience, and train them in the hotel business if necessary. This strategy reflected the broadening of hospitality education, and also the maturing of business education in general. Accounting, finance, and marketing had become full-fledged academic disciplines, on the same level as psychology, economics, or sociology. Hotel faculty who taught these subjects had to be at least as good as the faculty at leading business schools, for a simple reason: business schools put competitive pressure on the Hotel school whenever they emphasized management skills for service industries.

### Research That Produces

Another of Dittman's priorities was to increase the stature of research. "Hospitality management research is a key to the long-run preeminence of the school," he says. "The 3M Corporation has a goal: every year they introduce new products which are projected to account for 20 percent of their revenues in five years. We need to be thinking that way. The research we create today becomes the curriculum we teach tomorrow."

Several other excellent hospitality education programs included a school at the University of Houston, a strong department at Michigan State University, and hundreds of colleges offering courses in hotel and restaurant management. Clearly, the key to staying ahead of this pack was to hire the most talented teachers, do the best research, and attract the best students.

Research "gives us the chance to prove that the Cornell Hotel school is valuable to the industry. It also has direct benefits for our executive education efforts, because our executive students have high expectations. We have to provide them with hospitality-specific information that they can't get elsewhere, or they will go to another school for general business training.

"We also have a big advantage because Cornell University teaches everything. We can invite people from the Business school over to look at management issues. We can bring experts in sociology to look at issues on social drinking. We can bring people in urban planning together to look at site location. We can reach out into this great research university to augment our students' experiences."

In July 1992, the school formed a Center for Hospitality Research to develop topics important to the industry and academe. The center's first director was Prof. John B. ("Jack") Corgel, whose areas of expertise were real estate, property management, and finance. "For the most part, companies in the hospitality industry do not have their own in-house brain trusts or full-fledged research departments," Corgel said. "We will be the de facto research center for the industry."

The center soon attracted a lot of attention and support from major players in the hospitality industry. Founding partners included Procter & Gamble,

ECOLAB (a cleaning products manufacturer), Cini·Little (food service and hotel design), Banfi Vintners, Marriott Lodging and Resorts, Medallion Hotels, and Amedeo Hotels. Sponsors included Holiday Inn Worldwide, NHV Hotels International, and Choice Hotels.

The center was an immediate success because it listened to its corporate customers, says Dittman. It concentrated on projects that had been recommended and in most cases sponsored by the industry. One of its early projects, for a Fortune 500 company, was to determine the impact on guests of amenities in hotels. Other projects sought to determine how the franchise affiliation of a hotel affects its sale price; how brand names become a factor in a hospitality customer's purchase decision; and how yield management, a pricing strategy common in the airline industry, could be applied to hotels. In 1994, Corgel was succeeded by Prof. Leo Renaghan as the center's director.

## New Academic Programs

Dittman's first five years included a comprehensive redesign of graduate education programs. "Our original strategic plan called for determining whether we should stay in the business of educating graduate students. We determined to revise the graduate curriculum to make it more distinct from the undergraduate program."

## PASSING A TEST

Christopher Reynolds was a reporter for the *Los Angeles Times* on assignment at Cornell. But he didn't come for the gorges, the ivy-covered halls, or even to interview the university's new president, Hunter Rawlings. He came to make trouble for the Statler Hotel.

One day after the 1995 graduation, as the hotel was recuperating from its biggest weekend of the year, Reynolds checked in with his wife and proceeded to make a lot of unreasonable demands. "Cornell's hoteliers are still pups, and checking into the Ithaca Statler is something like taking a seat in a barber's college," he wrote. As "the hotel guest from hell," his assignment was "to give a few young hoteliers a chance to show grace (or the lack of it) under pressure."

There was just one problem. Every time Reynolds acted up, the students handled him perfectly.

When he arrived two hours before the specified check-in time and demanded a room with a view of the campus, a valet, and a bellman, he got all of them immediately. The bellman even hung up his coat without being asked. The next morning, he intentionally placed a breakfast order with room service that could be interpreted two ways. He complained when the order arrived exactly on time. "The waiter looked as if he had been struck by a nun with a ruler," wrote Reynolds. A few moments later, the order Reynolds insisted on arrived with a promise that he wouldn't be charged. "In my book, it was clearly a sign to throw in the towel (rather than stealing it) and acknowledge my failure as a troublemaker," he wrote. "Two hours later, we checked out."

In 1994, after three years of planning and development, the graduate faculty introduced a completely redesigned curriculum that would lead to a new degree, Master of Management in Hospitality (MMH). "Our graduates will be competitive with the graduates of any top management program," said Prof. Michael Redlin. "But they will truly shine in their ability to implement their visions and decisions."

Part of the planning included a survey of "stakeholders" in the new program, including industry figures, Hotel faculty, and graduate alumni and students. Respondents were asked to name the most important qualities of a successful hospitality manager. The seven themes that emerged were strategic orientation, or the ability to see the big picture; communications ability; management style, particularly the use of teamwork; leadership skills, or the ability to persuade, motivate, and encourage; ethical awareness; an international scope; and analytical ability, with sufficient mastery of technical skills and industry concepts.

Prof. A. Neal Geller led the effort to create the MMH degree to replace the Hotel MPS. He was assisted by Sandra Boothe, director of the existing Masters of Professional Studies Program, and seven faculty members: Professors Judith L. Brownell, a specialist in organizational and management communications; Jack Corgel; Chekitan S. Dev; Cathy A. Enz; Sheryl E. Kimes; Richard G. Moore *67; and Daphne A. Jameson.

Each student in the revamped graduate program is rigorously evaluated and given a program of study tailored to individual interests and skills. At the end of the second semester, students are given on-site consulting assignments by hospitality firms. Following the assignment, each student is matched with a high-level industry mentor who provides additional training and guidance.

In June 1995, the New York State Board of Regents authorized the MMH degree. As word spread of changes in the graduate program, the number of applications increased. More than 350 applications were received for 55 places in the class entering in 1995. The first MMH class was to be graduated in 1996.

In 1995, Dittman named a new academic affairs team. After eleven semesters as associate dean, Michael Redlin rejoined the faculty in the properties management area. Neal Geller was named associate dean for academic affairs and Judith Brownell was named director of graduate programs.

Timothy R. Hinkin, associate professor in the management of organizations and human resources, was named director of undergraduate programs. Geller and Hinkin immediately began working on a major revision of the undergraduate curriculum, the first since 1983. Their plans called for a survey of industry leaders similar to the one that informed the masters program. Geller said that the undergraduate survey's goal was slightly different, however. The planners wanted to look at how the hospitality industry will change between 1995 and 2020, and how the school could produce graduates who will lead those changes.

### Education for Executives

The school's executive education efforts for non-degree candidates, begun in 1928, were strengthened in 1993 by the appointment of David Butler as associate dean. One of Butler's earliest decisions was to hire Norm Peckenpaugh as chief of staff, thereby ending his second brief retirement.

In the next two years, Butler, Peckenpaugh, and a team of senior Hotel faculty reorganized the Professional Development Program (PDP). The result was a 20 percent increase in enrollment, and eighteen new

Eric Hilton, vice chairman of Hilton Hotels Corporation, gives the keynote address at HEC 70 in 1995. Hilton's father, Conrad Hilton, spoke at HEC 29 in 1954, on the occasion of Prof Meek's appointment as dean of the school.

professional certification programs were undertaken that enrolled 250 persons from across the hospitality industry. From 1993–95 the number of countries represented in PDP rose to eighty-one.

Similar progress was made in the General Managers and Advanced Management programs. The former program sold out for the first time in its eight-year history in 1994 and repeated in 1995. At the suggestion of the participants, the Advanced Management Program was redesigned in 1995 from a three-week seminar to a more concentrated two-week session. Custom programs continued around the world, with a greater emphasis on continuing seminars. In the mid-1990s the school made alliances with the National University in Singapore, NHV Hotels of Japan, Dusit Thani College of Thailand, Cresta Hotels of South Africa, Institut fur Hotelmanagement of Germany, and Ortels of Switzerland and Ecuador.

Dean and Mrs. Dittman attend a meeting of the Cornell Society of Hotelmen in Hong Kong in June 1995. *See Sources for names.*

The school was also making plans for further global expansion as the seventy-fifth anniversary approached. For example, the executive certificate program was a possibility for expansion into countries such as India and China. "It is a form of preemptive marketing when people see that all the leading managers in these countries are from the Cornell Hotel school. It increases our presence, the name, and the reputation of the school," says Dittman.

Dean Dittman says he hopes the day will come when the school can reduce faculty teaching loads in other graduate programs so as to offer more executive education. "And we may start to treat people who teach in executive education less as independent contractors for us and more as full-time instructors on the payroll."

## International Reach

The most ambitious aspect of the Hotel school by the mid-1990s was its renewed emphasis on international programs. In 1994, Cornell began a partnership with the Australian International Hotel School (AIHS) in Canberra. A team of Cornell faculty, led by Prof. Richard H. Penner, developed the Australian school's innovative three-year curriculum. Course sequences were designed to quickly build managerial, communication, and quantitative skills which could be applied to a wide range of global hospitality topics. Many subjects incorporated case studies, team projects, guest speakers from the industry, and, in the last semesters, drew extensively from the students' varied externship experiences throughout Australia and the Pacific region. First-year students are also required to live and work at the Hotel Kurrajong, an historic landmark in Canberra.

Australia was a logical choice for the school to establish an Asian base for several reasons: English is Australia's native language, and many students in the Asia–Pacific region go to Australia and New Zealand for higher education. Tourism in Asia was booming in the mid-1990s: the number of visitors to Australia was estimated to exceed 5 million by the year 2001, and hospitality jobs were projected to increase 20 percent between 1995 and 2000. These needs were magnified by the Olympic Games, scheduled for the year 2000 in Sydney. Similar gains were projected for tourism in Korea, Thailand, India, and other Asian countries.

The Cornell-Canberra connection included many alumni and faculty. Jerry Vallen '50, dean of the UNLV hotel school for twenty-two years, went on to serve as the founding dean of the Canberra school in 1994–95. Hannah Messerli, PhD '93 became the school's assistant dean of academic affairs.

Plans were also set to strengthen the school's presence in Europe. In 1994, a new agreement between Groupe ESSEC and the Hotel school made the IMHI (Institut de Management Hôtelier International), started by Bob Beck in 1979, a true partnership. Student exchanges were encouraged, and IMHI was to hire a permanent faculty to teach and do research, which would facilitate student

Dean Dittman and the Cornell athletic mascots in 1994.

as well as faculty exchanges. The Hotel school's faculty were to take a more active role in the affairs of IMHI through specific initiatives to be developed by a seven-person faculty committee led by Prof. Thomas P. Cullen '66, PhD '83, who has an international reputation in strategic management—efficiency and troubleshooting for the hospitality industry. The committee also included Professors Cathy Enz and Mary H. Tabacchi from Cornell, and Gérard Guibilato, director of IMHI, and his colleagues, Adjunct Director Mike Nowlis, Jean-Marie Choffray, and Alain Bernard.

The school's fourth dean may not, as he said, have known the hospitality industry or Cornell's place in it when he arrived at Statler Hall in 1990. But by 1995 he

At the 1995 Commencement.

The Statler Hotel was generating income for the school. Another revision of the undergraduate curriculum was in the works, a new Masters of Management in Hospitality program was off to a strong start, and the caliber of entering classes was at an all-time high. Dean David Dittman presided over teams of faculty who were expanding research programs and overseas operations. Behind all of these efforts was a worldwide network of powerful and passionately devoted alumni.

In seventy-five years, the Hotel school had grown from an enterprise directed from one office "under the stairs" to a global player in the hospitality industry. The school organization was directed by area specialists with strong management skills whose efforts were coordinated by the dean, just as the many branches of a multinational hospitality business are coordinated by a chief executive officer.

The base for these efforts was laid by Jock Howie, Prof Meek, and the American Hotel Association in 1922. It was expanded by Bob Beck, Jack Clark, and three generations of dedicated faculty, staff, students, alumni, and friends. In the twenty-first century, the Cornell Hotel school will provide global leadership to a huge, multifaceted industry. But the bottom line will always be the same. Hotelies will always keep looking for ways to offer a little more, a little better service.

had proven to be a quick study in both, so that under his leadership the school was poised to continue its place as a most important player in hospitality education.

### Ready for the Future

As the Cornell School of Hotel Administration approached its seventy-fifth anniversary, the message of E. M. Statler—"Life is service, the one who progresses is the one who gives his fellow men a little more, a little better service"—was its overarching principle.

An evening view of the new entrance atrium to the School of Hotel Administration.

Aerial view of the Cornell campus, in 1989. The newly completed nine-story hotel and Statler Hall are at right center, in front of the large, pitched-roof Barton Hall.

# Sources

## Notes on the Text

The materials used to write this book are located in Cornell University's Department of Manuscripts and University Archives, the Stouffer Hotels Library in Statler Hall, or elsewhere as noted. Recommended are:

"Life Is Service: A History of the Cornell University School of Hotel Administration," by Dian Olson Belanger and Joan M. Zenzen of History Associates, Inc., Rockville, MD (1991, 156 pages), an uncorrected draft which covers the years from the founding to 1990.

"The Founding of a Profession: A History of the School of Hotel Administration at Cornell University" by Helen Recknagel (1983, 80 pages), an uncorrected draft which begins with the nineteenth century and ends circa 1930.

*The Cornell Hotel and Restaurant Administration Quarterly*, Vol. 26, No. 1 (May 1985), a special issue devoted to the history of hospitality industries, with special emphasis on industry and Hotel school events since 1961.

*From a Closet Under The Stairs* by Charles I. Sayles '26 (privately published softcover, 1988), an anecdotal history and memoir by a charter student and 40-year faculty member of the Hotel school.

*The Best Ever! Memories of Hotel Ezra Cornell* by Joy Sheridan Nichols '90 with Kimberly Joy Sanders '92 and Allison Jeanne Morris '92 (Ithaca, NY: The Grapevine Press, 1990), which contains brief descriptions, photographs, and lists of the HEC Boards of Directors from 1925 to 1990.

*Statler: America's Extraordinary Hotelman* by Floyd Miller (1968: The Statler Foundation, New York, NY), a semi-fictionalized biography of the hotelman.

Photocopies compiled in 1988 by Joan Livingston *75 from originals stored in the University Archives. These are organized into two loose-leaf binders in the Hotel school library. Many of the most significant documents relating to the school from 1914 to 1979 are represented, including annual Dean's Reports to the University Provost.

The following is an informal list of sources.

**Epigraph**  Page v: "What is a hotelier?" an unattributed quote distributed by the late John Stewart Foote '64.

 A PROJECT
TOO BIG TO REFUSE

**Opening**  "John McFarlane Howie: The Forgotten Godfather of the Cornell School of Hotel Administration" by David Warren Howell, Associate Professor, Institute of Travel, Hotel, and Restaurant Administration, Niagara University, New York (1993); "The Origin of the School of Hotel Administration (as I have heard it related by Neal)" by Mrs. Cornelius Betten (2-page typescript).

**The Science of Hotels**  *Palaces of the People: A Social History of Commercial Hospitality* by Arthur White (1970: Taplinger Publishing Co. Inc., New York, NY); "American Hotels in 1848" by Doris Elizabeth King, in "Never Let People be Kept Waiting: A Textbook on Hotel Management," (1973: The

First students in Hotel administration, fall 1922. *From left, seated:* John M. Dockery '25; Cornelius Betten, director of resident instruction, College of Agriculture and Home Economics; Prof. H.B. Meek; and Alfred Olsen '25. *Second row:* Howard M. Zinram *25, Harold P. Gundersdorf *25, Kenneth M. Wilson *25, Herbert J. Marchand *25, A. Winston Dunlap '25, Clyde A. Jennings '25, and Albert Lang *26. *Third row:* John F. Hamill *26, Arthur P. Hanlon *26, John M. Crandall '25, William H. Lodge '27, Arthur V. Taft '26, and Loyal Gibbs '26. *Fourth row:* Clermont Hanlon '25, John H. Platt '26, John Courtney '25, Lewis H. Combs *26, and Robert W. Boggs *26.

Graphic Press, Raleigh, NC); "75 Years: The Odyssey of Eating Out," *Nation's Restaurant News*, January 1994; *Cornell Hotel and Restaurant Administration Quarterly*, Vol. 26, No. 1.

**The Greenbrier's Early Days**  *The History of the Greenbrier* by Robert S. Conte (1989: Pictorial Histories Publishing Co.).

**Statler: Faster, Better, and Cheaper**  *Statler: America's Extraordinary Hotelman.*

**Wanted: An Innovation Foundry**  "A Brief History of Unionism in the Hospitality Industry" by Robert M. Kok, School of Hotel, Restaurant, and Recreation Management, Pennsylvania State University (working paper 93–03, February 1993); Sayles manuscript; Belanger and Zenzen manuscript; Henry Bohm to John Howie, August 30, 1913; Howie to Elmore Green, December 19, 1919; Frank Dudley to Jacob Schurman, January 20, 1921; Albert Mann to Flora Rose, June 24, 1921; Martha Van Rensselaer to Albert Mann, February 12, 1921; *New York Hotel Review*, January 14, 1922; "Report of Frank A. Dudley, Chairman of the Educational Committee," February 24, 1922; "Telegrams Relating to the Appointment of Howard B. Meek," transcript dated September 12, 1922.

**A Man Of Many Menus** and **Heavy Dining**  Oscar Tschirky Menu Collection, Stouffer Hotels Library, Statler Hall.

 MEEK CAN HAVE ANYTHING HE WANTS

**Meek Inherits The Challenge**  Sayles manuscript; interview with Howard Meek by Sharon Carroll, May 14, 1964 (80-page transcript).

**Scrounging and Borrowing**  "Cornell—Ten Years After" by W. R. Needham in *Hotel Management*, February 1935; interview with Joseph Nolin by Ira Apfel (from notes); Sayles manuscript; Meek interview.

**The Story of Martha and Flora** "Milestones in History" compiled by Vivien N. Warters, 1965 (4-page typescript); unsigned Flora Rose obituary (2-page typescript); Biography of Martha Van Rensselaer for "Notable Women" by Edith M. Fox, 1963 (7-page typescript).

**Help From Hotelmen** Sayles manuscript; correspondence cited in "Money" section, below; Cornelius Betten in *Cornell Daily Sun*, September 20, 1922.

**Creating a Course of Study** *Register of Ye Hosts,* May 7, 1926.

**Where's the Money?** Interview with Lois Jean Meek by Dick Brown, April 12, 1995 (18-page transcript); Sayles manuscript; Howie to Dudley, November 28, 1922; F. W. Bergman to Meek, May 12, 1923; Mann to Meek, August 27, 1923; "Memorandum of Understanding between the American Hotel Association and Cornell University," January 23, 1924; Mann to Livingston Farrand, July 26, 1924; Meek to Mann, December 22, 1926.

**Early Hotel Curriculum** *Announcement of the Program of Hotel Administration,* 1925–26.

**Hotelmen and Prohibition** *Ye Hosts,* May 7, 1926; interview with Vinnicombe by Apfel (from notes); *Ithaca Journal,* June 6, 1922.

**The First Hotel Ezra Cornell** Sayles manuscript; "Thumbnail Sketch of the Origin of the Cornell Society of Hotelmen" by John Courtney, June 1952 CSH *Directory; Ye Hosts,* May 7, 1926; brief memoir by Alexander MacLennan in *The Best Ever! Memories of Hotel Ezra Cornell.*

**Ellsworth Comes to Ezra** Alice Seidler to Meek, February 2, 1926; Meek to Mann, February 4, 1926; Ellsworth Statler to Meek, March 22, 1927; Statler biography; Sayles manuscript; Meek interview.

 THE FULFILLMENT OF A PROMISE

**Opening** The Best Ever! *Bulletin of the Cornell Society of Hotelmen,* Vol. 6, No. 2.

**How the Industry Endured** Recknagel, pages 69–80; *Nation's Restaurant News,* January 1994; "A Brief History of Unionism in the Hospitality Industry."

**Hard Times on the Hill** Recknagel, pages 61 and 63; Meek's reports to Provost, 1930–1941; Vinnicombe interview; Sayles manuscript.

**Struggling With Statler** Belanger and Zenzen, pages 28 and 40; Frank McKowne to Meek, May 13, 1931, February 22, 1935; Meek interview, interview with Lois Jean Meek, 1995 (tape and transcript); Mann to Betten, February 22, 1930; Meek interview; Meek to Mann, September 1, 1933; Howie to Meek, March 27, 1934, August 19, 1934; Howie to Walter C. Heasley, May 20, 1943; Howie to W.I. Hamilton, October 29, 1947.

**Women in the Hotel Program** Interview with Dorothy Daly Johnson by Apfel (from notes); Hilda Longyear Gifford quoted in Sayles manuscript; interview with Mary Wright by Apfel, November 1994 (13-page transcript); Margaret Kappa to Michael Chiu, October 1995; Elizabeth Harlow '85 quote in *Cornell Daily Sun,* May 5, 1985.

**Page 16** (detail): Hotel faculty and students as guests of the Hotel Pennsylvania November 1929, at the opening luncheon of the annual New York hotel show, identified by Kevin Howard '31: **1** William N. Davis *31, **2** H. Glen Herb '31, **3** George V. McKay '31, **4** Raymond Milks '31, **5** John McGinn '31, **6** Alton Morris '31, **7** William Carroll '31, **8** Maurice W. Jackson '31, **10** Lloyd Knauss *32, **11** Ernest Clarenbach Jr. '31, **12** Alfred Merrick '30, **15** Prof. Frank Randolph, **16** Prof. A.B. Recknagel, **18** Robert Timmerman '31, **19** Martin Hess '31, **20** James Knipe '31, **27** Kevin Howard '31, **29** Edward Ramage *31, **33** R. Augustus Nulle '33, **34** James B. Smith '31, **35** Prof. Alfred Olsen '25, **36** William Needham '25, **37** Prof. John Courtney, **40** Robert Stieglitz '31, **41** Herbert F. Dill '31, and **42** Carrie Meyer '31.

**How To Haze a Hotelie** Sayles manuscript; Vinnicombe interview.

**The School Gets Stronger** Mann to Meek, June 12, 1931; Meek interview, pages 78–81, 52, 58; Meek to Mann, May 2, 1929, June 4, 1937; Sayles manuscript; James P. Duchscherer to Chiu, October 1995; Meek interview, pages 63–66; *Announcement,* 1935 (faculty list).

**Early Faculty Contributions** Archives of the Cornell Dean of Faculty.

**The Cornell Society of Hotelmen** Needham in *Hotel Management*; Belanger and Zenzen, pages 53 and 46–7; Sayles manuscript; Meek to Provost, September 1941; Meek interview.

**Needham & Grohmann** Interview with Heinsius by Apfel (from notes).

**The War Years** Anonymous alumnus quoted in Sayles manuscript; Meek to Provost, 1942–45; Meek to Sarah Blanding, February 10, 1942; Navy to Meek, February 28, 1943; Meek to Battles quoted in Belanger and Zenzen, page 51; shipwreck story in Sayles manuscript.

 A MAGNIFICENT ADDITION ... AN ENDURING LEGACY

This and subsequent chapters were enhanced by the responses of twenty-nine alumni to an October 1995 letter from Michael Chiu asking for answers to these questions: What and who meant the most to your Hotel school education? What stories do you tell about your years at Cornell? Why did you choose the Hotel school? What were your career goals on graduation? and, How has the school or its alumni made a difference?

All twenty-nine responses are with the author's files.

ANNUAL DINNER
CORNELL SOCIETY OF HOTELMEN
IN THE EMBASSY ROOM OF
HOTEL AMBASSADOR · NEW YORK
WEDNESDAY · NOVEMBER 17, 1937

Annual dinner dance of the Cornell Society of Hotelmen in the Embassy Room of the Hotel Ambassador in New York City, November 1937. Identification by Kevin E. Howard '31. **2** Stephen W. Allio Jr. '29, **4** James R. McKowne '32, **10** Harry Jackson '32, **11** Frank A. Ready '35, **12** Mrs. St. Laurent, **15** E. Truman Wright '34, **16** Bruce Parlett '32, **17** Mrs. Ready, **19** Kevin Howard '31, **27** Georges St. Laurent '33, **34** John Shea '26, **37** H. Victor Grohmann '28, **39** Mrs. Shea, **41** John P. Stack, *25, **43** Arthur C. Hunt '29, **45** William Needham '25, **46** Loyal Gibbs '26, **47** Hubert E. Westfall '34, **55** Martin Hess '31, **59** Tom C. Deveau '27, **62** Arvine C. Bowdish '26, **65** Robert Stocking, **66** Milton Smith '32, **67** Peggy Smith *32, **68** Prof. Frank Randolph, **70** Arthur Buddenhagen '27, **71** Prof. John Courtney '25, **73** Mrs. Morrison, **74** James A. Morrison '30, **77** Everett E. Burdge '30, and **79** Ernest Clarenbach '31.

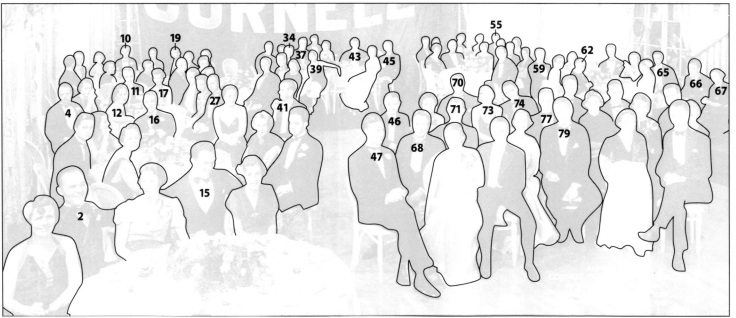

# Notes on the Illustrations

In these listings the page number of the illustration is followed by the name of the photographer or original owner, if known, and the lender of the illustration in italics.

---

Lender abbreviations:

*Cornell Hotel School = School of Hotel Administration, Cornell University*

*DRMC, CU = Division of Rare and Manuscript Collections, Cornell University Library*

*University Photography = Cornell Department of University Photography*

---

ii *Cornell Hotel School*

vii *Cornell Hotel School*

xvi Harry B. Settle. *George S. Bolster Collection, Historical Society of Saratoga Springs*

 A Project
Too Big to Refuse

2 Left: W. A. Drennan. *Buffalo and Erie County Historical Society;* right (detail): John Troy. *Cornell Hotel School*

3 J. W. Taylor. *Chicago Historical Society (ICHi-00748)*

5 Parsons. *DRMC, CU (E. M. Statler papers, 3879)*

7 *Santa Fe Railway Collection, Kansas State Historical Society*

8 *Cornell Hotel School*

11 *DRMC, CU*

14 Left: *Cornell Hotel School*

14–15 Menus, *clockwise from top left:* Hudson and Manhattan Railroad Company, celebrating the opening of the first tunnels under the Hudson River, Sherry's, New York, February 25, 1908 (Tiffany etching, gold emboss, and hand-tinting—signed by the governors of New York and New Jersey); American Paper and Pulp Association, thirty-third annual banquet, Waldorf-Astoria, New York, February 10, 1910 (seven-color printing including metallic inks); New York State Chamber of Commerce, one hundred and fifty-first annual banquet, Waldorf-Astoria, New York, November 13, 1919 (calligraphy and foil-stamped emboss); Hudson-Fulton Company, Staten Island Banquet, Municipal Ferry Terminal, St. George, September 30, 1909 (color etching and gold foil-stamping); Ohio Society of New York, twenty-fourth annual banquet, Waldorf-Astoria, New York, January 10, 1910 (calligraphy and engraving—Orville and Wilbur Wright were at the head table); Bancroft Hotel, New Year's Eve dinner, Worcester, Massachusetts, 1914 (twelve-color lithograph). *Oscar Tschirky Menu Collection, Stouffer Hotels Library, Cornell Hotel School*

The student body poses on the slope where Mann Library now stands, in 1948.

A formal organization of Hotelies was inevitable. From the earliest days of the program at Cornell, Hotel students and alumni banded together for camaraderie and to help one another. Early students met on campus as the "Coffee Hounds," later forming Ye Hosts and then the Cornell Hotel Association. Soon alumni and students were meeting at the annual hotel shows in New York and Chicago. In 1928, at Ithaca, alumni formed the Cornell Society of Hotelmen with John M. Crandall '25 as president, and Prof. John Courtney '25 as secretary-treasurer.

Early activities of the society included placement committees in Ithaca, New York, and Chicago, a *Bulletin*, receptions and dinners at the main hospitality industry gatherings, a loan fund and scholarships for students, and the formation of local chapters. The number of chapters grew from 6 in 1935 to 48 in 1995, moving across the Pacific to Hawaii and Japan at first, then to the Caribbean, Central America, and to Europe in 1962. By 1995, 39 chapters existed in the U.S. and Canada, and 9 abroad, in twelve regions.

From 1,000 alumni in the late 1940s, the number of former students had grown to 9,000 by 1995. Graduates qualify automatically for membership. Others taking courses in executive education and summer programs can become affiliate members after satisfying certain course requirements.

As the years went by, the society produced an alumni directory and took on admissions interviewing, high school recruitment, mentorship, counselling, fundraising, and other activities in support of the dean and Hotel school, including publication of this history.

The men and women who have been president of the Cornell Society of Hotelmen since its founding are:

John M. Crandall '25, 1928–30
Arthur C. Hunt '29, 1930–31
Clyde Jennings '25, 1931–32
William R. Needham '25, 1932–33
John L. Shea '26, 1933–34
Albert E. Koehl '28, 1934–35
Kenneth W. Baker '29, 1935–36
Joseph P. Binns '28, 1936–38
Richard B. Shanley '32, 1938
Howard L. Dayton '28, 1938–40
Frank H. Briggs '35, 1940–42
H. Victor Grohmann '28, 1942–44
Charles I. Sayles '26, 1944–46
Henry B. Williams '30, 1946–48
H. Alexander MacLennan '26, 1948–50
Joseph H. Nolin '25, 1950–51
Robert M. Brush '34, 1951–52
Ruel Tyo '27, 1952–53
Wallace W. Lee Jr. '36, 1953–54
Lynn P. Himmelman '33, 1954–55
Lee E. Schoenbrunn '40, 1955–56
E. Truman Wright '34, 1956–57
Henry A. Montague '34, 1957–58
Jerome B. P. Temple '38, 1958–59
James Barker Smith '31, 1959–60
Roy Watson Jr. '48, 1960–61
Frank J. Irving '35, 1961–62

J. Frank
Edward J.
Richard
William
James P.
Richard
Thomas
Philip Pis
Milton C.
Maurice
John F. C
Richard
Robert M
Michael
J. William
James V.
Richard
Richard J
Margaret
William J
M. Theo
Bjorn R.
Thomas
Donald
William J
Frank T.
Kevin P.
Burton
James E.
Richard
William
Caren W
Michael

Past presidents of the Cornell Society of Hotelmen receive gavels from Dean Meek in 1957 at the Plaza Hotel in New York City. *From left, first row:* Clyde Jennings '25, Henry B. Williams '30, Joseph H. Nolin '25, Henry A. Montague '34, Dean Meek, John Shea '26, and John Crandall '25. *Second row:* Robert M. Brush '34, Lee Schoenbrunn '40, E. Truman Wright '34, Wallace W. Lee '36, H. Alexander MacLennan '26, Joseph P. Binns '28, Frank H. Briggs '36, Albert E. Koehl '28, Lynn P. Himmelman '33, Kenneth W. Baker '29, and H. Victor Grohmann '28.

# Extended Captions

The following are fuller captions for selected photographs that appear in chapters 1–7.

27  First full class in Hotel Administration to graduate, 1926. *From left, all Class of 1926, except faculty. First row:* Fred L. Miner, William Lodge '27, Arthur Taft, John Shea, John L. Slack, and John M. Welch. *Second row:* Prof. Frank H. Randolph *17; Prof Meek; Director Martha Van Rensselaer of Home Economics; John Howie, "AHA member, supporter of program;" acting dean Cornelius Betten of Agriculture and Home Economics; Hilda Longyear; and Walter Bovard. *Back row:* H. Alexander MacLennan, Arvine C. Bowdish, Raymond M. Stearns, Herbert L. Nickles, Robert Boggs *26, Loyal Gibbs, and Albert Lang *26.

34  HEC board members for 1929 meet in Willard Straight Hall. All are Class of 1929 except as otherwise indicated. *From left:* Donald F. Savery, Charles A. Krieger, Frederik Groenveld '31, Robert A. Rose, Harry A. Smith '30, Arthur C. Hunt, Kenneth W. Baker, Clement Rynalski, Frank W. Case Jr., B. Franklin Copp, Edgar A. Whiting, and Stephen W. Allio Jr.

35  *Top:* Among those identifiable helping register an HEC guest in the late 1920s: John Sullivan '30, left; John P. McGinn '31, third from left; and Harry A. Smith '30, fourth from left.

46  *Bottom:* Identifiable among HEC guest couples in 1935 are Harry S. Jackson '32, *left;* Albert J. McAllister '29, *seventh from left;* John A. Bullock '32, *tenth;* Milton C. Smith *32, *eleventh;* and Margaret Wilkinson Smith '32, *twelfth.*

47  Directors of the 1942 HEC at the Hotel Seneca in Rochester in April 1942 who are identifiable are, *from left around the table, class of* 1942 *unless otherwise noted:* Reed Andrae, James S. Patterson, Robert K. Jones, Hugh D. Leslie, Jerome A. Batt '43, James H. Barrett '43, PhD '51, Roger M. Merwin, Frederick R. Haverly, ——, ——, ——, ——, James C. Muth, either twin Henry or John Wannop, Herbert G. Eldridge, and the other Wannop twin. Among the unidentified directors are Charles W. Jack, Edward C. Callis, Albert P. Mitroff, Ernest Holcombe Palmer, David E. Beach, and David Estes '43.

60  Waitresses' derby for '44 HEC included Mary R. Wright '45, Jane Ingram '46, the winner Joan Blaikie '45, Amy Mann '45, Jacqueline ("Johnny") Rogers '46, Janice O'Donnell '44, Patricia Will '45, Joyce Heath '47, and Elvira Mattucci '48, not necessarily in that order.

74  Learning to photograph food for a menu. *From left,* Norman H. Cochrane '66; Prof. Raymond Fox *44, PhD '56, floriculture; Wernaldo David Temel '64, Prof. Myrtle Ericson of the food faculty; and Maclean Dameron, director of university photography.

78  Faculty in 1952. *From left, front row:* John Courtney, Louis Toth, Frank Randolph *17, Dean H. B. Meek, John Sherry, Thomas W. Silk '38, and Paul R. Broten *47. *Second row:* Librarian Blanche Fickle, Helen Recknagel, Elizabeth Kaiser, Myrtle Ericson, Florence George '34, ——, Nita C. Kendrick, and Allan H. Treman *21. *Third row:* James Barrett '43, Fred B. Mills *48, Leonard Van Lent, George McHatton, and Gerald W. Lattin, PhD '49. *Back row:* Jeremiah Wanderstock *41, Charles E. Cladel '29, and J. William Conner '40, MS '56.

101  European Chapter meeting of the Cornell Society of
     Hotelmen in Berlin in October 1967. *From left, front row:*
     David A. Berins '66, Patrick F. Brocato '60, two brewery
     workers, Wolfgang Haenisch, and Hans Oppacher. *Second
     row:* David Nailon *ss* (for special student), Lalit Nirula '66,
     Willem J. Bijl '66, Renate Kenaston, Pamela Troutman '66,
     "Billie" Starke, Arenda Spicle, Dominik Betschart *ss*, Jutta
     Oppacher, and Mr. Dauge. *Third row:* ——, ——, Heinz
     Roget *ss*, John G. ("Terry") Kenaston '63, Rudolf W. T.
     Muenster '62, Sven Akerstrand *ss*, Ralph M. Starke '52,
     Christian K. Petzold *70, Prof. Eben S. Reynolds '47,
     Rudolphe W. Schelbert '55, Elsbeth Schelbert, and Matti L.
     Sarkia '64.

103  *Top:* Japan Chapter meeting of the Cornell Society of Hotel-
     men in Tokyo in July 1972. *Kneeling,* Yuji A. Yamaguchi '61;
     *from left, front,* Mrs. J. Inumaru, Mrs. Gamo, Mrs. K. Suzuki,
     Mrs. Yamaguchi, Kaoru Suzuki '53, and Jiro Inumaru '55;
     *standing,* guest, K. Okado, Dean and Mrs. Beck, guest,
     Yoshikatsu Gamo '53, and Takahisa Nagashima '59.

     *Bottom:* Southeast Asia Chapter of the Cornell Society of
     Hotelmen meets in New Delhi in July 1972. *From left are,
     standing,* Sewa Ram Arora '68, Naresh K. Khanna '69,
     Prithipal S. Lamba '56, Ramesh K. Khanna '62, Rudolf
     Muenster '62, Roy A. Cretton '59, Robindro N. Rekhi '68, and
     Lalit Nirula '66. *Seated,* Mrs. N. Khanna, Mrs. R. Khanna,
     Mrs. Arora, Mrs. Muenster, and Mrs. Lamba.

105  Alumni sing at a hotel gathering in Carefree, Colorado,
     in January 1961. *From left,* Kenney E. Mallory '52, Lynn
     Himmelman '33, John F. ("Jack") Craver '52, Edward H.
     Carrette Jr. '61, Robert W. Dupar '49, Howard C.
     Donnelly '47, and George Nicholas North '52.

106  Prof. Robert M. Chase *59 speaks to guests at the 1970 Hotel
     Ezra Cornell. *From left in the foreground are* Peter Balas,
     Conrad Engelhardt '42, and Thomas V. Pedulla '60.

112  Prof. Charles I. Sayles '26 and data processing boards.
     Others, *from left,* Emil Cipolla *60, MBA '63, a lab instructor;
     Carl W. Vail Jr. '61; and another person.

113  Discussing a research study in 1962 on the thawing of frozen
     foods are faculty, including, *from right,* Hotel professors
     Charles Sayles, Robert Chase, Jeremiah Wanderstock, and
     Paul Broten. Others are Emil Cipolla *60, *left,* and Nicholous
     Schneider *57, an instructor in Hotel engineering.

153  Sharing a meal in the new McLamore Cafeteria in 1992, *from
     left,* Calvin Stovall '93, Jewel Ayres '94, Dennis Byron, Nikki
     Bryant '93, and Leo Yen '94.

163  Members of the 1995 Student Committee for Continuous
     Improvement, all members of the Class of 1996 except
     as shown otherwise: *From left, front row,* Kathleen N.
     McDonnell *98, Amy E. Broderick, Michael S. Dukart,
     and Alessandra K. Murata; *second row,* Jeffrey M. Blumer and
     Eric Sinoway; and *back row,* Imre Hild '97, Kirsten P. Knipp
     '97, Mark C. Canlis '97, Theodor J. Keilholz, Philip A. Baugh,
     and Damianos Damalitis.

172  Dean and Mrs. Dittman attend a meeting of the Cornell
     Society of Hotelmen in Hong Kong in June 1995.
     *From left,* William S. Hsu, MPS '83, Hong Kong chapter presi-
     dent; Albert I-M. Wu '76, Asia Pacific regional vice president;
     Rudolf W. Muenster '62, CSH first vice president; Michael W.
     N. Chiu '66, CSH president; and Maureen and David
     Dittman.

**1**

The Freshman at Cornell is first confronted with many problems, but with great confidence he steps forward to meet them . . .

**2**

. . . He must first scientifically pick his course of study from the many offered . . .

**3**

Once decided, he is carefully indoctrinated and slowly introduced to his chosen field . . .

**7**

. . . activities within his school are a valuable part of his education, as is . . .

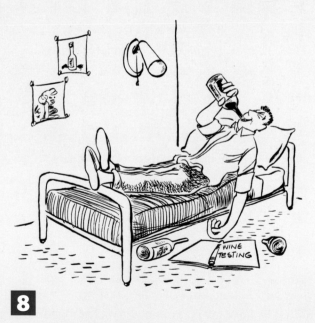

**8**

. . . a strict adherence to study schedules . . .

**4**

...He is carefully trained; mentally...

**5**

...spiritually...

**6**

...and physically for his profession...

**9**

but all is for good reason and eventually will come graduation, followed by...

**10**

...a noble life where his accumulated knowledge will be utilized to enrich the life of his fellow man.

Cartoons from *The Cornell Innkeeper,* Spring 1957, by Fred Thomas, Arch. '57

THE HOTEL SCHOOL

HOSPITALITY · MANAGEMENT

CORNELL

U N I V E R S I T Y

# Index